Tenth

PRESBYTERIAN
CHURCH *of*
PHILADELPHIA

Tenth

PRESBYTERIAN
CHURCH *of*
PHILADELPHIA

175 Years of Thinking and Acting Biblically

EDITED BY PHILIP GRAHAM RYKEN

WITH CONTRIBUTIONS BY
ALLEN C. GUELZO, WILLIAM S. BARKER, PAUL S. JONES

FOREWORD BY LINDA M. BOICE

PUBLISHING
P.O. BOX 817 • PHILLIPSBURG • NEW JERSEY 08865

Page design and typesetting by Lakeside Design Plus

Printed in the United States of America

Library of Congress Cataloging-in-Publication Data
Tenth Presbyterian Church of Philadelphia : 175 years of thinking and acting biblically / edited by Philip Graham Ryken ; with contributions by Allen Guelzo, William S. Barker, Paul S. Jones.
    p. cm.
    Includes bibliographical references and index.
    ISBN 0-87552-571-7
    1. Tenth Presbyterian Church (Philadelphia, Pa.) I. Ryken, Philip Graham, 1966- II. Guelzo, Allen C. III. Barker, William S. IV. Jones, Paul S., 1969-

BX9211.P5T448 2004
285'.174811—dc22

                       2003065624

To all who are spiritually weary and seek rest;
to all who mourn and long for comfort;
to all who struggle and desire victory;
to all who sin and need a Savior;
to all who are strangers and want fellowship;
to all who hunger and thirst after righteousness;
and to whoever will come—
this church opens wide her doors
and offers her welcome
in the name of the Lord Jesus Christ.

CONTENTS

ILLUSTRATIONS

Illustrations appear on eight pages between pages 128 and 129.

FOREWORD

Tenth Presbyterian Church. The big old dark-stoned structure dominates the corner of Seventeenth and Spruce Streets in
Center City Philadelphia, just a few blocks from the businesses
and shops in the heart of the city. The church is flanked by cen-
tury-old four-story row houses that serve as expensive private
homes, collections of student apartments, and paneled offices for
lawyers and realtors. Tenth is truly a city church.

I knew of Tenth Church before I first came to Philadelphia
because Dr. Donald Grey Barnhouse, the senior pastor, had spoken more than once at my home church in Montclair, New Jersey. But Tenth did not become a part of my life until the fall of
1955, when I entered the University of Pennsylvania and moved
into a small women's dorm at Thirty-Fourth and Chestnut Streets.

"When you get to Philadelphia, you should go to Dr. Barnhouse's church—Tenth Presbyterian," my parents urged, as did
several older Christian friends. So I did.

Two absolutely vital experiences—experiences that have
shaped and sustained my Christian life for the past forty-eight
years—occurred in my first days as a freshman at Penn. Even
before classes began, I found the small Inter-Varsity Christian
Fellowship group that met on campus. And on the first Sundays
in September, I and another Christian girl from my dorm took
the Chestnut Street bus across the Schuylkill River to downtown
Philadelphia, where we hopped off at Seventeenth Street and
walked five or six blocks south to attend morning and evening
services at Tenth Presbyterian Church.

My friend Elsie and I drank in the truths of God's Word that Dr. Barnhouse taught so effectively and so forcefully. I had never heard such preaching. It was preaching that made the Bible come alive. It was preaching that stretched our understanding of our great, almighty, redeeming God, known to us through his revelation in the Scriptures and through the incarnation and atoning work of his Son, Jesus Christ. How could we not want to love and obey and serve such a great God?

What I didn't realize at the time was that as I was being taught the Scriptures in all their depth and richness, I was also being grounded in the great Reformation doctrines. The truths of the Bible and the insights and formulations of the Reformers could not be separated. I remember, for example, what Dr. Barnhouse said one spring Sunday in 1958, shortly before he was to leave on a lengthy speaking tour in South America. He was preaching on Genesis 50:20, in which Joseph addresses his terrified brothers, acknowledging their sin against him, but also putting that sin right in the heart of the plans of the Lord: "Ye thought evil against me; but God meant it unto good, to bring to pass, as it is this day, to save much people alive" (KJV). Dr. Barnhouse knew that he would be flying on small planes as he hopped over the Andes, and there was certainly the possibility that he would never return to his congregation. But he exhorted us not to doubt the wisdom and sovereignty of almighty God, because no matter what the future held, God's purposes are good and his plans cannot be thwarted. That message continues to be a help and comfort to this day.

Because the teaching of the Scriptures informed every aspect of the worship services, the offering at Tenth was not collected until the congregation had been admonished, in Dr. Barnhouse's rumbling bass, that "if you are not a believer, you are not invited to give." Rather, visitors were urged to receive—that is, to receive the gospel of the forgiveness of sin and new life in Jesus Christ. Then they would be ready to give to God's work. An even firmer warning was delivered before the Lord's Supper was distributed. Besides soaking up the Bible teaching, I was absorbing the other benefits of a church that sought so consistently to be guided by Scripture alone.

My Christian life was nourished by a weekly dorm Bible study, a morning prayer group, and weekly Inter-Varsity meetings that featured speakers from local churches. A favorite was the Rev. Edwin Houk, a much-loved associate minister at Tenth Presbyterian. For four years I was never far from Tenth's influence.

When the Lord took me to Cambridge, Massachusetts, for graduate work in education, I knew where to go to church. Park Street Church in downtown Boston was considered a sister church to Tenth in Philadelphia. Both city churches had expository pastors (Dr. Harold John Ockenga at Park Street), both had strong ministries to students, and both had a strong interest in missions.

On my first Sunday in graduate school I took the subway to Park Street Church. Returning on the subway after the evening service, I asked a young man who was carrying a Bible whether he knew of an Inter-Varsity group at Harvard. He gave me the time and place, and the following Friday evening I trekked across the Harvard Yard to find my spiritual home on campus. In the course of that academic year (1959–1960), through involvement in Inter-Varsity activities, I met a graduating senior—also an English major—named James Montgomery Boice.

That spring, with most of his undergraduate work completed, Jim Boice called and invited me to dinner and the theater. We talked over a meal in a small restaurant in the Back Bay area of Boston. What soon became clear was that Dr. Barnhouse's Bible teaching had exercised an enormous influence on each of us. By dessert we were saying, "Did you hear him give this sermon illustration . . . ?" And then the other picked up with, "Yes, and what about . . . ?" I have always felt that in the Lord's providence, Dr. Barnhouse brought Jim and me together, albeit unknowingly!

By September 1960, Jim and I were at Princeton Theological Seminary—he preparing for the pastorate, and I preparing for some less well-defined Christian service. During that same fall the Lord took Dr. Barnhouse home to Glory. Jim's father, Dr.

G. Newton Boice, was a board member of the Evangelical Foundation, which sponsored The Bible Study Hour and *Eternity* magazine, ministries that had been instituted and carried forward by Barnhouse. Newton and Jean Boice drove from their home near Pittsburgh for the memorial service at Tenth, and Jim and I drove from Princeton to join them. Later, Jim's father purchased the big desk that Dr. Barnhouse had used when he did work at the Foundation office on Spruce Street, and Jim had the desk for many years.

In June 1962 we were married, and while Jim finished his last year of seminary, I taught English in a nearby high school. Then we headed overseas for three years in Basel, Switzerland, where Jim earned a doctorate in theology and began to teach Romans to a small English-speaking congregation that grew out of a weekly international Bible study group. Dr. Barnhouse's volumes on Romans were well-used resources, then and in later years.

During those six years of advanced study, Jim was sure of two things: one, that following Dr. Barnhouse's pattern he needed the best education possible; and two, that his education was preparation for an expository ministry in a city church. After Basel, Jim worked for a year and a half as an assistant editor for *Christianity Today* in Washington, D.C. But this was only a stop along the way, never the destination.

Then came that unforgettable Sunday evening in January 1968. Jim was asked to preach at Sixth Presbyterian Church in Washington by the gracious pastor, Dr. Ben Sheldon. Members of the pulpit committee of Tenth Presbyterian Church had arranged for the invitation, though we did not know that until they introduced themselves after the service. They asked Jim whether he wanted to pursue a possible call to the pastorate at Tenth.

On the way home, after Jim's brief conversation with the Tenth elders, we talked about the possibility of being pastor and wife at Tenth Presbyterian Church. In one way it seemed unbelievable. But somewhere down deep—and it wasn't presumption—we both knew that night that the Lord was taking us to

Philadelphia to serve at Tenth, the very church whose ministry had made such an impact on each of us individually.

Jim's first sermon as the new pastor was on Easter Sunday 1968, though we didn't move into the old manse on Delancey Street until May. Our three-year-old Elizabeth quickly made friends with both young and old in the congregation, and as a family we regularly visited church members who were bereaved or confined to nursing homes. Hospital visits meant that Elizabeth and I read books in the lobby while Jim went to the patient's room.

The church did not have many programs or meetings in those early days of our ministry, and there weren't many young couples or families. So we opened our home and threw ourselves into building a young couples' group, encouraged home Bible studies (one of which we attended weekly for three years), and hosted young adults for meals and meetings. Jim worked very hard to prepare the expositional sermons that he knew would feed and strengthen those who were filling the pews. And he and some elders brought Dr. Robert Elmore to change the whole music program, introducing a new Allen organ and a multi-voice choir.

Soon Heather and Jennifer were born, and when Jennifer was a toddler I was asked to teach the senior high Sunday school class. It was exactly what I most wanted to do, and that class has been a joy ever since. Tenth grew and the staff grew, and our concern for the city and its great needs led to the establishment of various ministries. My training was in secondary education in the area of English. As our two younger daughters approached high school age, we sensed the city's great need for a Christian high school that would be affordable for city families but also academically challenging. Since its founding in 1983, City Center Academy has been under the umbrella of Tenth Church and has been my major ministry focus.

Dr. Barnhouse had preached on Jesus' reaching out to the rejected, unacceptable, and ignored members of society. He applied that message to our city culture, as did Jim. Whether he was preaching on Hosea and his wife or on Jesus' interaction with the woman at the well, he made clear our Christian calling to minister to the city, to the people in the place where the Lord had placed us. As members of Tenth, we have had no choice but to put our doctrine into action. A city church cannot simply bask in its good teaching; it must put that teaching into active ministry that reaches well outside the sanctuary walls. I have seen this become much more of a reality during my years at Tenth, both in the increased number and support of missionaries of extraordinary caliber who serve all over the globe and in the concern for and support of ministries to the socially and spiritually needy in Philadelphia's urban neighborhoods. City Center Academy is one of Tenth's many efforts to make a difference in our own community.

In April 2000—when Jim's preaching and writing were flourishing, and when he and our gifted organist and choir director, Dr. Paul Jones, were writing hymns of exceptional quality—Jim was struck with an aggressive liver cancer. Just eight weeks later, on June 15, he slipped quietly into the Lord's presence.

During the weeks of Jim's illness I had not attended the worship services—when he was too weak to be in church it seemed selfish for me to go, even when our daughters were by his bedside. We knew about and were sustained by a tremendous outpouring of prayer from Tenth members and from others all over the world. Cards and e-mail messages were amazingly thoughtful and heartening. I had not intended to go to the morning worship service the first Sunday after losing Jim. But then I learned that Dr. Philip Ryken—at that time our associate minister of preaching—was going to speak on Psalm 23, and I learned what hymns were to be sung. I said to my daughter Heather, who was staying with me, "I have to go to this service." She and I went together, and though tears welled up, it was a great blessing and comfort to be back with our Tenth family.

Yes, the congregation that I have loved has become my family. The outpouring of shared grief has been overshadowed by shared love, practical support, and ongoing encouragement for me and my daughters. In one sense, Tenth Presbyterian Church is a big old stone building planted on a city corner. But in the truest sense, Tenth is a body of believers, far from perfect, yet drawn together by a love for the faithful preaching of God's Word. And because that Word has been clearly preached and faithfully applied, God's people have grown and flourished and shared their knowledge of the Word with others through deeds of love and service. I am blessed to call Tenth my home, and its people my family.

Linda M. Boice
Philadelphia, Pennsylvania

PREFACE

A church is a community of people who profess faith in Jesus Christ. And since a church is a community, it should not be surprising that this book—which tells the story of one particular church—has been a group effort, with many individuals contributing to it over many years.

The book is a history of the Tenth Presbyterian Church of Philadelphia. It is really a revision of a 1979 book called *Making God's Word Plain: One Hundred and Fifty Years in the History of Tenth Presbyterian Church of Philadelphia*. As its subtitle indicates, *Making God's Word Plain* was published to coincide with the church's 150th anniversary. It was edited by Tenth's senior minister at the time, the late Rev. Dr. James Montgomery Boice.

In the book's preface, Dr. Boice was careful to acknowledge the community of scholars, pastors, and others who had worked to produce it. The chief historian was Allen Guelzo, who was then lecturing in American church history and apologetics at the Theological Seminary of the Reformed Episcopal Church in Philadelphia, and who has since gone on to have a notable career as a historian. Dr. Guelzo currently serves as Grace F. Kea Professor of American History and Dean of the Templeton Honors College at Eastern University. Among his outstanding achievements are a masterly religious biography entitled *Abraham Lincoln: Redeemer President* (Eerdmans, 2000) and a more recent book called *Lincoln's Emancipation Proclamation: The End of Slavery in America* (Simon & Schuster, 2004).

16

Dr. Guelzo wrote the chapters in *Making God's Word Plain* that recounted Tenth's history through 1967. He was helped by the work of several other young men who were preparing for pastoral ministry at the time. Ray Burton Lanning did special research on the life of Henry Augustus Boardman. Robert W. Patterson interviewed Margaret Bell Barnhouse and Mariano Di Gangi to provide perspective on the Barnhouse and Di Gangi years. Another valuable resource was Tenth's unofficial archivist, William H. Pascoe, a longtime elder who preserved memories and documents that dated back to the period of Marcus Brownson and, before that, to John McNeil.

This volume represents a substantial revision of *Making God's Word Plain*. Dr. Guelzo's material has been kept in its entirety (chapters 1 through 4), except in one or two minor instances in which the intervening years required a factual update. Several sections have been removed (chiefly the book's foreword and a chapter on foundations for ministry), primarily because they have since become somewhat out of date. The new foreword is written by Linda M. Boice, who brings a unique perspective from her many years as a college student, pastor's wife, and servant in ministry at Tenth Church.

But the primary change is the addition of two major chapters. Chapter 5 ("Boice") updates Tenth's history by surveying the life and ministry of my immediate predecessor, Dr. James Montgomery Boice. This chapter was written by Dr. William S. Barker, who holds his doctorate in church history from Vanderbilt University and has had a distinguished career as a churchman and church historian. Dr. Barker has served as president of Covenant Theological Seminary in St. Louis, editor of the *Presbyterian Journal*, academic dean of Westminster Theological Seminary in Philadelphia, and moderator of the General Assembly of the Presbyterian Church in America (PCA). His published work includes *Puritan Profiles* (Christian Focus, 1996), a biographical handbook to the Westminster Assembly.

Dr. Barker is the ideal person to have written an account of Dr. Boice's ministry at Tenth and beyond. Although the two men did not work together closely, Dr. Barker knew Dr. Boice and sat under his preaching during his years in Philadelphia. This experience, coupled with his superb grasp of the Reformed and evangelical landscape during the late twentieth century, has enabled Dr. Barker to place Dr. Boice's ministry in its local and national contexts.

I served as the book's editor and contributed the final chapter ("A Church for the Twenty-First Century"), in which I attempt to review Tenth's congregational commitments to biblical teaching, the evangelical church, Reformation theology, Presbyterian church government, and the city of Philadelphia. I also show how the seven priorities expressed in Tenth's mission statement remain relevant in the twenty-first century.

The appendixes contain some new material, including a history of music at Tenth. This material, which is virtually a chapter in its own right, was written by Dr. Paul S. Jones, who now serves as Tenth's organist and music director, and who worked closely with Dr. Boice during the final three years of his ministry. Dr. Jones received his doctorate in choral conducting from Indiana University and has begun what promises to be a significant career as a conductor, composer, and church musician. In the seventh appendix, he surveys the history of worship music at Tenth with a view to charting a course for its future.

This book is for everyone who loves the Christian church, and especially for anyone who has been blessed by the ministry of Tenth Presbyterian Church. On behalf of the session and congregation of Tenth Presbyterian Church, I wish to express our gratitude to Allan Fisher and the staff at P&R for partnering with us to produce this congregational history. Royalties from its sale will be dedicated to City Center Academy, the college preparatory school for urban students that was started at Tenth and remains closely associated with its ministry to this day. For more information about the school, see appendix 9.

On the happy occasion of our 175th anniversary as a church, we give praise to God for his sovereign grace and for the amazing privilege of reaching our city and our world with the love of

Jesus Christ. Our prayer is that this book will help you to do the same, wherever God has called you to serve. It is dedicated to "him who is able to do far more abundantly than all that we ask or think, according to the power at work within us, to him be glory in the church and in Christ Jesus throughout all generations, forever and ever. Amen" (Eph. 3:20–21 ESV).

Philip Graham Ryken
Philadelphia, Pennsylvania

ACKNOWLEDGMENTS

Contributor William S. Barker wishes to thank Phil and Lisa Ryken for kind and helpful arrangements; the following for granting most useful interviews: Manfred Garibotti, Carroll Wynne, Linward Crowe, Clive Stockdale, Linda Boice, Glenn McDowell, Jay and Jane MacMoran, Elmer and Sherry Snethen, Nancy Hala, Marion Clark, R. C. Sproul, C. Everett Koop, Norman Koop, Erna Goulding, and Cora Hogue; and the following for additional assistance: Dot Boersma, Patricia Russell, and Ed Mutzer.

Contributor Paul S. Jones wishes to thank the following persons for their assistance with interviews, information, and editing: Manfred O. Garibotti, who served for 50 years as an elder; Gordon Palmer, who served as a trustee and then elder from 1961; Nancy Bucklin, soloist for many years; Robert Carwithen, former organist and music director; Hughes Oliphant Old, Tenth member and Princeton Seminary professor, for access to the Boardman hymnal; Barbara T. Harder, Dennis & Cheryl Sanfaçon, and Martin Troutman, long-serving choir members; Linda Boice, member since 1968 and wife of former senior minister James Montgomery Boice; Donald Grey Barnhouse Jr., Russell Bird, and Dot Boersma for research assistance; Elizabeth Mosebrook, who found the helpful article on Louis Benson; and Philip Moyer and Philip Ryken, who did the final editing. The author also acknowledges the assistance of staff at the Presbyterian Historical Society in Philadelphia.

20

ROOTS

Allen C. Guelzo

Sometime during the year 1701, Francis Makemie came to Philadelphia to preside at an ordination. In those days, ordinations in the American colonies were still rare enough to be important events, but this ordination was particularly important because Francis Makemie, the first Presbyterian missionary to the New World, was to preside over the first ordination of an American Presbyterian on American soil. There were other Presbyterian ministers in most of the colonies so that adding one more to the list was not in itself remarkable. The significant difference was that the others were all foreign-born and foreign-educated. There was little to hold such men in America when the wilderness proved overwhelming. The ordination of a native American in an American city was the ordination of one who had nowhere else to call home and who was, in fact, already starting to talk in accents strange to English ears.

To ordain an American was to raise up the standard of American Presbyterianism, not merely a transplanted English or Scottish Presbyterianism. Looking back, people would see that ordination as a high point in Makemie's rough-and-tumble career.

21

Beginnings

Rough-and-tumble it had been, almost from the beginning. Born in 1658 in Scots-Irish Ulster, Makemie had a knack for getting into dangerous situations. His Presbyterian parents had been targets for Anglican harassment during the Restoration, at which time the local Presbyterian minister lost his pulpit for refusing to conform to the state-decreed ceremonies. Makemie himself, banned as a Dissenter from Trinity College, Dublin, was forced to seek his education at Edinburgh, just in time to endure the great Scottish "Killing Time," which made Scotland even more unhealthy than Ulster for Presbyterians. Makemie took what must have looked like the ultimate risk when, shortly after his ordination in 1682, he volunteered to answer a call from a Presbyterian plantation in Maryland, in those days at the far end of nowhere.[1]

Makemie went to Maryland to "submit to the sovereign providence of God who has been pleased very unexpectedly to drive me back to this poor desolate people, among whom I design to continue until God in his providence determine otherwise."[2] But Maryland was not quite that poor and desolate, as it turned out. In 1698 Makemie married the daughter of a rich merchant and wound up running his father-in-law's sloop to the West Indies. Still, his heart was in preaching and church planting, and going into trade for his father-in-law was just another way of supporting himself while preaching to those who could not afford to pay him.

From 1684 to 1705, Makemie ministered to a tiny congregation on the Elizabeth River in Virginia, toured the Carolinas, wangled a license to start a church in his own house in Accomac County on Virginia's eastern shore, and started or assisted in running six new churches across the line in Maryland.[3]

Makemie's one lingering disappointment was a visit paid to Philadelphia in 1692. William Penn's Quaker experiment on the Delaware was then less than ten years old, but already it was home to more than three hundred brick or frame houses,[4] a bustling business community—and a massive and disastrous doctrinal schism within Quakerism. Makemie had arrived hoping to rally Reformed believers in the area and perhaps pick up a few converts from the badly divided Quakers. But it did not prove to be that easy. Makemie, for his own reasons, had developed a distaste for Quakerism and reserved a particular disgust for "the instability of many who are so earthly, and soon drawn to embrace and espouse that persuasion."[5] The Quakers, therefore, greeted his missionary efforts by accusing him of using "the invented words of man's wisdom, not according, but contrary unto the Holy Scriptures," and baldly asserting that Presbyterian ordination and baptism were "from the Church of Rome, which they call the whore of Babylon."[6] Makemie probably preached the first Presbyterian sermon in Philadelphia's history during his stay, but nothing seems to have come of it, and he went on to Boston unrequited. It took three more years before Protestant dissenters of any stripe actually pulled themselves together and organized a meeting.

What they did eventually organize was an ungainly compromise. Nine Baptists and perhaps half a dozen Presbyterians met together in the cramped and decrepit storehouse of the Barbados Company, a West Indies trading firm at Market and Second Streets. Since the Presbyterians lacked leadership, the Baptists arranged for one of their own neighboring ministers, John Watts, to preach to the group on alternate Sundays. The choice for the intervening Sundays was left to the Presbyterians, but this was little more than a gesture since there were no Presbyterian preachers nearer than Maryland. Usually the Presbyterians could find no one but another Baptist to preach for them.

In the summer of 1698, an itinerant preacher named Jedidiah Andrews arrived in Philadelphia from Hingham, Massachusetts, and presented himself as a Presbyterian willing to take up the Presbyterian half of the preaching, even though he was as yet unordained and only fresh out of Harvard College. Andrews had arrived at a propitious moment—although why it was Jedidiah Andrews who showed up and not one of Makemie's Maryland protégés is a mystery. Very likely, Makemie was at work in this, but from afar. He was on good terms with Puritan Massachusetts in general, and with Cotton Mather in particular. Cotton had called Makemie "that brave man,"[7] and Increase Mather, along with Samuel Willard, James Allin, Cotton, and other moguls of the Bay, had supplied a preface to Makemie's pamphlet against the Quakers. Mather, as it turned out, was also well acquainted with Jedidiah Andrews, and it is possible that Andrews's arrival was the product of a plea from Makemie to Mather for Philadelphia.

The appearance of Andrews rapidly complicated matters in the storehouse, because Andrews was evidently long on dogmatics and short on patience with Baptists. Within three months, the union congregation had become divided, the nine Baptists listening to John Watts in the morning and the Presbyterians waiting until afternoon to come defiantly trooping in to hear Andrews.[8] By October, the exasperated Baptists had worked themselves into a fit (fueled, doubtless, by Andrews's suggestion that Baptist ordinations were something less than valid) and warned that they would only

> freely confess and promise for ourselves that we can and do own and allow of your approved ministers . . . if you can also freely confess and promise for yourselves that you can and will allow of our approved ministers . . . so that each side may own, embrace and accept of one another as fellow brethren and ministers of Christ.[9]

The Presbyterians solemnly replied that such an interest in "unity and communion in the things of God" was commendable, and Andrews invited the disgruntled Baptists to set a date for a conference. The Baptists agreed, set the date and place, and showed up—only to find none of the Presbyterians there. Andrews afterward insisted that he had misunderstood the time, but the Baptists were convinced that the absence was deliberate, and they notified him that they would have to meet apart. Off they went to worship at Anthony Morris's brew house, leaving the Barbados storehouse to the Presbyterians.

How much of this was a sincere collision of legitimate interests and how much the clever maneuverings of Jedidiah Andrews was never clear. Years after, Morgan Edwards, compiling materials for a history of the Baptists, said that the Presbyterian answer to the Baptist request for a meeting had not been "in sincerity, how goodly soever their words may be."[10] Andrews, for his part, exulted with a rather indiscreet glee that "we have got the Anabaptists out of the house,"[11] and Edwards glumly remarked that "this was what the Presbyterians wanted in reality."[12]

The secession of the Baptists did not end Presbyterian difficulties. We may date the founding of the first Presbyterian church in Philadelphia from Andrews's *fait accompli,* but it was by no means certain that the church was there to stay. Andrews did not have a formal ordination, and without any other disciplinary machinery but his own presence of mind, people were just as likely to follow the example of the Baptists if Andrews did something that failed to suit them. For three years Andrews labored, preaching and (apparently without authority) baptizing infants born of Presbyterian parents.

In proper circles, news of Andrews's actions might have gotten him into trouble. But Francis Makemie was not the sort to let want of formal procedure stand in the way of the growth of the Philadelphia church. Accordingly, he arranged for the company of the Reverend Josias Mackie of Norfolk and two recent University of Glasgow graduates whom he had recruited on a recent visit to Britain, John Hampton and George MacNish, to form the first Presbyterian ordination council and technically the first temporary presbytery in America. They would ordain Jedidiah Andrews and in so doing make a beginning for American Presbyterianism—which is why, sometime during 1701, Makemie was coming up to Philadelphia.

A GROWING CHURCH

Whatever Makemie's original reservations may have been about Quaker Philadelphia, they were soon balanced by the almost unlimited potential for growth that Philadelphia presented to the new Presbyterian church. For all the hardship that Andrews had endured in getting something started, his first thoughts turned optimistically to expansion. He confided to a friend that even with uncontested possession of the storehouse, "our continuance there is uncertain; and therefore we must think of building, notwithstanding our poverty and the smallness of our numbers."[13]

Poverty, however, was probably precisely what caused the Presbyterians to wait until 1704 before erecting "a frame church building at the southeast corner of Market Street and Bank Alley," which Peter Kalm, the Swedish naturalist, would describe in the 1740s as being "of middling size."[14] The delay certainly could not be blamed on "smallness of numbers," for the one thing that delighted Andrews's heart was the extraordinary numbers of Scots-Irish that were pouring out onto the Philadelphia wharves, bags in hand.[15] His rejoicing at the prospect of so many Scots-Irish immigrants was a well-founded one, for Andrews knew that Scots-Irish immigrants were almost man for man Presbyterian, and that in turn meant a constant supply of Presbyterians for Philadelphia's first Presbyterian church.

In 1725, 3,500 Ulstermen alone immigrated. In 1728, 2,000 left from Dublin especially for Philadelphia. The next year the number jumped to 4,000, and by 1740, 12,000 were leaving annually from Ulster.[16]

Makemie rightly foresaw that to handle the influx of immigration something more organized than a straggling handful of loosely knit churches was needed. So back he went to Philadelphia, collected five other ministers from New Jersey, Maryland, and Virginia, along with three elders, and met with Jedidiah Andrews and his elder, Joseph Yard. In the spring of 1706, they organized the first presbytery in America

to meet yearly, and oftener if necessary, to consult the most proper measures for advancing religion and propagating Christianity in our various stations, and to maintain such a correspondence as may conduce to the improvement of our ministerial ability by prescribing texts to be preached on by two of our number at every meeting, which performance is subjected to the censure of our brethren.[17]

If anyone feared that the multitude of immigrants was going to swamp the American identity of the church, they wasted their fears. The free air of the New World had a startling effect on those who had known nothing but the bonds of the Old World, and the immigrants Americanized themselves with happy ardor. Far from the immigrants' detracting from the Americanness of the Presbyterian church, Makemie and Andrews could congratulate each other on how much the newcomers actually worked to bolster that identity. On the other hand, that fact spelled trouble for those who came to Philadelphia expecting to run the church in the old Scots-Irish fashion, for they found that, once in Pennsylvania, the Scots-Irish immigrant no longer felt bound to play by Scots-Irish rules. The ministers and elders who had been brought up to the "proper" ways of doing things found that it was one thing to make fine pronouncements about organizing new churches, founding new presbyteries, and ordaining Americans; it was quite another to realize that American Presbyterianism would have to be administered and nurtured according to the harsh realities of colonial America.

The presbytery in Philadelphia was not indifferent in the face of rowdiness and immorality, especially among its ministers. But the swelling numbers of independent-minded colonists and the almost unlimited expanse of land stretching westward, plus the simple shortage of ministers available to cover it all, added up to an inability to control what was going on by the old rules of order. The presbytery was reluctant to remove ministers when it became apparent that there were too few to go around. Always complicating the picture was the sheer size of the American wilderness. In England, one rebuked a man and he was suitably cowed. In America, one rebuked a man and then watched him move ten miles away, start his own rival church, and print a number of vilifying pamphlets. The presbytery shortly discovered that in America it was best to suffer with unruly ministers and congregations as long as possible. The unfortunate consequence was that, like every other religious group that came to American shores, the Presbyterians seemed willing to look the other way when a minister floundered or a congregation became defiant.

A leader who understood America well enough to measure discipline and ingenuity in right quantities might have been able to control things better. But Makemie was not an administrator by choice, and he tended to look on the presbytery as being nothing more official than a meeting of ministers. Moreover, the strain of missionary work told heavily on his health, and in the spring of 1708 his strength failed. He slowly declined and was dead before the leaves turned. Makemie would be honored as "the father of American Presbyterianism." But American Presbyterianism was only an infant at his death, and it would have to grope around the problems of being an American church in its own way.

Multiplying Churches

At least the presbytery was growing. In 1710 there were only five Presbyterian churches in Pennsylvania, but in a few more years a number of other congregations had either been started or attached themselves to the presbytery. By 1715 there were Presbyterian churches from Long Island to Cape May, and these were dutifully sending representatives to Philadelphia. The next year, "it having pleased divine Providence so to increase our number,"[18] the presbytery decided to form four subordinate presbyteries—Philadelphia, New Castle (Delaware), Long Island, and Snow Hill (Maryland)—and reorganize itself as the Synod of Philadelphia.

But the joy of growth was limited. The physical growth of the synod only exacerbated the problems of keeping far-flung ministers and congregations under discipline. What was worse, the Scots-Irish immigrants, who were looked upon as the chief supply of members for the churches of the synod, never amounted to more than one-third of the total immigration passing through Philadelphia. The other two-thirds was made up of a seething crazy quilt of denominations, all looking to make Philadelphia their personal possession. William Penn's novel policy of religious toleration proved a magnet for everything from Moravian pietists to Rosicrucian monks, and far from encouraging the growth of Christianity, the multiplicity of sects only made other settlers hesitant to commit themselves to any one. Each boatload of immigrants had to deal with the pleas, demands, and cajoleries of the sectaries that had preceded them, and in the midst of so much mental tumult it was easier to sink down into indifference than to struggle.

Many of the immigrants were unlikely even to be impressed with religion, no matter what shape it came in. Henry Melchior Muhlenburg came from Germany in 1742 as the new pastor to three Lutheran congregations outside Philadelphia. He soon shuddered at

> how few good and how many exceptionally godless, wicked people have come into this country every year. The whole country is being flooded with ordinary, extraordinary and unprecedented wickedness and crime. Surely the rod of God cannot be spared much longer. Our old residents are mere stupid children in sin when compared with the new arrivals! Oh, what a fearful thing it is to have so many thousands of unruly and brazen sinners come into this free air and unfenced country![19]

Kept up day after day, the jeers of the ungodly and the persuasions of the sects could erode even the most substantial congregation, and the erosion would go all the more swiftly if a congregation contained a number of apprentices or indentured servants (who might have pressures of a disapproving master to cope with) or if one encountered an ambush of wily Quakers or Moravians who waited only for the first doctrinal fuzziness to catch a person in some creedal intricacy.

The Philadelphia Presbytery and the synod had found stability and order hard to achieve. What they did not need in their second decade was an assault on that fragile stability from outside, which is exactly what the sects represented. Not surprisingly, the first reaction of the presbytery was to barricade its doors against the sects. The second reaction, paradoxically, was to leave the back doors unlatched by making membership requirements easy and attractive. What this amounted to in practice was preaching that offered a legalistic code of correct denominational behavior coupled with a tendency to go easy on the more difficult (and more necessary) business of true spiritual regeneration. Makemie had been a little guilty of this himself, but Jedidiah Andrews proved to be notorious for it. Benjamin Franklin went to hear Andrews on one occasion and quickly found that Andrews, to begin with, was not a good preacher. Furthermore, since Franklin had been "religiously educated as a Presbyterian," he immediately recognized that "his discourses were chiefly either polemic arguments or explications of the peculiar doctrines" of Presbyterianism "and were all to me very dry, uninteresting and unedifying, since not a single moral principle was inculcated or enforced, their aim seeming rather to make us Presbyterians than good citizens."[20]

Legalistic preaching, as Franklin could have told Andrews, was a poor cure for almost any problem. And in fact, the desire to have people pay "a due respect to God's ministers" backfired in Andrews's face. In 1735 Andrews took as an assistant an emigrant Scots-Irish minister named Samuel Hemphill. Hemphill turned out to be a Deist, and when Andrews moved to have him ousted by the synod, one faction in the Philadelphia church (including Franklin) heeded Andrews's injunction and paid its due respect—to Hemphill. They actually defied Andrews for some time, until Andrews was able to catch Hemphill plagiarizing heretical works in his sermons. That "at once chilled enthusiasm for him, and soon scattered his admirers."[21]

Legalism produced other crises less easy to discern. Many Scots-Irish had taken to immigrating as whole congregations, leaving their ministers to find something else in Ireland (which usually meant conforming to the state church) or else coming to America with the congregations. The situation might have worked out neatly had the congregations stayed together once they reached the New World; the ministers could simply have taken up their old duties within the community. But the congregations did not stay together, and the ministers who did come to America often found themselves with nothing to do. The synod was increasingly suspicious of the sudden abundance of unattached ministers and tried to slap an embargo on emigrant ministers by requiring subscription to the Westminster Confession before permission to preach in America was granted.

That decision sparked a division within Andrews's congregation between the Scots, who were eager to make the subscription a test of orthodoxy, and the English and Welsh, who protested on the grounds of Article XX of the Confession that "God alone is Lord of the conscience"—not the Synod of Philadelphia. "What shall we do?" wailed Andrews in a letter to Boston's Benjamin Colman, as he surveyed the prospect of trying to hold together "divers nations of different sentiments."[22] An interdenominational war would be a gift to the sects, and Andrews probably dreaded the possibility of having the tables of the Barbados storehouse turned on him.

Eventually a compromise was worked out in the Adopting Act of 1729. No foreign minister was to preach without an American call or without testifying letters from his own people; and even with these, he must candidate within the synod for half a year before synodical approval would be given. On the other hand, those who objected to subscribing to the Confession were to specifically state what they objected to, and if that was judged to be inconsequential, they would be passed. It was a convenient and careful decision, especially since the first condition virtually ensured that no foreigner would be able to apply, and the other conditions ensured that no foreigner would want to.

THE GREAT AWAKENING

One problem of ministerial discipline had been solved, but its place was taken by the old dilemma of where proper ministers were to come from.

A minister needed some type of formal education, and most Presbyterian ministers had come to America with suitable degrees from Glasgow or Edinburgh. But if under the Adopting Act preference was to be given to homegrown material, where were the colleges to send it to? Quaker antipathy to education had prevented the building of anything beyond the secondary level in Pennsylvania. To send young men back to Britain was to risk that settled Europe might prove more alluring than colonial America. In any case, the young men usually came back more foreign than American. But the only colleges in America were those established by the Congregationalists in New England (such as Harvard or Yale) or the Anglican institutions, both of which meant subjecting Presbyterian sons to anti-Presbyterian propaganda.

While Jedidiah Andrews was trying to compensate for the lack by making some fumbling arrangements with Yale College, another Presbyterian tried to fill the vacuum with an institution that came close to destroying the Presbyterianism it had been built to perpetuate. The Presbyterian in question was William Tennent, who had renounced his ordination in the Church of Ireland and with his four sons, Gilbert, William Jr., John, and Charles, joined the Scots-Irish procession to Pennsylvania in 1716. In 1718 he was ordained a Presbyterian and in 1726 settled in Neshaminy. Tennent, according to Elias Boudinot, "was well-skilled in the Latin language, . . . could speak and converse in it with as much facility as in his vernacular tongue, and . . . was proficient in the other languages."[23] Besides, good parent that he was, Tennent wanted something of the same for his sons and, seeing that there was nothing in Pennsylvania to provide it, decided to build his own. It was a simple log structure, about twenty by twenty feet. From what went on inside it was called "The Log College."[24]

Although Tennent taught his sons and several others largely from his own fund of classical and theological learning, he was also instilling into the heads of his students a warm evangelical spirit. In contrast with the polite, legalistic formalities with which Jedidiah Andrews was trying to hold together the Philadelphia church, Tennent was trying to put evangelical life back into a ministry that, since the death of Makemie, had given up trying to do anything more than observe proprieties.

Others, looking uncomfortably over their shoulders, saw in Tennent a threat to their own security and decided that something had to be done about the Log College. So in 1738 the synod acted to prevent the licensure of any preacher who did not first undergo an examination by a synodical committee "in the several branches of philosophy and divinity and languages." This was not intended to be an ordination examination. It was "a public testimonial from the Synod, which, until better provision be made, will in some measure answer the design of taking a degree."[25] All this did not mean very much, except to the Log College people, who saw it as a deliberate attempt to make things just hard enough to fail Log College graduates while persuading others that the synod did not regard a college as an immediate necessity.

The presbytery of New Brunswick in northern New Jersey, the home presbytery of Gilbert Tennent and something of a Log College enclave, protested with the thinly veiled suggestion that the synod would be better off examining the spiritual credentials of some of the men already in its pulpits. The synod apparently turned a deaf ear. So the New Brunswickers promptly defied the restriction by licensing Log College graduate John Rowland. Rowland was an excellent preacher and in every way a good minister—except that he was a Log College man. And that aroused a storm of rebuke in Philadelphia when the synod met in May 1739. The New Brunswickers maintained their position as best they could, but when it became obvious that they could not prevail against entrenched interests in the synod, they simply walked out.

The matter might have ended there and remained an incident of local proportions to be settled when hot tempers cooled off. But it actually became part of a much larger movement throughout the colonies called the Great Awakening. The Great Awakening overtook Philadelphia just in time to transform the Tennent–New Brunswick–synod skirmish into a full-scale war.

The catalyst of this transformation was a twenty-three-year-old Anglican named George Whitefield. Neither boy parsons nor

Anglicans tended to get good hearings in the eighteenth century, but Whitefield had a Samson-like power of voice that, matched with the fervent evangelical zeal of his message, set his fellow Englishmen quivering in terror of the judgment. The ready wit, the direct challenge, and the powerful preaching of Whitefield rocked even the sermon-proof cynics. They also rocked his complacent superiors in the Church of England who envied his successes, resented his reproofs, and did, in some cases, whatever they could to make things difficult for him.

Whitefield came to America in 1739. He stopped in Philadelphia in November, whereupon the city went wild over him. He preached in the churches and streets to six and eight thousand at a time and had them all wailing for their sins.[26] More important, old William Tennent paid him a visit and, by drawing a close analogy between Whitefield's difficulties within the Anglican church and the Tennents' difficulties within the Presbyterian churches, soon won the evangelist as a powerful ally. The feeling was intensified when Whitefield heard Gilbert Tennent, William's oldest son, preach in New Brunswick. "He is a son of thunder and does not fear the faces of men," Whitefield marveled approvingly.[27]

Indeed, Gilbert Tennent did not. Ordained in 1727, he had made it clear from the start that he had no compromises to make with formalism or legalism. Thomas Prince, the chronicler of the Great Awakening in New England, heard Tennent preach in Boston and recorded that

> his preaching was as searching and rousing as ever I heard. . . . He seemed to have such a lively view of the divine Majesty—of the spirituality, purity, extensiveness and strictness of the law; his glorious holiness and displeasure at sin; his justice, truth and power in punishing the damned—that the very terrors of God seemed to rise in his mind afresh when he displayed and brandished them in the eyes of unreconciled sinners.[28]

He was not being called "Hell-fire" Tennent for nothing.

Whitefield's successes in Philadelphia emboldened the Tennents. They proposed to take the offensive. Gilbert himself fired the opening salvo in "The Danger of an Unconverted Ministry," a sermon that, except for Jonathan Edwards's "Sinners in the Hands of an Angry God" (which would be preached the following year), has to be the most important sermon ever preached on the North American continent. He used it for the first, and not the last, time on March 8, 1740, and he deliberately and publicly smote the legalism of the Synod of Philadelphia hip and thigh. Pointing only an indirect finger at Jedidiah Andrews, Tennent ignored the dubious authority of the synod and appealed directly to the people to "look into the congregations of unconverted ministers and see what a sad security reigns there, not a soul convinced that can be heard of for many years together; and yet the ministers are easy, for they say they do their duty! . . . These caterpillars labour to devour every green thing" and their chief object is not to preach the new birth but to "keep the people in their interests." Gilbert's most dangerous assertion in the context of 1740 was that "natural men have no call of God to the ministerial work." So if a godly man finds himself in a church or denomination where such "natural men" hold rule, "then it is both lawful and expedient to go from them to hear godly persons."[29]

For Andrews and the synod this was unrelieved disaster, the destruction of the neat, intricate, and spiritually hollow mechanisms they had built up to get people into the church and keep them there. Tennent was telling the world that the thing that was needful in a man's life was the one thing that the church had stopped preaching, and he let the people know that if the ministers—for this read "Synod of Philadelphia"—did not mend their own fences, then the people were justified in leaving. They were even *obliged* to leave.

Reactions to Tennent's sermon were extreme. When it was printed in Boston, one writer declared that it had "sown the seeds of all that discord, intrusion, confusion, separation, hatred, variance, emulations, wrath, strife, seditions and heresies that have been springing up. . . ."[30] In Philadelphia the synod finally made up its mind to do something, and when it met on May 27, 1741, it became clear that what it intended to do was rid itself of Tennent. With Andrews as moderator and Andrews's assistant, Robert Cross, leading the attack, a protestation was entered against the New Brunswickers, and a resolution was put to exclude them from the synod. There was no trial, no examination, no debate. One quick vote, and the New Brunswick Presbytery found itself no longer welcome. Upon this they withdrew, and the synod proceeded to other business.[31]

The exclusion of the New Brunswickers was a blunder of colossal proportions. It made the past actions of the synod appear to be exactly what Tennent had claimed them to be—attempts "to prevent his father's school for training gracious men for the ministry."[32] It also drove a number of influential moderates, who were angered at the synod's highhandedness, into outright sympathy with Tennent and eventually resulted in so many secessions from the synod that the "secessionists" were able to form their own "New Side" Synod of New York in 1745. Closer to home and more insulting for Jedidiah Andrews was the indignant departure of many members of Andrews's own church. The departing members made it apparent that they took Tennent's warnings about an unconverted ministry quite seriously and rubbed it in even harder by calling Tennent to come and preach to them.

A building had been erected at Fourth and Arch Streets by Whitefield's sympathizers for Whitefield's use whenever he came to Philadelphia. With permission, the New Siders now moved into this new, spacious, and ready-made church. Since the building was due to be turned over to the new Pennsylvania Academy in 1749, they soon built their own church, Second Presbyterian, near the Delaware at Third Street.

Whatever the Synod of Philadelphia might have had in mind by way of retaliation was foiled by the influence of Whitefield, who lent his awesome prestige to Gilbert Tennent's efforts. With each of his nine visits to Philadelphia, Whitefield swept the city before him, to the great delight and benefit of the New Siders. If the reports are true, he also swept some part of New Jersey with him at the same time, since he could be heard on the Jersey side of the Delaware at Gloucester while preaching across the river (two miles away) on Society Hill.[33] With Whitefield as their spearhead, the New Siders advanced victoriously, and the "Old Side" synod could respond only by filling Philadelphia with vitriolic pamphlets against Tennent. One of these was written by John Thomson, who had been ordained by the Presbytery of Lewes in Delaware in 1717 but had drifted from church to church since then. He wrote *The Government of the Church of Christ,* which accused Tennent of bad conduct, Whitefield of lying, and the whole Awakening as being "many wicked profane reveries which are borrowed from Bilingsgate rather than from the Holy Scriptures."[34]

In the meantime, the New Siders moved to put the Log College on a more respectable and less vulnerable footing. A new college was founded under the aegis of moderate New Sider Jonathan Dickinson, who began to conduct classes in his parsonage in Elizabethtown, New Jersey, in May 1747. The Old Side made a feeble attempt to found its own academy under the distinguished classicist Francis Alison, but it made poor competition with the New Side college. Within ten years the New Side institution would be settled at Princeton as the College of New Jersey and would have the finest facilities in the American colonies. When in 1758 it called as president the great philosopher-preacher of the Awakening, Jonathan Edwards, the ultimate justification of the Tennents seemed to have arrived.

The Synod of Philadelphia still tried to wave its flag, but the waving became progressively more feeble. Jedidiah Andrews died in 1746. John Thomson disappeared into obscurity. Robert Cross took over the weakened Old Side stronghold of First Presbyterian until he in turn died in 1758, whereupon the pulpit passed to the mild-mannered and unassuming John Ewing. (Ewing also doubled as professor of mathematics at the new College of Pennsylvania and diverted himself with such projects as observing the transit of Venus from the State House yard in tandem with Captain James Cook's observations in Tahiti in 1769.)

On the other hand, William Tennent Sr. died in 1743, and most of his combative sons and students relocated in New Jersey. Jonathan Dickinson lived only five months after the first classes of the new college met in his parsonage. Whitefield remained the popular evangelist he had always been, but the enthusiasm for revival died off after 1750, and Whitefield came to Philadelphia less frequently before his death in 1770. Gilbert Tennent alone remained in Philadelphia at Second Presbyterian, and as he grew older his sermons grew less fiery and even a little dull. Gilbert Tennent died in 1764, living long enough to see the Old Side–New Side division healed. He had gone a long way toward effecting that reconciliation, especially by writing such conciliatory tracts as his *Irenicum Ecclesiasticum.*

But he could afford to. By 1758 the evangelical New Side had clearly triumphed, founding their own successful college and increasing their numbers in the ministry from twenty-two to seventy-two, while the Old Siders had lost, slipping from twenty-four to twenty-three.[35] When the Old Side and New Side synods finally rejoined in that year to form the Synod of New York and Philadelphia, the New Side had it pretty much on their own terms.

The victory of the New Side also closed a phase in Philadelphia's Presbyterian career that had begun with Makemie's ordination of Jedidiah Andrews. Then, the idea of an American church had been only a hope. The New Siders embodied American realism detached from the formalistic methods and left on Presbyterianism a mark of deep spirituality and a dedication to biblical honesty and fidelity that in turn left a profound and beneficial impression on Philadelphia and the nation for another century and a half.

CONFLICT AND REVOLUTION

Whatever the immediate casualties of the Old Side–New Side division were, the losses were quickly made up. The Presbyterians found themselves the chief beneficiary of the large-scale con-

versions that occurred in Philadelphia during the Great Awakening. But prospects of Presbyterian ascendancy were not pleasant
to the old Quaker groups or to the emerging Anglican party at
Christ Church, Second and Market Streets. Nor did Presbyterians
do anything to assuage anyone's fears, especially when Ewing
made comments about the swelling numbers of Presbyterians and
Presbyterian ministers becoming "the dominant force" in not just
Philadelphia, but all America.[36]

Denominational suspicions came to a political head in the
wake of the French and Indian War. The Quakers in the Pennsylvania Assembly, true to the Quaker peace testimony, defied the
governor and his Proprietary Party and refused to vote either
arms or men for defense. This meant that Philadelphians had to
wait only a short time—after the disastrous defeat of Braddock
in western Pennsylvania and mounting Indian attacks on conve-
niently undefended settlements—for the fur to begin to fly. In
particular, it was Presbyterian fur. In 1755 the whole Scots-Irish
frontier began to cave in. "Our country is in utmost confusion,"
wrote John Steel, who combined his ordination in the Presbyterian church with a captain's commission in the Pennsylvania
militia. "Great numbers have left (Cumberland) County, and
many are preparing to follow."[37] What enraged men like Steel
more than watching their homes go up in smoke was the knowledge that the Philadelphia Quakers had been adamant in their
refusal to defend those homes or punish those who did the burn-
ing. The Scots-Irish felt that it was part of a deliberate anti-
Presbyterian campaign. Lazarus Stewart, a Presbyterian elder,
wrote that the Assembly sitting in Philadelphia was "more solic-
itous for the welfare of the bloodthirsty Indian than for the lives
of the frontiersmen."[38]

In 1763, during Pontiac's Rebellion, the Assembly finally
made a grudging allotment, but it was enough for only 700 men
and accomplished little more than to further shorten Scots-Irish
tempers. In December tensions snapped, and a group of Scots-
Irish from Paxton ruthlessly murdered six Christian Indians at
Conestoga and then killed fourteen more at Lancaster two weeks

later. It was an indefensible act of savagery. But to the "Paxton Boys" Indians were Indians, and the memory of too many of their own dead kin crowded out the niceties of inquiring after the spiritual condition of their victims.

The Paxton affair blew the lid off the simmering mess of politics and religion in Philadelphia. Israel Pemberton, a leading Quaker, denounced the Scots-Irish as "bloodthirsty Presbyterians." Samuel Folke, a Quaker from Bucks County, accused the Presbyterians of being "tainted with the same bloody principles as the Indians" and "disaffection to the government."[39] "Presbyterianism and Rebellion are twin sisters sprung from faction, and their affection for each other has been so strong that a separation of them could never be effected," declared one pamphleteer.[40] The Presbyterians replied by accusing the Quakers of deliberately encouraging the Indians to kill Presbyterian settlers.

> Pray, worthy Friends, observe the text,
> Get money first, and virtue next . . .
> Go on, good Christians, never spare
> To give your Indians clothes to wear,
> Good name, good beef, pork and bread,
> Guns, powder, flints, and store of lead
> To shoot your neighbors through the head.[41]

Meanwhile, the dissatisfied Paxton Boys marched on Philadelphia, determined to right all wrongs and, in particular, demand equal representation for the frontier counties in the Assembly. Some 250 of them reached Germantown but were turned back by a delegation headed by Benjamin Franklin, after leaving two of their number to present a petition of grievances. The real battle started in the press and pamphlets. In *The Paxton Boys: A Farce,* city Presbyterians were lampooned by showing them closing up their churches on the Sunday the Paxton Boys were marching in order to go out and supply them with arms and ammunition. The Presbyterians replied that for all they saw the Paxton Boys were "brave, loyal and discreet"; the Quakers, on the contrary, "often spent their time in debating, whilst our poor frontier inhabitants have been suffering."[42]

The whole controversy gradually degenerated into a mudslinging free-for-all. *The Quaker Vindicated* was answered by *The Quaker Unmasked,* which was replied to by *The Author of the Quaker Unmasked Stripped Naked* or *The Delineated Presbyterian Played Hob With,* which was followed by *Cloathes for a Stark Naked Author.*

The dispute might have burned itself out on that level had not Franklin and the Assemblymen proposed that the only way Pennsylvania could be restored to order was by its being made a Royal colony. Franklin was no friend to the Presbyterians, and as a Deist he was thoroughly frightened at the expanding influence of Presbyterianism in Pennsylvania. He thought the introduction of direct Crown rule would get the establishment of the Church of England in Pennsylvania and with it an Anglican bishop to keep the Presbyterians down.

Threat of an established church was enough to send shivers up and down the collective spine of colonial Presbyterians, as Franklin undoubtedly knew. Most Presbyterians had fled Britain or been taken from there by their parents to avoid the restrictions and disabilities laid on their backs by an established church, and the freedom they enjoyed in Pennsylvania only made them more determined than ever to resist Anglican encroachments. What Franklin underestimated was the amount of unity that determination could summon.

Franklin pushed the issue to a vote by standing for election to the Assembly in 1764, along with a sizable block of anti-Proprietary candidates. That election amazed observers for the sheer numbers that turned out to vote, and at least one foreign observer thought that it was made that way by Presbyterians who "turned their pulpits into ecclesiastical drums for politics and told their people to vote according as they directed them at the peril of their damnation."[43] Gilbert Tennent, Francis Alison, and John Ewing, in a surprising show of unanimity, jumped into the fray by circulating a letter during the adjournment of the Assembly, affirming that the Presbyterians here, upon mature deliberation, are of the opinion that it is not safe to do things of such importance rashly. Our privileges by these means (i.e., making Pennsylvania a Royal colony) may be greatly abridged but never will be enlarged. . . . The affair is in all probability a trap laid to ensnare the unwary and then to cast an odium on the Presbyterians for ruining or attempting to ruin the province.[44]

Tennent, Alison, and Ewing exhorted sympathetic readers "to lose no time in advising all under your influence" to oppose Franklin's move and Franklin's election to the Assembly. In the fall, the election was lost by Franklin and the anti-Proprietary party, and when Franklin tried to circumvent the Assembly by presenting a petition for transfer of the government to the Crown in London the next February, he got nowhere. Pennsylvania had been made safe for Presbyterianism.

But the threat of establishment continued to haunt the Presbyterians, and it was hardly a case of seeing ghosts for bedsheets. In the eyes of many Americans, Anglican tactics were all part of the increasing pressure that England under George III was bringing to bear to curb the broad liberties that Americans had enjoyed for almost a century.

In Philadelphia the great trumpeter of resistance, especially Presbyterian resistance to these "plans of power," was George Duffield. He demonstrated his pugnacity the first Sunday he preached in Philadelphia.

Duffield had been in Philadelphia in 1764 and, as a pronounced New Sider, had been invited to succeed Gilbert Tennent at Second Presbyterian after Tennent's death late that year. Duffield declined. Instead, he did missionary work and visitation on the frontier. But in 1771 another call came from Philadelphia, this time from a new congregation meeting on Pine Street, and Duffield accepted it. The new congregation was a branch church of First Presbyterian built "for the sake of peace and harmony."[45] Officially, the new church was for those who found First Presbyterian's quarters too cramped on Sundays and for those who lived in Southwark who found the distance to Market Street too great to travel on foot in foul weather. But in truth it was an attempt to hold together unreconciled New Side and Old Side factions by giving each its own meetinghouse. The compromise eventually broke down, and the Pine Street branch, which was mostly moderate New Side in sympathy, issued a unilateral call to Duffield as pastor and began to advertise itself as the Third Presbyterian congregation in the city. First Church tried to have an injunction placed on the Pine Streeters, on the grounds that the Pine Street meetinghouse was the legal property of First Church.

To Duffield the smell of combat was a sweet savor, especially when it came to championing evangelical causes. When he showed up in Philadelphia ready to preach, First Church's elders locked the doors of the Pine Street meetinghouse to keep him and the Pine Streeters out. But they neglected to bar the windows, and some enterprising Pine Street men climbed in, hauled Duffield through a window, unlocked the doors, and let the faithful in. A good number there were, too, to the embarrassment of First Church—so many, in fact, that when First Church learned that Duffield intended to preach again that day, the leaders frantically appealed to the city magistrates to do something. The magistrates responded by deputizing an Old Side nonentity named Jimmy Bryant. Bryant strode into the packed Pine Street meetinghouse and, since Duffield had already started preaching, hit on the not-very-bright idea of interrupting Duffield by reading the Riot Act. He had gotten through a few sentences when Robert Knox, one of the prime movers of the Pine Street congregation, rose up, seized Bryant by the scruff of the neck, and deposited him none too gently on the paving stones outside. "Take that and begone!" roared Knox grandiloquently. "And disturb us no more."[46]

First Church gave up its claims very reluctantly, however, and it was not until after the Revolution that they were finally persuaded to accept a cash settlement. But even before that, whether First Church liked it or not, the Pine Street congregation was functioning with the full approbation of the synod as the Third Presbyterian Church.

Duffield lived up to this colorful beginning by becoming one of the most popular ministers in the city. From 1775 to 1790 he baptized 1,340 persons, an average of 90 a year, and from 1785 to 1790 married 728 couples—160 couples a year.[47] He made himself even more popular by his vivid denunciations of British episcopacy and British tyranny.

In 1774, when the First Continental Congress met in Philadelphia, John Adams attended Duffield's preaching. "I have been this morning to hear Mr. Duffield," Adams wrote home to Abigail, "a preacher in this city whose principles, prayer and sermons more nearly resemble those of our New England clergy than any I have heard."[48] Whether Adams was speaking as one of the sons of the Puritans or as one of the sons of liberty is not certain. Duffield would have fit the bill in either case.

When the war for independence came, the Presbyterians rallied to the patriot cause almost as a body. In their eyes, said Carl Bridenbaugh, "no distinction between religious and civil liberties any longer existed; liberty itself faced extinction, and they rushed to its defense."[49] Whether taxes or bishops, the Presbyterians wanted no more of British rule. The British also noted how eagerly the Presbyterians rushed to revolution. Joseph Galloway, the Philadelphia Tory chieftain, wrote that the insurrection was led by "Congregationalists, Presbyterians and Smugglers." A Hessian captain who fought in Pennsylvania denounced the whole war as "nothing more or less than an Irish-Scotch Presbyterian rebellion."[50] The Quaker historian, Isaac Sharpless, later sighed that "the revolution was three-fourths at least a Presbyterian movement."[51]

The Presbyterians in Philadelphia did their best to justify those judgments. The Philadelphia patriot leaders—such as Thomas McKean, James Wilson, and Benjamin Rush (all signers of the Declaration of Independence), and Charles Thomson (secretary of the Continental Congress)—were largely Presbyterians or Presbyterian-educated. And laymen were not alone in their zeal. When the synod met in May 1775, a "pastoral letter" was drawn up, hailing the Congress as "delegates chosen in the most free and unbiased manner, by the body of the people." Not only was the Congress to be respected and encouraged, but "let your prayers be offered up to God for his direction in their proceedings" and "adhere firmly to their resolutions."[52] Disgusted, one Tory wrote, "I do not know one Presbyterian minister, nor have I been able after strict inquiry to hear of any who did not by preaching and every effort in their power promote all the measures of the Continental Congress, however extravagant."[53] Worse still for Tory peace of mind, the president of the College of New Jersey, John Witherspoon, was actually sitting in the Congress as representative for his state.

The individual congregations in Philadelphia had their part to play. From Third Presbyterian Church, Robert Knox, muzzler of the hapless Bryant, became the major of Philadelphia's first militia regiment. William Shippen, who taught medicine at the College of Pennsylvania, was appointed director-general of all hospitals in 1777. William Hurrie rang the state house bell (now the Liberty Bell) for the adoption of the Declaration of Independence on July 8, 1776. In addition to five colonels, three captains, and other assorted officers, Third Church contributed George Duffield.

Four months before the Declaration of Independence was adopted, Duffield had been at work prodding the delegates toward severing ties with England.

> Can it be supposed that that God, who made man free and engraved in indefaceable characters the love of liberty in his mind, should forbid freedom, already exiled from Asia and Africa, and under sentence of banishment from Europe—that He should forbid her to erect her banners here and constrain her to abandon the earth? As soon shall He subject creation and forbid the sun to shine. . . . When that day shall come—if ever come—then, and not till then, shall she fall also, slain with them that go down to the pit.[54]

Not surprisingly, four days after the Declaration was adopted Duffield was commissioned as a chaplain in the Pennsylvania militia and went off to the war. He witnessed many major battles and had some narrow escapes—made all the more frightful by the fact that the British, fully realizing how valuable Duffield was to the morale of the patriots, had put a price on his head. By ingenious hooks and crooks he eluded capture and stayed with the armies throughout the war.

At war's end Duffield and many of the other Philadelphia Presbyterians returned to the city to find that the British, who had occupied the patriot capital during the winter of 1777–78, had singled out Presbyterian churches as object lessons of the king's displeasure. Pews had been ripped out for firewood. Sanctuaries had been used as hospitals. In one case, as a particular mark of British affection, a church had been used as a stable. More than a hundred Hessian soldiers who had died of disease or wounds had been dumped into the graveyard of Third Presbyterian.

But with the war over, Americans in general (and Philadelphians especially) had energy to spare, and much of it went into rebuilding the churches. In 1794 First Church tore down its old, much-repaired building and erected an imposing new church with a broad porch and four massive Corinthian columns fronting Market Street. Second Church was already remarkable for the prodigious steeple that jutted up over the quaint roof-rows of Arch Street. Duffield's Third Church was a plain, two-story structure, surrounded on three sides by its graveyard and facing the fourth side onto Pine Street. Duffield had his pulpit redecorated. It stood along the west wall crowned with a crimson velvet cushion and hangings and overtopped by a great sounding board. After his death in 1790, the church underwent a massive rebuilding program. The church was raised bodily, a basement was installed, and a new entrance was added facing Pine Street.

TENTH PRESBYTERIAN

Apart from congregational worship, the visibility of the churches was limited. But in time new ideas for furthering their public influence were put forward, especially by Archibald Alexander, who pastored Third Church from 1806 to 1812. Alexander organized a proto-Sunday school for neighborhood children and held regular catechism sessions for the children of the church. One student spoke of Alexander's sessions long afterward:

> We assembled on Saturday afternoon in the main aisle of the church. Our seats were the baize-covered benches used by communicants when sitting at the Lord's table. The aisle was paved with bricks. . . . A large tin-plate stove in the main aisle was the only heater. Near it the pastor took his seat and put the class through the Shorter Catechism. The older children were required to bring written proofs of certain points assigned.[55]

Alexander was a brilliant and mercurial scholar and a successful pastor. In his six-year tenure at Third Church, he baptized 306 persons and received nearly 140 into communion. He left 353 members on the rolls when he resigned to take up duties as the first professor at Princeton Theological Seminary.[56]

On May 29, 1788, in First Presbyterian Church, the Synod of New York and Philadelphia finally broke the last ties with its colonial and Old World past by revising chapters XX and XXIII of the Westminster Confession (taking away the powers granted by those articles to governments for restricting freedom of religion) and reorganizing the synod as the "General Assembly of the Presbyterian Church in the United States of America."[57]

The cocoon of the European past that Francis Makemie had set about to pry open was shed at last, and nothing could have been more significant than the timing. Only three weeks before the first official meeting of the General Assembly at Second Presbyterian, George Washington had been inaugurated as the first President of the new Federal Union. A fully American perspective had arrived in the churches and states, and the Presbyterians—177 ministers, 111 probationers, 431 churches, and some 20,000 members—were already beginning to look westward.[58]

In their own way, so were the Presbyterians of Philadelphia. In 1770 there had been between 25,000 and 30,000 people in Philadelphia, with three Anglican and three Presbyterian churches and a scattering of Baptists, Moravians, Methodists, Lutherans,

German Reformed, Quakers, and Roman Catholics. By 1810, there were almost 89,000 Philadelphians, and as the city's population multiplied, so did the churches. A Fourth Presbyterian Church was organized in June 1799, in a rented house at Third and Lombard Streets. It quickly grew large enough to require the services of a regular pastor and, in 1802, a new building.[59] Arch Street (Fifth) Presbyterian opened on June 7, 1823, after having occupied a "somewhat dilapidated chapel on Locust Street." A Congregational Tabernacle at Fourth and Chestnut Streets came over to the presbytery to form the Seventh Presbyterian Church (a short-lived Sixth Church had been started by a secessionist group from Third Presbyterian, but it eventually merged with Seventh Church in the 1800s).[60] The union of the local synod of the Associate Reformed Presbyterian Church (a small denomination that traced its origins to a division within the Scottish Kirk in 1773) with the Philadelphia Presbytery gave the presbytery two additional churches: Scots Presbyterian (the eighth) and a smaller church at Thirteenth and Market Streets, then on the outskirts of the city. It became the Ninth Presbyterian Church.

But even this enlarged spread of churches could scarcely keep pace with the growth of Philadelphia's population. By 1827, Philadelphia boasted 31,000 buildings and 133,000 inhabitants with, besides the Presbyterian churches, thirteen Episcopal, eight Baptist, and fourteen Methodist churches, accompanied by others representing virtually every denomination then known. The pace of growth showed no signs of slacking.

Accordingly, Furman Leaming, a Presbyterian layman and city hardware dealer, proposed that still another Presbyterian church be built, at Twelfth and Walnut Streets. On March 16, 1828, Leaming was joined by John Stille, Solomon Allen, George Ralston, James Kerr, and William Brown in the session room of Sixth Presbyterian to organize the church that Leaming envisioned.[61] On July 13, 1828, the cornerstone of the new building was laid, and early in December 1829, the doors were opened for services at what was to be known in Philadelphia as Tenth.

THE FIRST THREE "B's"

Allen C. Guelzo

In 1838 the Presbyterian churches in America were wrenched by a denominational schism. The issue at stake was acutely similar to the issue that had split Presbyterians almost a century before. Once again, revivalism was the matter over which men raged, and once again the denomination was torn apart by revivalism's partisans and enemies.

But the revivalism that had split Old Lights and New Lights, the revivalism of George Whitefield, Gilbert Tennent, and Jonathan Edwards, was a far cry from what passed for revivalism in the early nineteenth century. In Kentucky, Presbyterians such as James McGready and Barton Stone presided over tumultuous camp meetings full of "bodily agitations or exercises" such as "the jerks" and "dancing," "barking," "laughing," and "running" exercises.[1] In upstate New York the arch-druid of revivalism, Charles Grandison Finney, was violently denouncing Calvinistic theology, assuring his hearers that if they did not will themselves into salvation, then neither man nor God could save them. Ironically, Finney had been ordained a Presbyterian. But as he afterward confessed, he had at the time of his ordination never yet read the Westminster Confession of Faith.[2] By the time he did read it, he was successful enough to ignore it—and ignore it he did.

With civil war raging in Zion, the founding of each new Presbyterian church became a contest to see to which side the congregation could be won over: "New School," as Finney and his cohorts became known, or "Old School," as his horrified opponents were called. Thus, when the new Tenth Presbyterian Church opened its doors at the northeast corner of Twelfth and Walnut Streets on December 13, 1829, the waters of controversy promptly began to wash around it. To begin with, the cornerstone-laying ceremonies were handled by the august Old School preacher, Ashbel Green, who had spent the greater part of his life hunting down fugitives from Reformed orthodoxy. He had cleaned the Deists out of the College of New Jersey (now known as Princeton) in the early years of the century, and he had very nearly toppled the New School pastor of Philadelphia's First Presbyterian Church, Albert Barnes. If Green had anything to say about it, Tenth Presbyterian would be an Old School foundation.

It is tempting to suppose that it was Green's fertile brain that supplied the Old Schoolish message sealed up in a bottle and placed behind the cornerstone for the edification of posterity:

> The house of which this is the corner-stone is ever to be considered as dedicated to the worship of the one only living and true God, Father, Son and Holy Ghost. In it no doctrine ought ever to be taught, no worship ever attempted not consistent with a belief of the unity and personality of the Godhead, the natural and deep depravity of man, the atonement and intercession of the Lord Jesus Christ, the indispensable necessity of the renewing and sanctifying influences of the Holy Spirit in life, sincere obedience to all the commands of God, and a future state of endless rewards and punishments.[3]

To what must have been Green's mighty mortification, the first pastor to be called to Tenth Church was Thomas A. McAuley,

like Finney a New Yorker and like Finney a New School Presbyterian. He had been professor of mathematics and natural philosophy at Union College, New York, for eight years before being
licensed to preach in 1822 by the presbytery of Albany (another
upstate New York revivalist group). After that, he had settled in
New York City as pastor of the Rutgers Street Church. He was
officially installed in the pastorate of Tenth Presbyterian on
December 17, 1829, and six months later got himself elected president of the Presbyterian Board of Education.[4] What was more,
McAuley successfully engineered the attachment of Tenth Church
to the Second Presbytery of Philadelphia, a New School presbytery that for the sake of peace the Synod of Philadelphia had
allowed the New Schoolers to organize.

Nevertheless, McAuley stayed at Tenth Presbyterian for only
four years, and the reasons for his departure are ambiguous. Perhaps he encountered too much pressure from outside the church.
Perhaps he sensed mounting opposition within the church. Perhaps his interests were wandering back to New York City, to which
he shortly returned to become founder and president of the New
School institution known as Union Theological Seminary.

In any case, the pulpit was open for likely candidates
throughout 1833. This time the balance swung back to Old School
men, and on November 8, 1833, a youthful graduate of Princeton Seminary (which in that time was synonymous with Old
School theology) named Henry Augustus Boardman was installed
as pastor. For forty-three years, Boardman would occupy the pulpit of Tenth Presbyterian, stabilizing it in the midst of denominational controversy and solidifying its allegiance to Reformed
theology. He would make it (and himself) a city institution.

HENRY AUGUSTUS BOARDMAN

The Tenth Church that Boardman inherited was not an over-
whelmingly impressive sight, even though the city's leading architect, William Strickland, had been engaged to design it. Strick-

land was in the midst of creating his best-known architectural works—the Second Bank building on Chestnut Street and the graceful Merchants Exchange at Third and Dock Streets—but he apparently employed none of his genius on churches, and the result was an exceedingly plain-looking Tenth Presbyterian. Outside, the walls were blunt and undecorated, featuring the same monotonous Corinthian porch and pillars that almost every other Presbyterian church in Philadelphia possessed. Inside, the pews were arranged in two blocks, divided by a single main aisle, while the pulpit, standing at the head of the aisle, was only a simple lectern on a platform mounted by two sets of steps on either side.

On the other hand, the church at least had the advantage of location. In the decade before the building of Tenth Church, Philadelphia had been a city of merchants, grocers, and clerks, and as Joseph Watson remembered, "the smart quarter of the city was in the vicinity of Third and Spruce Streets." By 1830, and still more by 1840, Philadelphia was ceasing to be a city of small shopkeepers, and the influx of immigrant labor into Southwark was driving "the smart quarter" farther westward.[5] As a result, in the same year that Tenth Church was opened, the University of Pennsylvania moved from its old quarters at Fourth and Arch to a solid, dull-looking College Hall on the corner of Ninth and Chestnut—only a corner and three blocks away from Tenth. The Academy of Fine Arts was located even closer (at 1029 Chestnut Street), and in 1833, the year Boardman was installed, the Second United States Mint was built within a quick walk's distance (at Chestnut and Juniper). The "New Circus" at Ninth and Walnut was transformed into the famous Walnut Street Theater in the 1820s, and behind it the Herkness Bazaar opened in 1847 to house a cyclorama of the city of Jerusalem.[6]

More important were the long lines of fine brownstone row houses expanding westward around the church. They were the residences of the wealthy and newly wealthy who would provide the bulk of Tenth's congregation. No church directories of Tenth Church survive from this period, but since the church was located in what was fast becoming the most highly assessed ward in the city, it is hard to doubt that Tenth had an increasingly prosperous and well-to-do congregation.

Whatever the church lacked in aesthetic appeal was more than made up for in the person of Boardman. Born at Troy, New York, on January 9, 1808, Boardman graduated from Yale College in 1829 and passed under the tutelage of Old School Presbyterianism at Princeton Seminary. He emerged from that tutelage, degree in hand, in 1833, just in time to step into the vacated pulpit of Tenth Church.[7] Oddly enough, he had previously resolved, "even should the opportunity present itself, not to go from the seminary to a large city." He preferred "a rural congregation," where he could learn the practical duties of the ministry far from the hothouse atmosphere of urban congregations.

In July, Boardman was prevailed upon to supply Tenth's empty pulpit, and with some misgivings he did so, preaching from Luke 6:45–46 ("A good man out of the good treasure of his heart bringeth forth that which is good; and an evil man out of the evil treasure of his heart bringeth forth that which is evil: for of the abundance of the heart his mouth speaketh. And why call ye me, Lord, Lord, and do not the things which I say?") and Isaiah 1:2–3 ("The vision of Isaiah the son of Amoz. . . . Hear, O heavens, and give ear, O earth: for the LORD hath spoken, I have nourished and brought up children, and they have rebelled against me.").[8] By the time he was finished, the only one in Tenth Presbyterian who had any doubts about what Boardman should do with his life was Boardman himself.

In August, a personage no less impressive than Ashbel Green implored Boardman to take up the ministry of Tenth Church and, incidentally, restore the church to the Old School fold. The session also invited Boardman to return, which he did, preaching there on August 18, 1833. Two weeks later, the entire church invited him to become their pastor. Boardman's reluctance crumbled piece by piece. "We are all led in paths which we knew not," he said twenty-five years later. "In the end, I did the only thing which I had made up my mind, in respect to a settlement, I would not do." After talking with his professors at Princeton (who "with one voice . . . said I ought to accept the call"), Boardman relented and was finally "satisfied that the pillar of cloud had moved in this direction and that there was neither peace nor safety except in following it."[9]

Not that all the qualms in Boardman's stomach were thereby stilled. There remained the unsettling business of Tenth's attachment to the New School Second Presbytery. That business was made even more unsettling when on the eve of his ordination and installation the Synod of Philadelphia finally lost its patience with the New Schoolers and ordered the Second Presbytery dissolved. Since this drastic action could not be made final until the General Assembly met the following May, the New Schoolers held onto a brief stay of execution. But that left Boardman in the unhappy predicament of having to seek ordination at the hands of a presbytery that was virtually an outlaw organization; nor could he wait until the following May to see where the chips would fall, since his ordination and installation had been set for November 8, 1833.

Once again, he began to question whether he ought to join a presbytery under such suspicion and when he had such little sympathy with its tenets. "Unquestionably," wrote Boardman, "it was a contest which involved both the purity of our faith and the integrity of our ecclesiastical polity. Two incompatible systems of doctrine and two no less irreconcilable theories of ecclesiastical authority and policy" were at stake. In Boardman's mind, there was no hope of compromise "between those whose training had made them decided and earnest Presbyterians and others who had adopted our standards in a loose and general way." Nor was it, he observed, "a mere war of words. It took hold upon the central truths of the Gospel, such as original sin, the atonement, regeneration and justification."[10] Nevertheless, Boardman decided to go ahead with the ordination, a move that was to set a precedent for later pastors of Tenth Church who found themselves with similarly difficult choices. In time, his decision proved wise. Boardman was able to sever Tenth's connections with the New School Presbytery, and in 1837 the General Assembly

removed the thorn of New School Presbyterianism from Boardman's side by moving to lop all New School presbyteries off its
rolls. Not until 1869 were Old School and New School Presbyterians reunited.

For the time being, the new pastor was content to preach a
series of carefully written sermons, one design of which was to
discuss the erroneous sentiments of the late New School Presbytery. Otherwise, Boardman threw himself into the work of the
church with youthful vigor. In 1833, Tenth counted some 292
members. Over the period of the next quarter century, 1,068 new
members passed through the church, so that by 1858 Boardman
could look out over a congregation of about 450 members and
numerous other visitors.

Boardman himself grew both in fame and in personal attachment to his flock. One appraisal ran: "Evangelical and elevated
in his thoughts and pure, simple and direct in his style, he
charmed while instructing his people and bound them to himself by the ties of a reverential love."[11] Even when in 1868 illness
prostrated him and forced a lengthy vacation, he could not for-
bear expressing his deep feeling toward the people:

> That I feel most deeply this long suspension of my labors and this
> protracted separation from my church, you will readily believe. The
> greatest of all privileges is the privilege of preaching the gospel. If
> there can be anything to enhance it, it is to be allowed to preach
> the gospel in the same pulpit and to the same people for a lifetime.[12]

There were other marks of the bonds that grew between pastor and people. In his first twenty-five years at Tenth, Boardman
was called to baptize 598 children and 105 adults. He performed
222 weddings. He made, on his own initiative and by his own
estimate, some 10,000 pastoral visits ranging from 300 to 500 a
year.[13] In 1847 the strain of these activities broke his health, and
the doctors decreed a year in Europe for recuperation. Accordingly, Boardman offered to resign. Not only was his offer declined,

but by a unanimous vote the church "made generous provision for the supply of the pulpit during his absence."[14]

That generosity enabled Boardman to spread his influence throughout Philadelphia society, especially when he moved in the early 1840s to begin putting his sermons and lectures into print. Boardman had a fascination with controversy, and his subsequent writing career gave him opportunity to air his opinions on what he considered to be the ills of America. One of his early volumes, *The Bible in the Family or Hints on Domestic Happiness* (1851), was full of oracular utterances and selected fulminations against the pope, the socialist Robert Dale Owen, and Men's Clubs.

He had something more substantial to say two years later in *The Bible in the Counting House: A Course of Lectures, to Merchants* (1853). Sensing the disappearance of the old small-scale economic order in Philadelphia before the juggernaut of industrialization, Boardman reminded the new class of industrial entrepreneurs that a merchant "is all the while dealing with questions not merely of loss and gain but of right and wrong" and that "the equipment he needs, the only equipment which will at all meet the exigencies of his position, is true religion."

> The chart he requires, the only chart which defines with accuracy the reefs and quicksands, the treacherous shoals and vagrant currents of the sea which he is traversing, is the word of God. The Bible in the Counting House—this is the only specific which will at all meet the moral necessities of the business world.[15]

Boardman, however, was not so fatuous as to believe that the big new Philadelphia merchants would merely on his urging be transformed into models of true piety. He bleakly sized up the business dealings of Philadelphia, saying, "Where war has slain its thousands, commerce has slain its ten thousands. It strikes not at the body, although this sometimes falls, but at the soul." At one point he shrilly denounced the practitioners of "criminal avarice":

Ye ruthless devotees of Mammon! Drive on your eager traffic. Roll up your ample profits. Rejoice in your expanding business. Array your households in purple and fine linen. And revel in the congratulations of a sycophantic world. But there is a curse in your prosperity. Your gains are the price of blood.[16]

Yet Boardman had no radical designs on the Philadelphia body economic. "Let the entire property of Philadelphia be thrown into a common stock and divided *pro rata* among its population, not a hammer would be heard in the shipyards. . . . The silence of death would replace the intolerable but productive clatter of the foundries and machine shops" and "our noble array of religious and charitable associations would be shorn of their efficiency, if not annihilated."[17] Instead, he offered the model of the ideal Christian merchant:

It will be his pleasure to help forward every prudent scheme which promises to contribute to the general welfare. He will be ready to assist with his advice . . . firms of tried character which need succour. He will have his eye upon young men of real merit and at the proper time put them in the way of doing something for themselves. . . . Remembering his stewardship, he cares not to augment his ample estate. No dollar of interest with him ever petrifies into principal. His entire income, after deducting personal and household expenses, goes to promote the happiness of his fellow creatures and the prosperity of religion.[18]

In all fairness, Philadelphia Presbyterianism did manage to produce men who conformed to Boardman's rosy portrait, such as John Wanamaker. But for the most part, such characters populated the novels of Horatio Alger more frequently than the streets of Philadelphia. If Boardman had hoped to inaugurate a crusade to soften the hard grip of industrialization, he did not get many volunteers, and *The Bible in the Counting House* stands as a lonely symbol of the unease so many evangelicals felt at the coming of the business age.

Boardman was more successful when he turned to volatile subjects. In the 1840s he denounced the ritualist party in the Protestant Episcopal Church for subverting what had heretofore been respectably evangelical. Not that Boardman was terribly exercised over the Episcopalians per se. What he resented was the High Church insistence that, apart from Catholic and Anglican ordinations, there "was no church, no ministry, no valid ordinances." That automatically branded all Presbyterian ministers as "unauthorized intruders into the sacred office, and their churches . . . schismatical organizations."[19] Therefore, Boardman took up his literary cudgels against the Episcopalian ritualists for the same reason he had taken them up against the New Schoolers: to preserve the purity and justify the existence of Presbyterianism.

In another campaign, Boardman very nearly took up literal cudgels, for he chose to march with the temperance armies in America's war with "demon rum." Boardman reserved his most scorching contempt for the saloon:

> Our locomotives and steamboats have acquired some distinction as slaughtering-machines, but they are inert and tame when compared with the grog-shop. The cholera and yellow-fever burst forth at times and shroud the land in mourning, but where these slay their thousands, strong drink slays its tens of thousands. . . . There are probably states in the confederacy where, if all the victims intemperance has slain since the American Revolution could be brought together, the representatives who live furthest off could walk every step of the way from the Capitol to their homes upon their dead bodies.[20]

The one crusade in which Boardman did manage to come out on the winning side was the irrepressible conflict over slavery, but he betrayed an unhappy ambivalence. Boardman was no friend to slavery. He said so from his pulpit: "I have never set myself to defend it, and by the grace of God I never will." Slavery was "a colossal evil." But Boardman was no abolitionist either. He denounced antislavery agitators as fervently as proslavery agitators—perhaps because so many of the antislavery agitators were New School men, but more likely because he prized the Union more than the antislavery cause. When the Fugitive Slave Law was enacted in 1850, providing for the capture and reenslavement of blacks who had escaped to freedom in the North, Charles Grandison Finney had openly advocated resistance, but Boardman counseled submission lest agitation "bring about a disruption." "We have," he averred, "no more right to dictate to South Carolina what she shall do with her slaves than she has to prescribe to Pennsylvania what railroads we shall construct or what banks we shall charter."[21]

Still, when the Civil War came in 1861, Boardman along with many other hesitant Old Schoolers, such as Charles Hodge, cast hesitancy away and indicted the South for its duplicity. Nevertheless, Boardman's accusing finger was leveled not at Southern slaveholding, but at Southern disunionism:

> And now that the treachery is laid open and they see that all the while the one cherished object of these men was to destroy the Union, they have the double mixture of personal wrong and public duty to inflame their zeal on behalf of the cause of their country.[22]

Boardman's zeal was sufficiently inflamed that he went to work as a member of the executive committee in Philadelphia for the United States Sanitary Commission, a nineteenth-century combination of Red Cross and USO for Union soldiers flowing to and from the war.

In the end Boardman was at his best as an expositor of Scripture, for he emerged as a clear and lofty exponent of the best Old School Reformed orthodoxy. Fundamental to all Boardman's preaching was his unswerving allegiance to an authoritative and inerrant Bible. "Shut up your Bible, and what do you know of that world?" he asked imperiously.

> What do you know of God, of yourself, of retribution, of the possibility of forgiveness? You have a witness within your bosom

which tells you that you are a sinner. But what does conscience, reason or the light of nature reveal concerning the pardon of sin and future happiness? Nothing, literally nothing. The insatiate craving of the soul for information on this vital question is met only by guesses and conjectures, baseless, illusive, without authority and, therefore, without consolation.[23]

Boardman was equally emphatic (and dramatic) about other Reformed doctrines. He defined the providence of God in the most unequivocal terms:

> He governs brutes, and he governs men. He governs individuals, and he governs nations. He governs angels, and he governs devils. His supremacy extends to every mote that floats in the sunbeam, to every tiny globule that sparkles in the foam of the sea, to every transient emotion that flits across the breast of man or angel. Nothing exists but by his ordination. Nothing happens but as he bids or permits it to happen. The same hand which upholds the universe and keeps the stars in their courses guides the falling sparrow.[24]

He considered election to be "one of the fundamental and most precious truths of Scripture, that the providential government of God comprehends all creatures and all events."

> From the loftiest archangel before the throne to the invisible animalcule in a drop of water, from the extinction of a sphere to the fall of a sparrow, no creature but owns his sovereignty. . . . There are no greater crimes recorded in the history of the race than the sin of our first parents and the betrayal and crucifixion of our Lord. And no one who acknowledges the God of the Bible at all will deny that the introduction of moral evil into the world and the providing of a remedy for it were comprehended in the divine plan and controlled by his all-wise purposes.[25]

Little wonder, considering the authority and vigor in which Boardman clothed these doctrines, that the plain-looking church at Twelfth and Walnut began to run out of seating for the multitudes that trooped in on a Sunday.

SEVENTEENTH AND SPRUCE

As early as the 1840s, Boardman was tinkering with the idea of expanding the church by planting a colony farther westward in the city. Before his health gave way in 1847, he had considered planting a church near Logan Square (now, thanks to the Benjamin Franklin Parkway, Logan Circle). But that fell through when his health collapsed. Boardman kept at it, though, constantly dropping hints from the pulpit and making discreet recommendations. By 1852, he had Tenth ready to give its assent to the task of establishing a new church on a lot at the corner of Seventeenth and Spruce Streets, eventually to be known as the West Spruce Street Presbyterian Church.

On January 20, 1852, Boardman invited several gentlemen belonging to the congregation to his house, where together they hatched plans for the founding of the new church. "Without such a church," the inaugurators of this plan wrote, "we could not maintain our proper relative position among the evangelical denominations of the city." The committee formed for planting the new church included James B. Ross, Singleton A. Mercer, Morris Patterson, James Murphy, Thomas Hoge, and James Imbrie. Animated by "a sense of divine goodness—a desire to give some permanent and public expression of gratitude for signal benefits received" at Tenth Presbyterian,[26] they confidently moved ahead and in June 1852 secured a lot "one hundred and fourteen by two hundred and twelve feet at the southwest corner of Schuylkill Sixth (Seventeenth) and Spruce Streets." They began to raise money for construction by subscription among the Tenth Church congregation.

From that point, everything promptly went wrong or threatened to. The subscriptions raised only $27,500, about half of what was needed to begin building, while the help of other Presbyterian churches, which the committee had heavily counted on, proved nonexistent. Moreover, in May 1853, the General Assembly voted Boardman into the vacant professorship of theology at Princeton, an action that the committee well knew would not only torpedo the new church but punch a sizable hole in Tenth as well. It had been planned by the committee that Boardman should spread his prestige around by exchanging pulpits between Tenth and its new colony on alternate Sundays. Both churches would be separate in all other respects—separate eldership, deacons, trustees, and even a separate pastor—but Boardman would be available to preach in both pulpits, presumably packing the aisles of both churches. Take Boardman away, and the best hopes for the success of the new church would disappear.

On June 7, 1853, the congregation met and adopted seven resolutions spelling out in the strongest terms why they believed it wrong to remove Boardman from his place in the life not only of Tenth Church but also of the city of Philadelphia. On the next day a letter was addressed to Boardman by 115 of the city's business and social leaders, stating that "your departure from Philadelphia would be a loss not easily repaired to the public Christianity of a great commercial metropolis."[27] It included such signatories as Thomas Biddle, George and John Cadwalader, Joshua Lippincott, and Russell Thayer. The church also dispatched a protest to the Assembly, claiming quite candidly that Boardman's removal "will entirely undo what has already been done, and in fact extinguish that important prospective church."[28] Mercifully, Boardman himself cut the knot by declining the professorship, and the day was saved. Boardman even managed to obtain a consolation prize: election to moderator of the General Assembly (Old Synod).

In 1854 financial disaster rocked Philadelphia, a presage of the Panic of 1857. Faced with an "extraordinary scarcity of money, coupled with extravagant prices for every kind of labor and building materials," the fund-raising campaign ground to a halt. Not until 1855 was it possible even to lay the cornerstone of what was to be known as the West Spruce Street Presbyterian Church, and

even then not until the committee required "the liberal subscriptions of a *large number* of individuals." They said, "We take
it for granted that after what has occurred, every member of this
congregation *will wish to have a stone in this building.*"[29]

As it turned out, the exertion was worth the effort. The architect, John McArthur, was just beginning a noted career that would
be crowned by his design of the magnificent Philadelphia City
Hall in 1871, and he more than outdid himself. Working at great
speed, McArthur had the entire structure of the new church standing and roofed by the end of 1855, and on May 18, 1856, the lecture room was sufficiently completed to allow conduct of the first
worship service. In June, the Sabbath school was organized, and
on the first Sabbath of 1857 the great sanctuary was opened and
dedicated. The total cost had been $88,000.

It was, as the insurers noted, "a brick church edifice" with "a
brick and frame tower or steeple" on the east front corner.
McArthur had designed the tower to be the tallest structure in
Philadelphia. And so it was, rearing 250 feet into the air, 130 feet
of brickwork and 120 feet of framework. Facing the east tower
was a shorter west tower, 105 feet high, made of white pine tim-
ber and covered with the best cedar shingles. Within were "three
aisles, forty-four pews in each middle block . . . all furnished with
paneled ends," and a "gallery on each side of the building and
across the front." It had "five cast-iron columns under each side
gallery, extending to the roof." In the rear was the lecture room,
containing "fifty pew benches with scroll ends, a recess at the west
end and a platform and neat desk or pulpit with paneled front to
it, a trustees room, and a pastors study."[30]

WILLIAM PRATT BREED

The pastor who was to fill that study, according to the separate arrangements designed for the West Spruce Street Church,
was William Pratt Breed. He had been selected in February 1856.
Breed was not the colorful pulpiteer that Boardman was, and that

was perhaps for the best since the overwhelming presence of Boardman in both Tenth and the West Spruce Street Church left little room for independence on the part of the man who would have to share the pulpit with him every other Sunday. Apparently Breed worked well with Boardman, and Boardman for his own part never tried to meddle in the strictly autonomous affairs of the West Spruce Street Church. From the beginning, even during the May 18 lecture room inaugural service, Breed and Boardman carefully observed the niceties of the peculiar relationship.

If Breed was less colorful, he was no less orthodox than Boardman. West Spruce Street Church, he announced, "has no sympathy with the vague indefiniteness that professes to believe the whole Bible without professing faith in any given doctrine of the Bible, and none with that no-system that rejecting and decrying all creeds exacts of the Christian world an adherence to its creed that man should have no creed." He could be as frank as Boardman, even more so in his adherence to Reformed doctrine.

He wrote that this church "finds in the Word of God certain doctrines and among these that of the sovereignty of God of whom, to whom and through whom are all things. . . . The world's a stage and human beings are the players. But God wrote the play, and he determines the entrances and exits of the actors. He overrules all their free actions to his own glory."[31] Prospective members were greeted with a letter informing them that "you have been brought, as you humbly trust by the Spirit of God to feel your misery, guilt, depravity and helplessness as a sinner."[32]

Far from repelling people, the vigorous proclamation of Reformed theology attracted them. From the 34 attendees of the Sabbath school in June 1856, the church grew to include 923 members by 1867. By 1876 the Sabbath school alone had gone through 4 superintendents, 247 teachers, and 1,898 scholars— despite the fact that the infants class, which accounted for 854 of that total, had been lodged perilously high in one of the towers. A Dorcas Society (to do visitation and benevolent work) was flourishing. A Woman's Missionary Society was organized in 1870. A Saturday morning sewing school for poor girls was begun in 1871. Young men's and young women's prayer meetings met before and after the morning services so that the Sunday services were "inclosed in a hallowed parenthesis of youthful prayer and praise," as Breed put it.[33]

Those hallowed services, following nineteenth-century practice, met first at 10:30 a.m. on Sunday and regathered at 4:00 p.m. one Sunday each month and at 8:00 p.m. on all other Sundays. In addition, there was a Wednesday-evening lecture at 8:00 p.m. and a prayer meeting on Friday evening, augmented by the monthly concert for prayer on the first Monday. The Sabbath school met twice on Sundays, first at 9:00 a.m. and again at 3:00 p.m.

Through it all, William Breed vigilantly maintained a Presbyterian sense of decency and order. "We have steadily avoided the tendency that in some cases has resulted in a sort of combination of the religious opera and horticultural exhibition. We have not yielded up our singing gallery to the musical artist, according to whose creed the chief end of the church is the organ loft and the chief end of the performers there is to display their accomplishments, sing their own praises and gratify a cultivated musical taste the effect of which is to fritter away the attention, thought and emotion due to the stupendous themes of righteousness, temperance and a judgment to come."[34] Breed organized a strictly pruned worship, especially when administering the communion:

> Our communion service is observed once in three months on Sabbath morning, after a sermon appropriate to the occasion. Just before the administration of the sacrament, those who come to it for the first time are called into the aisle before the communion table where the pastor reminds them of the obligations involved in their applications for and admission by a vote of the session to a place at that table. He gives them a word of welcome and admonition and also reminds the people already at the table of their duty to these newcomers among them.[35]

During these years, both Tenth and the West Spruce Street churches were undergoing fundamental and ominous changes.

West Spruce Street's membership was already ceasing to be a strictly neighborhood membership. The increasing ease of city transport and the takeover by businesses of many of the old central residential districts combined to reduce West Spruce Street's neighborhood membership to only 54 percent of the whole. At Tenth Church the change was even more drastic. By 1885 only 21 percent of the members came from anywhere near Twelfth and Walnut, and the total membership had slumped to below half that of the colony at Seventeenth and Spruce.[36]

Tenth had already suffered a blow in 1876 when the aging Henry A. Boardman was finally no longer able to maintain his ministry and so resigned the pulpit. He had held it for forty-three years. By vote of the church and presbytery, Boardman was designated pastor emeritus and thus continued to shed the aura of his fame over Tenth a little while longer. But on June 15, 1880, Henry Augustus Boardman died. As it proved, there was none quite capable of taking his place.

In succession, John R. DeWitt and William Brenton Greene Jr. were named to the pastorate of Tenth, and in quick succession they left to take up professorships at Princeton. DeWitt remained only seven years, Greene nine. In 1893, lacking a pastor and watching its numbers dwindle, Tenth wearily petitioned the presbytery of Philadelphia to dissolve the congregation.

The presbytery decreed not dissolution, but a merger with the West Spruce Street colony. Accordingly, on May 24, 1893, the remaining members of Tenth Church voted to discontinue, and two weeks later the congregation of West Spruce Street voted to accept a merger with them. In deference to its mother church, the new congregation abandoned the name "West Spruce Street Presbyterian" and gave to the building at Seventeenth and Spruce the honored name of "Tenth Presbyterian Church." Old Tenth Church was sold for $150,000 in the spring of 1894, and after thirty-five bodies had been disinterred from its diminutive churchyard, the plain old building was demolished.[37]

William Breed did not live to preside over the amalgamated Tenth Presbyterian Church. Retiring in 1887, he, like Boardman, was urged that "whilst God spares his life he shall continue to be connected with our church as pastor emeritus." He had, as the session of West Spruce Street Church confirmed, "so entwined himself into the very life of this church, as well as into the life of almost every one of its families, that to part with him wholly we cannot, for it is like parting with one of our own flesh and blood."[38] Yet part with him they must. Sixteen months later, on February 14, 1889, Breed died. His death, along with Boardman's, marked the passing of the original founding generations of the two churches.

In Breed's place, James D. Paxton was installed as minister (although not until two years of candidating had passed), and it was Paxton who presided over the merger. He remained at Tenth until 1896, when he left to become pastor of the American Church in Paris.[39]

MARCUS A. BROWNSON

In January 1897, the church called Marcus A. Brownson, and with Brownson arrived yet another in Tenth's series of long-tenured ministers. Brownson was significantly different from either Boardman or Breed. For one thing, he was older than either of them had been when they were installed at Tenth—thirty-eight years old. Moreover, although he was the son of a Presbyterian minister, Brownson had gone to Western Seminary, not Princeton, from which he graduated in 1881. Brownson did not come to Philadelphia as a stranger; he had done missionary and church-planting work in the city for two years before moving on to pastorates in Wilmington, Camden, and Detroit.[40] And whereas Boardman and Breed had been sons of thunder, the chubby-cheeked Brownson was very much a son of consolation.

Not that Brownson offered watered-down doctrine. In the last years of his life he was preaching that "the Bible is the source of authority for our creed, the substance of what we are to believe, and it is the handbook of our conduct, the directory of all our duties and obligations to our Lord, to our own souls and souls of others. . . . We believe the Bible to be inspired of God, absolutely and, therefore, inerrant, infallible, authoritative, with a dominant, a predominant influence upon our thinking and our manner of life."[41] But Brownson definitely sympathized with the efforts of the late nineteenth-century revivalists, whose preaching was anything but Reformed. What Boardman had been trying to keep out of Tenth Church in the 1830s, Brownson was willing to admit by a side door in the 1890s. He demonstrated that by having the celebrated evangelist J. Wilbur Chapman deliver his installation sermon at Tenth Church on March 30, 1897.

Along with a new pastor, the church had acquired a new look. The original interior, when it was still the West Spruce Street Church, had been done up in a popular Italianate style. Just before the merger of the congregations, however, architect Frank Miles Day was commissioned to remodel the interior, and by the time he was finished the church hardly looked the same. Day created something of a hodgepodge. He replaced the windows and paneling with neo-Byzantine designs and mosaics. He borrowed ideas for the capitals and a dome above the pulpit from the Romanesque churches of Ravenna, Italy. From the ceiling, "like a great Venetian lamp," Day hung a huge central chandelier weighing over 700 pounds, each link in its connecting chain weighing 5 pounds.[42]

Some things did not change, however. Communion was still closed to all but those who were issued communicant's cards, collected by the elders at each communion. As late as 1916, Sunday morning worship still began at 10:30 a.m., although the Sunday school had by that time been moved to 12:00 noon. The church continued to collect pew rents from those who were willing to pay to assure themselves of a proper seat. The Dorcas and Home Missionary Society (as its title had become) was still going strong. In 1902 it spent over a thousand dollars in various endeavors, such as a school in Utah and "work among foreigners in Philadelphia." In 1910 that figure was up to $1,328.28. Although the Men's League, Women's Guild, and Young People's Society of Christian Endeavor had replaced the older organizations, the young people were still meeting, at 7:15 p.m. before the evening service, as in Breed's day.[43] Even the urge to colonize remained strong. The Hollond Memorial Church grew out of a bequest of $10,000 left in 1870 by a Sunday school teacher named Harriet Hollond, and the aging Boardman had himself preached the dedicatory sermon.[44] The Patterson Memorial Church at Sixty-Third and Vine Streets was endowed through the will of Morris Patterson, one of the original committee that had led the building of the West Spruce Street Church. The Church of the Evangel at Eighteenth and Tasker Streets was established through the gift of Gustavus Benson, head of one of the most important Tenth families.[45]

But some of the more unfortunate facts of urban church life did not change either. Although membership did not fluctuate drastically during these years, the balance of neighborhood membership did, so that by 1895 only 34 percent of the members lived in the immediate vicinity. Most lived elsewhere in Philadelphia, clumped together either due west or east of the church. For the first time, suburban members amounted to a substantial 7 percent.[46] By 1911, neighborhood members were down to 30 percent of the total, while other city membership stood at 51 percent and suburban membership had doubled, to about 13 percent. The church membership was obviously picking up stakes and moving.

Brownson was increasingly forced to chide the congregation for not showing up at church services other than those on Sunday morning. "I greatly rejoice in the goodly number present at the Sabbath services and in the faithful company always to be found at the midweek prayer meeting," he wrote in a circular letter for New Year's Day 1904. "But I am always wondering why so many who have solemnly taken upon themselves 'the vows of God' are absent."[47] The answer lay in the increasing distance and time it took for people to come.

Meanwhile, the immediate neighborhood of the church was being transformed into apartments, hotels, and businesses. It was becoming "transient." In 1916 Brownson recognized the change by including on the front of the church bulletin: "A special invitation is extended to hotel guests, residents in apartment houses and students in the colleges of the city." That statement might as well have served as an epitaph to Tenth Church's role as a residential urban church.

As for Marcus Brownson, he continued to go on from strength to strength. He was elected a director of Princeton Seminary, a delegate to the Pan-Presbyterian Council in Liverpool in 1904, and a participant in the Calvin celebration in Geneva in 1909.[48] He remained in harness as pastor until 1924, when he retired. As with Boardman and Breed, the love he had engendered in the people led them to designate him the church's third pastor emeritus, which post he filled until his death on December 18, 1938.

For two years, until 1926, the Scottish evangelist John McNeil pastored Tenth Church, broadening the smile with which a post-Brownson Tenth was now looking on revivals and evangelists. McNeil had, in fact, been closely associated with Dwight L. Moody and was a notable conference and campground speaker—two things that Boardman had disliked in the 1820s and would have abhorred in the 1920s. McNeil was a symbol of how the style of American evangelicalism had changed. Reformed orthodoxy was in eclipse, and mass evangelism without much regard for doctrinal or creedal solidity was in fashion. McNeil, however, did not stay to establish revivalism at Tenth. In 1926 he departed for a more exciting climate where revivalism, showbiz, and strange religious enthusiasms were already swirling around. In a word, McNeil was going to California.

It would have been ironic if McNeil, going from Philadelphia to California, could have passed on his way a young man headed from California to Philadelphia, a man who was to become the new pastor of Tenth Presbyterian Church and raise both himself and Tenth to a plateau of international reputation. From out of the golden West came Donald Grey Barnhouse, the fourth of Tenth's famous "B's."

BARNHOUSE

Allen C. Guelzo

Donald Grey Barnhouse was born on March 28, 1895, but in every other respect he was a child of the twentieth century. He went on radio as early as 1928, when radio was still a babe in engineers' arms, and by the end of his life he had appeared on television and in color films. Whereas Breed and Brownson had contented themselves with using buggies, trains, and rickety motorcars to get around, Barnhouse used airplanes. Whereas Boardman had begrudged even a few months' recuperative vacation in Minnesota as a waste of time, Barnhouse hopped all over the world and once was gone from Philadelphia for sixteen months at a stretch. Boardman wrote books. Breed wrote discourses. But Barnhouse wrote a series of commentaries and a basketful of shorter devotional works. Moreover, he edited the magazine of a foundation that he himself had largely created.

Even his theology was a product of the times, for Barnhouse was an ardent advocate of dispensationalism, an American version of premillennialism (despite its British founder, John Nelson Darby) that swung into prominence about the time Barnhouse was first making his presence felt.

Barnhouse was a man of supreme paradox. He was dispensational, but he was also as eagerly Calvinistic as Boardman. Even if he did not toe all the lines drawn by traditional Reformed theology (on one broadcast he frankly repudiated the idea that any of Christ's works, apart from his death, were in any way a fulfillment of Old Testament law on behalf of the elect), he nonetheless thumped the drum for TULIP so loudly that he has to be given much credit for sowing the seed of the modern Reformed renewal in evangelicalism.

Despite his labors as preacher, writer, and administrator, Barnhouse fondly described himself as lazy, and his responses to even the best-intentioned suggestions could be harshly abrupt. If he preached revival, he certainly did not consider himself a revivalist, and he disliked "altar calls," pulpit salesmanship, and the other trappings of evangelical show business. Most paradoxically, he was capable of producing the most disparate reactions in people, from those who loved him to those who loathed him. The man who up to that time was probably heard by more people than any other preacher, except Billy Graham, was personally irked at those who idolized him, particularly "the little old ladies." Yet he basked in the adoration of the lawyers, physicians, and businessmen who lined up in every city to hear him. The enthusiastic zealots who joined up to work with him found that their hero could as easily trample on feelings and bumble through the most delicate situations as he could point men to the Wicket Gate. Many contracted "Barnhousitis," a chronic and sometimes infectious form of disillusion with the man. Yet others found him, for all his human weakness, a great instrument of God and worthy of support even in the hardest moments. Many loved him.

He was, after all, the pastor of Tenth Church who walked from pew to pew and kneeled at each praying for those who customarily sat there or who were soon to sit there. In those days nobody had sat in the gallery for years; the dust was thick on the carpets. Every time Barnhouse put his foot down, the dust went up and he sneezed. But he prayed by every pew, and it was not long before they began to fill up. Soon the front rows were filled and there were chairs in the aisles. Barnhouse was also the preacher who was wont to pray before each service, "Lord, put thy chosen flesh on the skeleton to which thou hast led my mind. Lord, thy strength is my weakness."[1]

To say that Donald Grey Barnhouse was complex and paradoxical is to say the truth—but still not enough.

THE EARLY YEARS

Barnhouse was thirty-two years old when he was installed as pastor of Tenth Presbyterian Church, and his career to that date was by staid Eastern standards highly irregular. Born in Watsonville, California, he was the only son in a family that included a devout father and mother and four daughters—meaning that from the beginning Donald Grey Barnhouse was the center of attention. In 1910, while attending the state convention of the Christian Endeavor Union, Barnhouse met a C.E.U. field secretary named Tom Haney who opened his eyes to the Scriptures so that, as he later said, "I received full assurance of forgiveness and knew that my sins were removed from me. I knew that I had been accepted by the Father . . . and was truly a child of God."[2] In 1913 Barnhouse graduated from high school and promptly went off to the school that Haney had graduated from, the Bible Institute of Los Angeles.

Bible institutes and Bible schools were a gift to America of the itinerant evangelists of the Gilded Age, men such as Dwight L. Moody and Billy Sunday. Having no particular theological training themselves and getting little cooperation from those who did, the Moodys and Sundays snorted that intense theological training was unnecessary for Christian workers and instead set up schools to teach "practical" things. In New York, Philadelphia, Chicago, and, of course, Los Angeles, Bible schools sprang up, unabashedly evangelistic, mostly Arminian, entirely dispensational, and with hardly a single intellectual credit to their names—of which things they were all quite proud.

Not that Donald Grey Barnhouse went to the Bible Institute of Los Angeles because he shared those characteristics. Quite to the contrary. The youth was already displaying a photographic memory and a singularly energetic intellect. What Barnhouse was looking for was what he needed most critically at that hour: personal guidance and biblical study. To have sent him to a secular college with the expectation that he would pick these things up later in seminary would likely have quenched his spirit. As it turned out, he found both the Bible study he craved and the leadership he needed in Los Angeles. Both were supplied by the chief luminary of the Los Angeles school, Reuben A. Torrey.

Torrey, along with J. Wilbur Chapman, had been a close associate of Dwight L. Moody, and when Moody retired from his evangelistic crusades in 1892, it was assumed that Torrey and Chapman would inherit his mantle. Things did not turn out that way. Until 1908 Torrey contented himself with being the first superintendent of Moody Bible Institute.[3] After that, until 1921, he divided his time principally between world preaching tours and the pastorate of the nondenominational Church of the Open Door in Los Angeles.

Torrey's one other responsibility was the Deanery of the Bible Institute of Los Angeles, a post to which he stuck until 1924, when he retired from the Bible Institute and the Open Door church (leaving the pulpit to be filled by none other than John McNeil, who had left Tenth Church in Philadelphia expressly to continue Torrey's work). In 1913 Torrey was energetic, evangelistic, and dispensational, and on all three of those counts he carried Barnhouse with him. Barnhouse eagerly adopted Torrey's dispensationalism, and Torrey was so flattered by the boy's enthusiasm that he even lent Barnhouse his personal class notes. And it would seem that Barnhouse imbibed more than Torrey's ideas. If a model is to be sought for Barnhouse's later activities—his transdenominational evangelistic campaigns, his incessant continent-hopping, as well as his dogmatic dispensationalism—that model can probably be found in Torrey.

The Bible Institute of Los Angeles asked only two years of its students' time. So in 1916 Barnhouse left Los Angeles for Princeton Theological Seminary, where for perhaps the first time in his life he was not the center of attention. No wonder—at Princeton his professors were the heavyweights of Reformed theology. Benjamin Breckinridge Warfield was professor of theology; Robert Dick Wilson was the Hebrew and Old Testament professor; J. Gresham Machen was a junior instructor in Greek. Some famous faces were even present from Tenth Presbyterian Church in the form of John DeWitt, professor of church history, and William Brenton Greene, professor of apologetics.

Barnhouse was the youngest in his class and, so far as academics go, one of the least well prepared. He found that a Bible institute education did not take one very far at Princeton, and for the next two years his photographic memory had everything it could do to catch up. On the other hand, what he learned—including how to be graciously cut down in class by B. B. Warfield—he learned well, and he got into his bones a healthy love of Reformed theology (or at least those parts of it that he could synthesize with dispensationalism). Thus, the paradoxes in his life were already appearing. He would always be thereafter a curious admixture of Bible institute enthusiasm and Reformed theological vigor.

Barnhouse did not take a degree at Princeton. Instead, World War I came to America in 1917, and Barnhouse wound up with a lieutenant's commission in the aviation section of the Signal Corps, which passed for an air force in the days of flying apple crates. That did not mean, unfortunately, that he was to dart through the skies above the trenches, machine guns hammering, squadron scarf aflutter. Donald Grey Barnhouse sat through the war as a flight instructor at Kelley Field in the baking-hot plains of Texas, itching all the while for a chance to get to Europe.

Surprisingly, he did get to Europe, but not until after the war and under very different auspices from those of the Signal Corps. Reuben Torrey, meeting Barnhouse in New York City near the end of the war, discerned Barnhouse's urge to move abroad and channeled that desire toward missionary work by putting Barnhouse in touch with the Belgian Gospel Mission. In 1919 Barn-house, newly demobilized, arrived in Brussels and mastered French so quickly that he was soon preaching in it. By 1921 he was able to undertake the pastorate of a French Reformed church in Fressinieres in the Alps.

The north of France had been economically smashed during the war, and the flower of an entire generation of French youth had been destroyed. The grim depression that these facts caused weighed heavily on the villagers to whom the buoyant young American was expected to minister, and his enthusiasm might very easily have viciously backfired. Instead, he lifted their spirits and taught them to have a hope and joy they thought they had lost forever. As one of the survivors said, "He had a natural faith in God and it gave him a buoyancy. We said, 'If he can believe it like that, we can too!'"[4]

What things Barnhouse had failed to learn in America were taught him in France, and for the first time his voracious, if indiscriminate, intellect came into touch with the ancient glories of European culture. For the rest of his life Barnhouse would love a Greek marble as easily as he loved a well-proportioned sermon, and he never stopped exhorting evangelicals to rise above artistic philistinism.[5]

Above all, France provided him with a wife, an American missionary named Ruth Tiffany, whom he married in September 1922. When Barnhouse returned to America at last in 1925, after having served yet another French Reformed church and having attended classes at the University of Grenoble, the two had become three, and Barnhouse had been stimulated to buckle down to the sort of academic study he had before shirked easily. Coming to Philadelphia to work at the University of Pennsylvania in ancient history, he swung into graduate work with gusto. He was helped by a university teaching assistant's grant that enabled him to hold forth on history before awed classes of undergraduates. Along with his studies and teaching, Barnhouse also accepted the pastorate of Grace Presbyterian Church (in September 1925), and only two years passed before he was called to the pastorate of Tenth Presbyterian.

For a youthful preacher, a call from Tenth Church might have been interpreted as a signal that he had arrived, that the uncertain struggles of youth were over, that the opportunity to lean back and settle in comfortably was at hand. If Barnhouse ever thought so, the moment contained the most erroneous thought his fertile brain had conceived.

LIBERALISM

Compared with the catastrophe that overcame American Presbyterianism in the years before and after World War I, the crises of New Light– Old Light in the 1740s and New School– Old School in the 1830s were but chivalrous and genteel joustings. The cause of denominational distress lay far deeper than wrangling over revival techniques and doctrine. It addressed the very nature of supernatural Christianity, and it became a matter that paralyzed not only Presbyterians but almost every other American denomination.

The religious impulse known as "liberalism" did not strike America until after the hurly-burly of the Civil War, even though the book that may be said to have been the catalyst of liberalism, Darwin's *The Origin of Species*, was published in 1859. For the first time in Western thought, an intellectually respectable alternative to Christian belief had been offered, since evolution proposed not only a logical answer about where man had come from but also an optimistic suggestion about where he was going to. By the time Darwin had published his second work, *The Descent of Man*, in 1871, Darwinism had made scientific investigation the declared enemy of religion, with scientific investigation increasingly looking like the winner.

At first, there were many who sought to defend Christianity from the frontal assault of Darwin by asserting the truth of the scriptural account of creation. But many of these were taken from behind by the works of Julius Wellhausen in the 1870s. Wellhausen, the father of "higher criticism" of the Bible, denied not only the supernatural authorship of Scripture but even any coherent authorship among the human writers, breaking the Old Testament up into various anonymous sources and editors. Caught between Darwin and Wellhausen, seminaries and churches alike often preferred to abdicate supernaturalism and desperately attempted to adjust their Christianity to science. Henry Ward Beecher, the most famous and fatuous spokesman of polite accommodation in the Gilded Age, warned that "the providence of God is rolling forward a spirit of investigation that Christian ministers must meet and join. There is no class of people upon earth who can less afford to let the development of truth run ahead of them than they."[6] That, of course, depended on what one construed as truth. For Henry Ward Beecher, truth was the belief that unless American Christianity jumped onto the evolutionary bandwagon, it might become "outdated." Out of that anxiety was born American religious liberalism. By 1900 the seminaries and divinity schools of Harvard, Yale, Union of New York, Andover, Bangor, Colgate, Rochester, Crozier, and the University of Chicago had gone liberal.

Those who remained faithful to the biblical standards found varieties of ways to respond—not always well or wisely. Dwight L. Moody began a tradition of aggressive revivalism that culminated in Billy Sunday. C. I. Scofield, James H. Brookes, and James M. Gray introduced dispensationalism to Protestant thought, where it served as a highly attractive alternative to the eschatology of evolution. Most significant, perhaps, in 1910 there appeared the first volume of *The Fundamentals*, a series of twelve booklets that enlisted some of the finest conservative spokesmen—such as B. B. Warfield and Bishop H. C. G. Moule—to defend the biblical position on the virgin birth of Christ, the atonement, the resurrection, and other cardinal doctrines. The publication of *The Fundamentals* was the most significant of all these responses because it provided a rallying point for conservatives who had heretofore lacked leadership and cohesion and so gave birth to that movement known as "fundamentalism."[7]

Fundamentalism was unable to stop the slide of Presbyterianism into the liberal abyss. The Presbyterians had long looked like the one outpost that would not surrender to liberalism. After all, in 1893 Charles Augustus Briggs, a professor of Hebrew at Union Seminary, was suspended from the Presbyterian ministry for condemning "the dogma of verbal inspiration," and as late as 1923 the General Assembly had declared that belief in the inspiration of Scripture, the virgin birth of Christ, the vicarious atonement, the bodily resurrection of the Lord, and the validity of the scriptural miracles were all "essential and necessary" for ordination. But the 1923 pronouncement was far from being a mandate for fundamentalism within the Presbyterian church. It had passed the General Assembly by the slim margin of only 80 votes. Indeed, before a year had gone by, a group of 150 Presbyterian ministers produced the "Auburn Affirmation," which blithely asserted: "We are united in believing that these (standards passed by the 1923 General Assembly) are not the only theories allowed by the Scriptures and our standards as explanations of the facts and doctrines of our religion."[8]

The gauntlet had been thrown down. In 1929 J. Gresham Machen was squeezed off the faculty of Princeton Seminary as the conclusion of a lengthy delaying action that he had been fighting against liberals in the seminary and on the board of trustees, and with him went the finest of the conservative minds yet remaining there. By the dawn of the 1930s, the balance of power within Presbyterianism was swinging inexorably toward the liberals. And the liberals, after having spent two decades pleading for tolerance for themselves, proceeded ruthlessly to smother conservative dissent with the pillow of denominational conformity.

In Philadelphia, long the bastion of conservative Presbyterianism, the dilemma was not quite so critical, although it was certainly serious. Philadelphia Presbyterian churches were up to their necks in problems, some on the high level of theological allegiance and some on the more mundane level of simply trying to keep their doors open. (Liberalism was succeeding, ironically, in closing more churches than it opened, since people who are told that there is nothing left for them to believe do not need to come every Sunday to have a well-salaried minister tell them that.)

Tenth Church especially was coming into dire financial straits. For one thing, John McArthur's great east tower had decayed so badly that it had to be removed and replaced with a simple hip roof at the level of the tower's brickwork. This cut more than a hundred feet from the tower's height. Inside, the bulky chandelier installed so ingeniously by Frank Miles Day was taken down, while the woodwork went in need of repainting and the trustees cast about for funds to rewire the lighting. Funds were the critical problem of the church, as the congregation began to dwindle in numbers and contribute less and less. Tenth Church had listed 487 members in 1915. That had slipped to 347 by 1927.[9] As a result, the church's income began to shrink, so much so that by 1922, only 12 percent of the church's income came through the weekly offerings, and the trustees had to rely more and more on fixed endowments and mortgages, such as the string of properties left to Tenth Church by Harriet Hollond. More and more also, the church was relying on the most anachronistic and distasteful form of income, the levying of pew rents, which in 1922 amounted to 37 percent of the church's income. These are not the marks of a thriving church, a fact that the trustees helplessly acknowledged by wailing that "there seems to be no way by which the board can reduce expenditure." Everything needed repair— hymnbooks, pew cushions, the heating system. There was simply no money coming in to pay for it.[10]

Things went from bad to worse. In 1923, a quarterly deficit began to creep into church financial statements. In 1924, that deficit had crept up from $22.37 to $410.29. By 1925, the trustees were reduced to the expedient of selling off the Liberty Bonds held by the church just to have cash in hand, and the financial secretary, Strickland L. Kneass, glumly reported that average plate offerings per Sunday had gone down from $128.00 in January of 1925 to $80.42 during November and December. For the fiscal year ending in March 1926, the church showed a whopping deficit of $2,758.91. And all this was happening during the Roaring Twenties, when America was in the greatest economic boom of its life! Somewhere, something had evidently gone wrong, and there was the distinct possibility that the man who would succeed McNeil to the pulpit of Tenth Presbyterian might have little else to do but preside over the disintegration of the church.[11]

This was the situation into which Donald Grey Barnhouse stepped in October 1927, although, true to form, it was a situation that Barnhouse promptly used to the furtherance of the most unlikely ends. There had been few volunteers for the pulpit of Tenth Church, considering the situation in which the church found itself, and Barnhouse doubtless realized very quickly that Tenth was even more eager to have him than he was to come to them. Therefore, with unprecedented boldness he insisted as preconditions to his acceptance of Tenth's call that the church agree to get its economic house in order, terminate Sunday-evening services so that he might do evangelistic work elsewhere in Philadelphia at that time, and support a radio broadcast of his preaching. Such cheeky demands upon a proud old church would have been met with scorn under normal conditions. But Tenth did not have the luxury of enjoying normal conditions in the 1920s. The session hesitantly agreed and stood back to see whether Barnhouse could part a way through the waters of their dilemmas.[12]

If anyone had dismissed Barnhouse as being merely a super-confident, overenthusiastic missionary, they had badly underestimated their new minister. Underneath the cocky self-assertiveness, Barnhouse had a rocklike faith in the providence of God and a sharp eye for the main chance. As risky as his propositions looked on paper, they turned out to be exactly what the church needed. Though Barnhouse called on the church for an outlay of $4,500 in 1928 for the radio broadcast—an outlay that it could ill afford—and even more money for new office equipment ($393.85), membership booklets, and advertising in newspapers, church papers, and hotel church directories, he compensated for that by boosting membership back up to 468 by 1929 and by taking upon himself a $2,000 cut in salary. Although 1928 still left the church with a deficit of $1,344.45, it was at least a dramatically reduced deficit

from previous years, and by October 1929, the church was showing quarterly credits again.

The reason for the rally was obvious. From the very first,
Barnhouse had made it plain that he intended to preach the Bible
well and faithfully, and the people simply flocked in to hear it. He
put Bibles in the pews, began reading the Bible in sequence in
Sunday morning services, rejuvenated the prayer meetings, held
services on Thursday evenings that crowded people in, reorganized the Sunday school with the help of Ruth Tiffany Barnhouse,
and, whether in person or over the airwaves of the Columbia
Broadcasting System, swept his hearers along with the crackly,
electric, and authoritative dogmatism of his preaching. Barnhouse
turned Tenth back into an urban preaching center and made himself a missionary from the city to the suburbs by using his free
Sunday evenings to preach in theaters in Germantown and at the
Tower Theater in Upper Darby.[13]

WARS WITHIN AND WITHOUT

One might say that it was Barnhouse's success in solving the
problems at Tenth that brought him into confrontation with the
problems plaguing the Presbyterian church as a whole. His radio
broadcasts, his pulpit manner, even his conversations had marked
him as a danger to liberals in the Philadelphia Presbytery. It is
tempting to accuse them of plotting against Barnhouse, but
whether they did or not, the unfortunate truth is that Barnhouse
very soon provided them with a rope with which they were only
too happy to hang him.

In the spring of 1929, several Upper Darby Presbyterian pastors complained about Barnhouse's preaching series at the Tower
Theater, claiming that he was violating the bounds of their
churches' jurisdiction. Then, in June, sensing an opportunity, seventeen other liberal-minded ministers of the Philadelphia Presbytery banded together to denounce Barnhouse not only for his
extracurricular preaching but for fingering them publicly as

heretics. Barnhouse was accused of describing one minister as more fit for a Unitarian than a Presbyterian church, of calling another a man who "did not feed his sheep," of telling another that he would die before allowing him into the pulpit of Tenth Church, and of saying on the radio that "within the sound of my voice there are two Presbyterian ministers who are treasonably disloyal to the gospel of Jesus Christ."[14]

It is regrettable that he did not realize why some of his listeners were writing these comments down and gleefully praying for more like them. When the matter was brought before the presbytery in March 1930, Barnhouse diplomatically offered a "voluntary statement of regret" to any offended members of the Philadelphia Presbytery, but the presbytery petulantly ignored his offer, forbade him any more meetings at the Tower Theater, and prepared to prosecute him for breach of the church's peace.

A howl immediately went up that made Barnhouse's liberal opponents quiver. The Christian Business Men's League of Philadelphia, a conservative group that had been underwriting the Tower Theater meetings, directed a formal protest to the presbytery, accusing it of being "un-Presbyterian, un-American and un-Christian." To the Upper Darby ministers, who appeared to the Leaguers to be more interested in their damaged pride than in saving souls, the League replied that "we believe that the Gospel of Jesus Christ cannot be dispensed too widely or too intensively" and that "the reclamation of even a very few who may have wandered out of the sphere of influence of our established churches is of more importance in the sight of God than any passing embarrassment which might attach to the ministers of such churches." After all, the Leaguers pointed out, the Tower Theater meetings had been drawing some 2,000 people every Sunday night, with numerous professions of conversion, and the very ministers who were nursing grudges against Barnhouse were the ones who were profiting from the influx of new members from those meetings.[15]

The presbytery backed down before the wail of protest. It was, to begin with, a presbytery very narrowly divided between liberals and conservatives, and while the original accusations against Barnhouse had been sufficient for a while to tip the balance toward the liberals, the cries of indignation rising in the wake of its actions against Barnhouse swung the presbytery's sympathies back the other way. The ban on the Tower Theater meetings remained in effect. But in May 1930, the presbytery hastily rescinded its first moves against Barnhouse and voted to accept his "voluntary statement of regret." To the unspeakable frustration of the liberals, they refused to prosecute him further.

Unwilling to lose their prey, the Philadelphia liberals appealed to the Synod of Pennsylvania, where they had more friends and more power, and the synod complied with their appeal in June by ruling the Philadelphia Presbytery in error and ordering Barnhouse to be tried by a judicial commission in Philadelphia. Now it was Barnhouse's turn to protest. If he was to be tried, it ought to be done by the whole presbytery and not by a handpicked commission. But the protests were to no avail, and Barnhouse went on trial before a commission of five ministers and four laymen in September 1930.[16]

Barnhouse might have saved himself the protests. The commission swiftly lost its nerve for prosecution—members resigned, the hearings were delayed from October 17 to November 7, and then to November 17—and finally concluded in December with the recommendation that Barnhouse be given the open trial he was asking for. The presbytery itself, offended at the highhandedness of the synod in decreeing an unwanted commission, angrily appealed to the General Assembly to have the synod's actions declared unconstitutional.[17] Nervous at the prospect of having to defend itself before the entire General Assembly, with its still-influential block of conservatives, the synod backed down. In a ten-page judgment handed out behind closed doors in the Witherspoon Building in Philadelphia on January 7, 1932, Barnhouse was convicted of a breach of the Ninth Commandment and violation of his ordination vows, and was officially admonished "to watch and pray that you enter not into temptation and to avoid the very appearance of evil." Beyond the admonition, the lowest form of church punishment, Barnhouse suffered nothing.

His lawyer, James F. Bennett, scorned the synod's judgment as "indecisive." It had merely talked airily of a breach of the Ninth Commandment without ever specifying which sins under the Ninth Commandment Barnhouse had committed, and without saying just what ordination vows he had broken. Barnhouse, unruffled by the decision, announced that he did not consider it worthy of an appeal to the General Assembly.

The force of the admonition was weakened even further when it was read in the presbytery on March 7, 1932, by a moderator who promptly apologized to Barnhouse for its contents, and it was weakened still more when the presbytery passed a resolution commending Barnhouse for not tangling matters with an appeal and "for his adherence to the doctrines of the church and his zeal in preaching the full gospel of salvation." Barnhouse himself grimly asserted that "I have appeared before the presbytery today to receive admonition in this case in the same spirit which animated my refusal to appeal the case. It must be understood that my attitude contains no admission of guilt. I have not been asked to retract any statement and do not retract any found in the records of this case."[18] In the end, the liberals had failed to engineer his disgrace. But for his own part, Barnhouse took twenty years to forgive them for trying.

From this point on until the 1950s, Barnhouse's contacts with the presbytery would range from the nonexistent to the nominal, and even then they were often hot with ill-feeling. On January 6, 1936, the presbytery met at Tenth Church and, without Barnhouse's knowledge, a communion service was arranged. When he learned of it, Barnhouse took the floor and informed the presbytery, "I know that this presbytery is certainly in no spiritual tone to take the communion of our Lord, the one with the other. . . . We are not at one as to whether Jesus Christ was supernaturally born. We are not at one as to whether Jesus Christ was eternally God. We are not at one as to whether the body of Jesus Christ was raised again on the third day."[19]

Such statements were not calculated to win Barnhouse friends, and he made even fewer of them in June 1936, when he defied the presbytery and opened the pulpit of Tenth Church to J. Gresham Machen, who by this time had left the Presbyterian church to form the Orthodox Presbyterian Church and Westminster Seminary. "I did this," Barnhouse boldly declared, "because of sympathy with his general doctrinal position and in defense of the freedom of speech."[20]

The question most often asked in the years after 1932 was, not surprisingly, why Donald Grey Barnhouse chose to remain a minister of a denomination that he was finding increasingly hostile and with which he was obviously disenchanted. The Presbyterian separatist Carl McIntire, so violent an advocate of separation that he even split with Machen when he suspected Machen of not separating enough, badgered Barnhouse incessantly in the *Christian Beacon* for his "half-heartedness." In February 1937, Barnhouse was sufficiently aroused to write McIntire a stinging letter that, in the course of much else, revealed Barnhouse's basic reasons for remaining within the Presbyterian church.

> Time and again I have pointed out from the pulpit and in the printed page that the risen Lord Jesus Christ said to the messenger of the church of Sardis that he was to stay in the church and strengthen the things that remained that were ready to die, even though the church had a name to live and was dead and even though the great majority had defiled their garments. You men who went out from the Presbyterian church to the new denomination had our respect and our support through the years of conflict, because we believed that you were sincere men, following your conscience. . . .

> I believe that God needs missionaries in the midst of our church today as much as he needs them in Africa. We believe that some of us who hold to the full doctrine of the Reformed faith as the expression of the truth taught in the Scriptures constitute the true Presbyterian Church in the U.S.A. denomination.
> The fact that robbers may enter a house at the far end of my block and may lay claim to ownership of the whole block is not going to disturb me in my full possession of my home. I pay no

tribute to them. As the church is in the world but not of the world, I can truly say before God that we, though in the church organization, are not of it in spirit as it is at present organized and believe that what we are seeing is a part of the prophetic tendency so clearly pictured in the Word of God that shows us all church organization running into the confusion of Babylon the Great, the Mother of Harlots.[21]

Otherwise, Barnhouse tried to be as friendly as McIntire would allow him to be. The second Mrs. Barnhouse reported that one time when they had been traveling and heard McIntire on the air in the car coming back, Barnhouse said, "You know, I'm going to call up that guy and tell him I'm praying for him." And he did. He got him on the phone and said, "Carl, this is Donald Barnhouse. I just want you to know that I'm still praying for you. I want you to know that I'm praying for your wife, too, and so is my wife, because these times must be difficult for her."

Barnhouse's conviviality did not heal the breach with McIntire, and his reasoning convinced few of his fellow fundamentalists. He eventually found himself in conflict with them more often than with liberals. In 1946 at a meeting of the Philadelphia fundamentalists, Barnhouse rebuked certain "good and godly ministers in this city whose names would strike terror to the lambs of the flock simply because they do not hold the same interpretation of the meaning of 'Come out from among them and be ye separate.'" Barnhouse had at the time only just returned from a tour of medical missions of Africa, and coming back to the separatist bickerings of Philadelphia made him "feel like a doctor who, having worked day and night in a plague center, returns to a satiated clientele who wish to discuss operations for face-lifting. Millions lie dying without the gospel and yet Christians in the city of brotherly love sit and bicker and gossip and backbite while the world perishes. God help us." By the end of the 1940s, Barnhouse was willing to declare a pox on both the liberal and fundamentalist houses and go his own way.

EXPANDING MINISTRIES

The antidote to Barnhouse's disgust was the national and international work which his radio broadcasts had been opening up. His broadcast, although unrenewed at CBS during the controversy in 1932, blossomed into the Bible Study Hour in 1949 and was shortly being carried by more than 100 stations in North America, Central America, the Philippines, the West Indies, and Africa. In 1933 Dallas Theological Seminary, the leading dispensational institution of America, conferred on him an honorary Doctor of Divinity, and in that same year he published his first book, with the possibly ironic title *His Own Received Him Not*. Barnhouse rapidly became in great demand as a speaker and preacher, whether for revivals, conventions, or whatnot, and the torrents of mail he received spoke eloquently, if often eccentrically, of the multitudes he was reaching.

One letter, received in 1940, sent him names and addresses of people the letter writer hoped Barnhouse would see fit to write to personally about their salvation. Another from a sixteen-year-old girl in Minneapolis asked whether she could open a correspondence with Barnhouse's daughter Ruth, also then sixteen. Others wrote to thank him fulsomely for a particular sermon that had moved them in a time of distress, such as one woman in Illinois who had lost both a sister and a mother to insanity in the space of four weeks and saw herself going the same way until hearing Barnhouse preach on "Calvary Covered It All." Still others sent him tedious, lonely letters about nothing in particular, addressed only to "Dr. Donald Grey Barnhouse, Philadelphia, Pennsylvania."

Barnhouse manfully tried to answer as many letters as he could. To a new convert in Bridgeport, Connecticut, he sent some practical advice:

> These first days of Christian life will have great difficulties because Satan, who has let you alone since he knew that there was sufficient in your old nature to keep you in his camp, will now bend every effort to destroy your witness and the reality of this new life.

You must not forget that he has an ally within your heart, your old nature, which like the wooden horse of Troy is within the walls ready to open the gates for the enemy. The only way to deal with the old nature is to judge it day by day and sometimes frequently during the day. Acknowledge before God that it is this old nature which crucified Christ. Condemn it in your heart and mind and yield it over to the Lord, asking that he keep it crucified with Christ, so that the risen life of the Lord may take control of your being.[22]

More often Barnhouse was forced to resort to a standard form letter to reply to the gushing correspondence flowing his way. "I am so happy to know that you received Christ as your Savior during my recent meetings in _____" began thousands of forms, to the delight of those who prized them as a "personal letter" from Donald Grey Barnhouse. Nevertheless, when the situation demanded it, Barnhouse happily went the extra personal mile.

One of the strangest and least known examples of Barnhouse's profound interest in people lies for the most part buried in the archives of the West German government. In 1939 Barnhouse was asked by the Hebrew Sheltering and Immigrant Aid Society to intervene in the case of one Kathe Meyersohn, a Jewish music teacher in Berlin who was trying desperately to get out of what was then Nazi Germany. Sometime in 1938 Barnhouse had begun writing to Meyersohn, offering to help her immigrate to the United States, and Meyersohn replied in December 1938, amazed "that there are such good friends in the world who want to help me and have already begun necessary preliminary measures." Those measures included an affidavit that was to be sent to the Nazi government by Barnhouse in Meyersohn's behalf. Using the Hebrew Aid Society, Barnhouse dispatched two copies of an affidavit to Berlin in April 1939. There, ominously, Barnhouse's file on Kathe Meyersohn stops. Whether she was able through Barnhouse's recommendation to escape the ensuing Holocaust is unknown from Barnhouse's records. But the incident clearly shows Barnhouse's determination to do good unto all people as well as his sensitivity to need, even of a stranger.

Barnhouse's other works multiplied with the passage of time. His radio broadcasts expanded, in spite of (or because of) the fact that he resisted the temptation to let them descend into vulgarity or sensationalism. Barnhouse was a stickler for good taste as well as good preaching, and he strongly insisted that programs ought to have "no pleas or requests for money, no giving away of premiums, no self-advertising, no mention of the names of any individual in dedicating a hymn to this or that person who may have sent in a few dollars for the broadcast. For the world could be listening in, and such things are an abomination to the culture of the world, and they should be an abomination to Christian culture, since these offenses hurt our witness and add nothing to it."[23] In a memorable broadcast in 1935, entitled "How Great Is Your God?," Barnhouse articulated his own motivation for resorting to electronic media. He took to the radio, he explained, because Christians "possess something that you do not possess" and the radio offered to him the best possible means of disseminating the news of that possession:

> What is it? Why, we have the knowledge of the true God. Our God is not a little God; our God is not a God in our own image; our God is not a God who is like unto ourselves, but he is the God of the Lord Jesus Christ; he is the God of the Bible; he is the God who is the Creator; he is the God who is the Redeemer; he is the God who is holy, and who, therefore, must come into being; the God of love who, therefore, came in Christ and took that punishment himself so that we might have eternal life through faith in him.[24]

Those animating facts led Barnhouse into the printed media as well, and in 1931, in the midst of the furor over his trial in Philadelphia, he found the time and stamina to begin the magazine he named *Revelation*. It took up much time, and his oldest son Donald quoted him as saying often, "There are five children in this family: Ruth, Donald, David, *Revelation* and Dorothy." For *Revelation* came between the births of the last two children and took a proportional share of the father's devotion.[25]

To support the work begun by the magazine, Barnhouse led in the organization of the Evangelical Foundation, which took up headquarters down the block from Tenth Church at 1716 Spruce Street. By the time *Revelation* was ready to be reorganized and expanded into *Eternity* in 1950, the Evangelical Foundation included fifty-three staffers, presided over by Barnhouse as editor of the magazine and president of the Foundation.[26]

Somewhere along the line, something in Barnhouse's cluttered list of responsibilities had to suffer, and many were only too quick to believe that the chief sufferer was Barnhouse's own Tenth Church. By 1940, Barnhouse was spending only half the Sundays of the year preaching at Tenth. He was doing very little pastoral calling, something that clashed sharply with the tradition of pastoral responsibility laid down by Henry Augustus Boardman. And it could not have sat well with the established segments of the church that Barnhouse was devoting so much of his attention to theater meetings, student groups from the University of Pennsylvania, conferences at Keswick and Cambridge in England, visits and lectures at the French Protestant seminary of Aix-en-Provence, and an on-again, off-again Bible study that he superintended in New York City on Monday nights.

In 1936 some of that disgruntlement boiled to the surface when Barnhouse clashed with Roland K. Armes, a member of the session at Tenth. Armes, irked at Barnhouse's insistence on hiring a full-time (and expensive) church secretary, accused Barnhouse of using church facilities for his own private, outside business. "I have wanted to tell you," Armes continued, "that it's a fine idea that men have that while they are paid a salary out of a church they can spend six days of a week elsewhere. They couldn't do that in any business organization." Barnhouse's reply, as it would be on every other occasion when criticism for neglecting the church was leveled at him, was that "I was under the impression that Tenth Church hired me to work for the Lord. That is what I am doing here and elsewhere, and whatever is done benefits the church."[27] That is where the conversation stopped in most cases. Nevertheless, it was not missed that Barnhouse, unlike every other previous pastor of Tenth, chose to live outside the city—he lived, in fact, on a farm near Doylestown—and it was more than once observed that he thought his pastoral duties were best discharged by how well he preached and not by how well he did visitation.[28]

If Tenth Presbyterian Church was suffering, as Barnhouse's detractors said, it was showing it in curious ways. By 1950 the membership stood at 765. Fifteen members of the congregation had gone into missionary work, which Barnhouse always thought was the best sign of a healthy church, and many more were studying at the various theological seminaries and schools that dotted the Philadelphia area.[29] Joseph Bayly, who later became, like Barnhouse, an evangelical magazine editor and writer, noted "the strong young men and women (but especially men) from Tenth Church who were active in the leadership of Inter-Varsity groups at some of the East's outstanding colleges and universities. They bore the stamp of Dr. Barnhouse's ministry, and it was a spiritually virile one."[30]

One pastor, Dr. Robert J. Lamont, wrote of his personal experience with Barnhouse:

> Mrs. Lamont and I had hoped for many years for a child of our own. And when that child came, a little boy named after a missionary surgeon, he turned out to be a Mongoloid boy, retarded, without any promise or hope that he would ever grow into manhood and usefulness in life. It was Dr. Barnhouse in tenderness and love who brought me to the place where I could thank God for Kenny. Dr. Barnhouse introduced me to these words in Exodus 4:11. "And the Lord said unto Moses, 'Who hath made man's mouth or who maketh the dumb or the deaf or the seeing or the blind? Have not I, saith the Lord?' "
>
> He said, "Bob, if you can believe this, your ministry will be the richer for it." And then he went on to say, "In everything give thanks, for this is the will of God in Christ concerning you." That night I learned to give thanks in a time of great personal crisis.[31]

Evidently, Barnhouse was doing something right at Tenth Presbyterian.

New Directions

On October 3–5, 1952, Barnhouse celebrated his twenty-fifth anniversary as the pastor of Tenth Church, and the festivities called for participation from a host of renowned evangelicals. Oswald T. Allis of Westminster Seminary and S. Lewis Johnson of Dallas Seminary delivered addresses on the significance of expository preaching. On the platform of Town Hall, where the first of the anniversary sessions took place, Barnhouse found himself in the company of such lights as the British fundamentalist E. J. Poole-Connor, the dispensationalists J. Dwight Pentecost and Clarence Mason of the Philadelphia Bible Institute, and a crowd of local pastors and leaders.

But whether anyone on that platform realized it, Donald Grey Barnhouse was moving into a new phase in his career, away from the period of the axe-swinging fundamentalist and toward something quite surprising. Barnhouse was, in fact, emerging from a long period of private emotional turmoil and was rethinking many of the ideas that had powered his ministry. In 1944 Ruth Tiffany Barnhouse had died, knocking one of the great props of his life out from under him. Moreover, he awoke at the end of the 1940s to the realization that, for all his fabulous popularity, he had few real friends. Presbyterian churches as they moved steadily into liberalism regarded him as a pariah. Fundamental churches were suspicious of him for not severing his denominational connections. Dispensationalists mistrusted him for remaining so ardently Calvinistic. Calvinists mistrusted him for his allegiance to dispensational eschatology. It is hard to say just how much pain each of these factors caused Barnhouse, but the combined weight caused something to happen in Barnhouse's thinking during 1952, and the result of it was his epochal "New Year's Resolution," which he printed in *Eternity* in January 1953.

The "New Year's Resolution" was a retreat from the militancy that had landed him in so much hot water in years gone by. "I want my circle of Christian fellowship on the basis of the fact that a man is going to be in heaven with me," Barnhouse wrote. "If he is, then why not get a little closer here and now? Give him the benefit of the doubt on the things we do not agree upon as soon as we find that we agree upon man's complete ruin in sin and God's perfect remedy in Christ. . . . I believe that the love of Jesus Christ must mellow a man."[32] Just what Barnhouse intended by this became more apparent in November 1954, when he appeared before the Philadelphia Presbytery with "a statement of humility" and an olive branch for the men he had once fought so bitterly.

> There have been personal differences over the years. In my youth I fought against anything that I thought had in it a small percentage of error. But while outwardly critical of some of the church's program, I have always considered myself to be a Presbyterian, and I am in the Presbyterian church because I think that its theology and policy are closest to that which is set forth in the New Testament. . . . On my part, I want to work in much closer fellowship with you of the presbytery and to use what influence the Lord has given me to strengthen the hands of all the brethren.[33]

To allow him to be about his presbytery's business, Barnhouse resorted to the calling of co-pastors—Dwight Hervey Small in 1953 and C. Edwin Houk in 1955—and offered their presence as evidence of his new commitment to pay more attention to his Presbyterian duties.[34] That the presbytery noticed this—indeed, that the whole Presbyterian church noticed it—became manifest in 1955 when the National Council of Churches offered to make a series of television programs featuring Barnhouse. The olive branch had been accepted.

To make matters rosier, in 1954 Barnhouse remarried to Margaret Nuckolls Bell, and in 1956 the National Broadcasting Company agreed to pick up the Bible Study Hour, with the result that Barnhouse's network was spread even further.

Beginning in 1956, Margaret Barnhouse often accompanied the new Barnhouse on his preaching tours, and she noted a difference in style. For one thing, Barnhouse had never liked the

Masonic order, and he dismissed the Masons with the caustic observation that "if the Masons want to have funny handshakes and sit up with a sick friend, God bless them. But if they tell me those things will take them to heaven, I'll *fight* them all the way to the gates of hell and watch them go through." Now he said the same things about the funny hats and the handshakes, but he added, "If you tell me that those things will take you to heaven, I will *plead* with you all the way to the gates of hell and *weep* as you go through."[35]

None of this change of style and temper in any way slowed his pace. A new building program was begun under the chairmanship of Leslie Brooks, featuring as vice-chairman a physician who would presently become one of the most celebrated surgeons in Philadelphia, C. Everett Koop. Church membership continued to hover in the 700s. Barnhouse, for his own part, never slackened the punishing schedule of preaching tours, broadcasting, and writing. He was engrossed in his monumental series on the epistle to the Romans, and by the summer of 1960 had completed his 455-broadcast sequence of verse-by-verse expositions, leaving only the last four unrecorded. At the same time, he produced a series of films featuring his teaching on such subjects as "The Geography of Salvation," "3 Equals One," and "Why Christ Had to Die."

FROM DEATH TO LIFE

In Costa Rica he began to feel ill. Donald Grey Barnhouse had only rarely been ill in his life, blessed as he was with an iron physical constitution, and his confession of illness was a serious symptom to begin with. But he had diabetes (though he denied it), and when he came back up to Philadelphia, his first tests led to a diagnosis of uncontrolled diabetes. For a time he went back to the farm. Then more serious symptoms developed. He began having problems thinking out crossword puzzles, and began to forget which was the horizontal and the vertical. Suspicious, the doctors began testing for other things, and eventually he was diagnosed as having a tumor on the brain. He was operated on for removal of the tumor on October 8, 1960. For a month he recovered well, holding out hope that his strength and alertness might yet surmount the dread onslaught of cancer. But on November 5 Barnhouse took a swift turn for the worst. Unexpectedly his condition rapidly declined, and in less than two hours he was gone.[36]

Several months before his death, he had been working with his research assistant and right-hand man, Ralph Keiper, at the Doylestown home. The two were sitting around the dining-room table working on a number of manuscripts. After several hours of work they stopped and began to banter. Nearby was a book on biography. Keiper pointed to it and said, "'B,' I believe your biography would be most interesting." Barnhouse replied, "Ralph, if you ever attempt to write my biography, I will haunt you, I will haunt you, I will haunt you."

Keiper asked, "What would you like me to do?"

Barnhouse turned to the Word of God and said, "What I would like you to do is to teach, preach and live my text." He then read Philippians 3:10—"That I may know him, and the power of his resurrection, and the fellowship of his sufferings, being made conformable unto his death. . . ."[37] Now Keiper was to have the unhappy opportunity of doing that as a memorial in *Eternity* magazine.

Other eulogies poured in from the most respected names in evangelicalism—and even non-evangelicalism. Bernard Ramm, Eugene Carson Blake, Billy Graham, William Culbertson, Harold John Ockenga, Wilbur M. Smith, E. J. Carnell, John F. Walvoord, Vernon C. Grounds, F. F. Bruce—all extolled the virtues and commended the work of the man who had for thirty-three years filled the pulpit of Tenth Church and occupied the attention of the evangelical world. Ironically, Barnhouse had provided his own eulogies, for he left among his papers an unpublished article on the subject of death that, as much as was possible, could have served as the eulogy he would have delivered on himself:

This great hope of being forever with the Lord is the high privilege of every believer. To you who love our Lord Jesus Christ, I say, you enter into this privilege, realizing that by his own death he robbed death of its fear for you. But to you who do not know the Lord Jesus Christ as your own personal Savior, death means doom. Death for you means eternal separation from God who loved you and from the Savior who died for you. Oh, heed the words of the Savior and accept him today! Then you will pass from eternal death into eternal life to be forever with the Lord. For this is his promise: "Truly, truly, I say unto you, he who hears my word and believes him who sent me, has eternal life; he does not come into judgment, but has passed from death to life."[38]

It was a final paradox. Even after death, Donald Grey Barnhouse reached out, as in life, for the salvation of souls.

CHAPTER 4

CITY CHURCH AGAIN

Allen C. Guelzo

"The Lord took Donald before he could undo the work of his early years," explained one member of the Evangelical Foundation.

Brusque as that judgment may have been, it said what many people at Tenth Presbyterian had only dared to think: that the final years of Donald Grey Barnhouse jeopardized the long-standing evangelicalism of Tenth by creating a détente with Presbyterian liberals. Even if Barnhouse's protestations of renewed love for the Philadelphia Presbytery had contained more words than sub-stance, they had still introduced the possibility that the church's strong evangelicalism was about to be shelved. Those who had all along assumed that Tenth had been safe for orthodoxy woke up after Barnhouse's death to find a sharp division between those who wanted to "continue" the work of Barnhouse (by this, they meant "continue it into a more liberal attitude in many areas") and those who were determined to wrench the church back onto a more definitely evangelical track.

Barnhouse's death also revealed other problems. While Barn-house had restored Tenth to its preeminence as an urban preach-ing center, he had not made it into an urban community church.

Worse still, it became swiftly apparent that the place people were flocking to was not really Tenth Presbyterian Church at all but only the pulpit of Donald Grey Barnhouse, and when Barnhouse was gone, so were the people. Above all, an undercurrent of dissent that had run through the church throughout Barnhouse's thirty-three years now surfaced. People said in open echo of Roland Armes that Barnhouse had spent too much time on the Bible Study Hour, *Eternity* magazine, Bible conferences, and worldwide junketing, and too little on Tenth. Thus, when the session set itself to find a new pastor, it was corporately muttering one prayer: Thank you, Lord, but no more Barnhouses.

Mariano Di Gangi

That was a harder rule of thumb to follow than it seemed. For if the session wanted to avoid the faults of Barnhouse, it certainly did not want to sacrifice his virtues as a preacher, and it was not completely sure that the one could be had without the other. It is surprising, then, that the church waited little more than eight months before calling to its pulpit a Canadian Presbyterian named Mariano Di Gangi. It was not that the church had gone desperate with haste. Far from it. The pulpit commission that screened Di Gangi was agonizingly deliberate in its motions. Quite simply, it was evident that in Mariano Di Gangi the session had found someone it could trust to wean Tenth from the heavy influence of Barnhouse and at the same time maintain the high level of preaching that Barnhouse and his predecessors, stretching back to Boardman, had set up as the church's peculiar standard.

Just how much a departure Mariano Di Gangi was from Barnhouse, and the whole history of Tenth's ministry, was obvious just from his name. He was the first ethnic name among Tenth's list of pastors. Born in Brooklyn in 1923, his theological education had been had at Westminster Theological Seminary—a sure sign that so far as education went, Di Gangi was not likely to share Barnhouse's warm feelings for the Philadelphia Presbytery. Moreover, at the very beginning of his work at Tenth, Di Gangi gave Philadelphia liberalism short shrift by scrapping the standard denominational Sunday school literature that "progressives" in the church had slipped into usage. He went on to nail his personal colors to the mast:

> I accept the full truthfulness of the Bible, inerrant in the original languages, as the Word of God. . . . Next, let me affirm my conviction that the gospel centers in Jesus Christ. Concerning him, I believe that he was conceived of the Holy Ghost, that he was born of the virgin Mary, that he died in sacrifice for the sins of men so that they might be reconciled to a holy God, that he arose bodily from the dead on the third day, that he ascended to the right hand of the majesty on high, that he is Lord of all life and that he shall return to judge the quick and the dead.[1]

Di Gangi also quietly rejected Barnhouse's dispensationalism and began touching on topics that his predecessor had either ignored or been untroubled by—such as the racial turmoil of the fifties and sixties. Most important, Di Gangi worked at being the pastor of Tenth Presbyterian Church in order that Tenth might become a community church once again.

Of course, Di Gangi was not a complete antithesis of Barnhouse. "I think that in message I shared a great many of Barnhouse's convictions," Di Gangi recalled. These included "the sovereignty of God, salvation by grace, an emphasis on justification by faith alone without the merit of human works or ritual, belief in the plenary inspiration, authority and finality of the written Word." In all these things Di Gangi was indistinguishable from Barnhouse.[2] Like Barnhouse, Di Gangi could also attract a sizable following. His previous work at St. Enoch's Presbyterian Church in Hamilton, Ontario, had served to triple the church's membership to nearly 1,100 people.[3] Like Barnhouse again, he had moved widely in Keswick and Gideon convention circles in Canada, and although the session had long before decided to sever any connection between the Bible Study Hour and the pul-

pit of Tenth Church, they relented sufficiently to raise $4,000 pri-
vately to create a local broadcast named "Time and Eternity" for
Di Gangi. For all intents and purposes, it was a duplicate of Barnhouse's broadcasts.[4]

Di Gangi was not inclined to spite Barnhouse's legacy. Coming from Canada where St. Enoch's Church had mainly been a
congregation of Irish, Scottish, and Dutch immigrants, Di Gangi
was profoundly amazed at the house that Barnhouse had built.
"The kind of session I had," he said of Tenth during his years as
pastor, "was the envy of the evangelical conservative ministers in
the presbytery. . . . I had people who were leaders in the fields of
medicine, law, financial analysis, and yet were deeply committed Christians, biblically knowledgeable and doctrinally articulate."[5] Di Gangi had a taste of just how well Barnhouse had taught
his people on the first day that he met Tenth's pulpit committee:

> Each member of the committee was permitted to ask three ques-
> tions—searching, perceptive, penetrating, necessary questions.
> The very first question was: What is your relationship to Jesus
> Christ? Then there were questions on: What is your view of edu-
> cation? The role of the minister in evangelism? Calvinism and
> Arminianism? What is your eschatology? How would you under-
> stand dispensationalism, premillennialism, amillennialism, post-
> millennialism? What is your view of the sovereignty of God and
> its relationship to evangelization? The questioning went on for
> about six hours. Then most of the committee adjourned. The chair-
> man and secretary, George Moffitt and Manfred Garibotti, went
> with me to my hotel room and continued the questioning: What
> is your view on the Mosaic authorship of the Pentateuch? What is
> your view on the documentary hypothesis? What is your view of
> the unity of Isaiah? I should have gotten a master's degree in the-
> ology at the end of the day.[6]

As the two meticulous elders left some hours later, one of
them apologized to the weary minister. "You know, this is the first
time we have had to choose a preacher in thirty-three years. You'll

have to forgive us if we haven't been sufficiently thorough." Mentally, Di Gangi's jaw dropped.

Nevertheless, while Di Gangi the theologian could admire the handiwork of Barnhouse, Di Gangi the pastor saw other things that he could not admire. At those he took dead aim. As early as a month before his installation in October 1961, Di Gangi was telling a church conference that he intended to steer into deeper waters than Barnhouse had, and within twenty months Di Gangi had laid foundations for a renewal of Tenth's work in the city: a visitation program that moved house by house, block by block through newly redeveloped urban areas; a full-scale program for college and university students that included counseling, instruction, and fellowship, instead of merely dropping by to hear a sermon; and a children's ministry to slow the flight of young families from the church.[7] To stress his own commitment to these plans, Di Gangi moved into the city, eventually living right around the corner from Tenth Church in a new manse on Delancey Place. He deliberately structured his time to give attention to the church's work. Fifty percent of his week he set aside for research and preparation of his sermons. The remainder was given over to administration of the church, visitation, and counseling.[8]

Not all of Di Gangi's plans caught fire at Tenth. Di Gangi had been particularly disappointed that Barnhouse had drained funds away from the church's music program in order to advertise how different Tenth was from liberal churches that lavished fortunes on choirs, organs, and soloists. What was worse, he found that the church in a burst of austerity had replaced its ancient pipe organ with a warbly Hammond that was more fit for a skating rink. What was left of a music program was in the hands of the organist and a quartet of singers whose singing sometimes gave more pain than edification. Di Gangi opened fire on this musical atrophy by proposing a new organ. To sweeten the pill for those who stuck by Barnhouse's philosophy, he disguised his proposal by calling it the "Donald Grey Barnhouse Memorial Organ." The plan fell ingloriously on its face, and Di Gangi was told, "DGB wouldn't want it, even if it is in his memory." Di Gangi was able to get new music into the church only by slipping around the flank of the ardent "Barnhousites" and reinstituting Good Friday services—with a string quartet from the Curtis Institute of Music.

Barnhouse had spurned Good Friday services as "funerals for Jesus," but Di Gangi argued that the "preaching of the word of the cross ought to be especially commemorated" and so got the service and the music. But it was, in the end, only a small victory. Tenth Church would have to wait until the arrival of organist and composer Robert Elmore before it would become one of the greatest musical churches, not only of Philadelphia, but of evangelical Christendom.[9]

Where Is Tenth?

One of the first tasks Di Gangi set himself was to ask, "Where is Tenth Presbyterian Church?" It was a simple question, but it suddenly lacked a simple answer. The death of Barnhouse had put attendance on the skids. In January 1960, Tenth had counted 948 heads on an average Sunday morning, whereas in January 1961, the average had shrunk to 679. People agreed that the slippage was only to be expected, and indeed church attendance began to pull itself back up into the seven and eight hundreds in 1962. People reassured themselves that they had lost only the occasional Barnhouse-seekers who had never really been a part of the church anyway.[10] But in 1963 things began to slip again. Within a year attendance was down to 450 on an average Sunday morning, and Di Gangi began prefacing the church's annual reports with cheery reminders that after all numbers were only statistics.[11]

Whatever it was that was causing attendance to falter, it could not be blamed on Di Gangi's neglecting his duties. He regularly preached either thirty-nine or forty Sundays of the year, as well as Good Friday and Thanksgiving; he presided over the administration of the communion five times annually. To cover any bases that his sermons might have missed, it became his custom on Sunday evenings to leave time at the end of the sermon for questions that were written out by the inquisitive, passed to the pulpit, and answered sight unseen.[12] Even when he was away, the pulpit was more than well filled, either by Di Gangi's live-wire assistant, William L. Hogan, or by a procession of evangelical worthies that included J. I. Packer, Ralph L. Keiper, E. M. Blaiklock, Douglas B. MacCorkle, Arthur Glasser, and Edmund P. Clowney.[13]

Di Gangi's aggressive notions about making Tenth an urban community church were having their fruit. Di Gangi and Hogan considered any visitor who signed the church register as fair game for visitation. "I have lived here for ten years," said one woman in an apartment house who received a visit from one of the visitation teams run by Hogan and T. William Richards. "You're the first persons who have ever come and invited me to church."[14] In 1962, Di Gangi imported Roger Green from the Children's Special Service Mission to conduct weekday children's missions in the neighborhood, running programs that included everything from chalkboards to puppet shows.[15]

One peculiarly long-range effect of Tenth's new work reached around the world to John J. Davis, a missionary with International Students who came down with a malarial seizure in Thailand. Deposited on the doorstep of a Thai military hospital, Davis was ignored by the hospital staff until his frantic wife attracted the attention of a Thai surgeon, who promptly left an appendectomy in the hands of an assistant to treat Davis. His attention saved Davis's life. Why had *he* bothered when no one else had? Because, the surgeon explained, when he was a medical student in America he had received nothing but prejudice from Americans until he was transferred to Philadelphia and met a family from Tenth Church. Unlike the others, they took him in, disarmed him of his bitterness by their affection, and finally, when he demanded to know the reason for their kindness, shared the gospel with him. He was converted and vowed that hereafter any American who needed help in Thailand would get his first priority. However sentimental the tale might have sounded in the telling, John Davis was one who profited richly, if unknowingly, from Tenth's city ministry.[16]

The lowered attendance figures also seemed to have had very little effect on the growth of service groups and activities within the church. Tenth was funding seventeen missionaries and making generous contributions to the Evangelical Foundation ($5,000 in 1962), Philadelphia College of Bible ($1,200 in 1966), Manna Bible Institute, Inter-Varsity Christian Fellowship, Stony Brook School, and others, and spending $1,625 in 1966 on Di Gangi's "Time and Eternity" broadcasts over WKDN in Camden. The Women's Association (a descendant of the old Dorcas Society) not only had its own offerings and its own investments in Standard Oil of New Jersey, but was regularly distributing over $2,000 to Tenth Church missionaries. A campus and career club was born that ran Bible studies, shuttled buses to nearby universities and colleges on Sundays, and managed its own affairs with the support of a membership estimated at well over 150. The missionary giving was aided by two yearly missionary conferences—spring and fall—and also by Di Gangi, who used vacation time to hop down to Mexico to visit work of the Wycliffe Bible Translators.

Closer to home, Di Gangi encouraged Edward Baldwin to organize an outreach to foreign students, and Tenth as a whole supplied money and volunteers for a Bible club and vacation church school at the Evangel Presbyterian Church at Eighteenth and Tasker Streets.[17]

But for all of Di Gangi's cheerfulness and the church's burgeoning activities, the statistics did not lie. Total communicant membership was down to 582 in 1967. At Barnhouse's death it had been 718. In 1966, morning worship attracted on the average only 425, and the evening service 275, half of what they had often been before 1961. Even the Bible school showed sharp declines. From a high of 235 students on the rolls in 1961, attendance had plummeted to 86 on a given Sunday.

The most unsettling statistics were financial. Barnhouse's last years had seen a deficit popping up. In 1952, 1953, 1956, and 1958–60, the church overspent by margins that ranged from $172 to $4,638. Not only did Di Gangi fail to stop the deficit, but it actually grew worse. In only two years of his tenure at Tenth did the church finish in the black.[18] If the question "Where is Tenth Church?" were asked solely of its statistics, the answer was bound to be a disappointment.

Part of the reason why the church was slumping could be had in the new ways Di Gangi was trying to answer the question of where Tenth was. "Tenth Church is in many places—wherever its members are," he explained.

> The church is not a building of brick with an imposing tower and leaded glass windows and an unusual stone pulpit. The church is people—people like you and me—people related to Jesus Christ. . . . The world will judge the church by what it hears us say concerning communism, economic injustice and racial prejudice. The world will measure what we do. As the apostle Paul reminds us, our words and works are like an open letter "known and read of all men."[19]

But there were many in the church who, like the statistics, refused to be charmed by Di Gangi's rhetoric about commitment. On the Sunday after he began assigning church visitation duties to church members, he had to announce, "I've received a letter that I would like to answer. I can't answer it privately because it's anonymous and I don't know where to send it. So I'm going to have to answer it from the pulpit." It went: "Dear Dr. Di Gangi, What do you mean by sending us out to do your work for you? What do you think you were hired for?"[20] Tenth Church was not so much slowing down as it was choking on the demands Di Gangi was making of it as a congregation.

There were still more gags over Di Gangi's stance on civil rights, and they came from all sorts of places—from those who wanted him to preach exclusively on civil rights *and* those who did not want to hear about them at all. Di Gangi tried to follow a firm, mediating, biblical course, and it cost him allies all over. In response, particularly to those who pressured him "to make declarations on the National Council of Churches, the World Council of Churches, the United Nations, this, that, and the other," Di Gangi icily replied, "I am here to preach Christ in the power of the Holy Spirit. I am here to emphasize the lordship of Jesus Christ. That lordship is the guarantee of the rights of racial minorities and the underwriter and guarantor of justice and stability in the civil order."[21] Di Gangi gladly served on Mayor James H. Tate's committee on civil rights, as Presbyterian representative for the Delaware Valley, and with equal gladness shared in the ordination of Tenth's first black elder and deacon. One wealthy member cut off contributions to the church in protest and then offered to reinstate his gifts if Tenth would rescind its open policy on membership. Di Gangi suggested that he either "repent of his racist sin" or "transfer to a country club with a chaplain where he could feel more comfortable."[22]

The man unfortunately—or perhaps fortunately—went elsewhere, as did others for various reasons. The unhappy statistical showing added to the resistance Di Gangi was encountering on visitation, social justice, and Good Friday services, and conspired to create a superficial impression that Di Gangi was failing to live up to Barnhouse's measure. Yet the standard by which Di Gangi deserves to be measured is not how unsuccessful he was compared with Barnhouse, but how undeniably successful he was compared with what almost anyone else could have done. Attendance dipped, but it did not disappear, and Tenth continued to top the attendance of the other, fashionable center-city churches. The budget went red, but in the sixties so did many others', and what was more, Tenth was shouldering the burden of paying for the new Delancey Place manse. Di Gangi was obstinate in his public position on civil rights and urban mission, but he was not obnoxious, and after the temperamentally touchy had gathered their skirts around themselves and departed, the church quietly contented itself with Di Gangi's moderation. Most important, Di Gangi continued to educate and edify his flock with consistent biblical preaching.

Ultimately it was neither the statistics nor the resistance that caused Di Gangi to resign the pulpit of Tenth in 1967. That would be caused by a problem beyond the power of either Di Gangi or Tenth Church to control.

CONFESSION OF 1967

During the years that both Barnhouse and Di Gangi were hewing their own ecclesiastical paths, the denomination to which both of them owed at least nominal allegiance was running further and further into theological and organizational anarchy. The advent of the Presbyterian age of chaos was heralded in the year of Barnhouse's death by H. Richard Niebuhr's essay "Radical Monotheism" and in 1961 by Gabriel Vahanian's *The Death of God: The Culture of Our Post-Christian Era*. Faster than the possessed swine had run down to the sea, there followed Bishop J. A. T. Robinson's *Honest to God*—whose content belied every syllable of its title—and Harvey Cox's *The Secular City* (1965).[23] As theology was emptied out and replaced by a gospel of radicalism, denominations that liberated themselves from the intellectual responsibility of believing anything began to shake off the restraint of their ancient creeds and embrace each other in an ecstasy of woolly-minded ecumenicity.

The United Presbyterian Church waited until 1967. But in that year, it too went the way of all liberal flesh and added to the Westminster Confession of Faith and its attendant catechisms the Confession of 1967. It was not that the new Confession was outrageously radical. It was merely vague, and the vagueness rightly set alarm bells ringing in the mind of every evangelical in the church. The new Confession stated that "the Scriptures (are) given under the guidance of the Holy Spirit"—which might or might not mean the same thing as inspiration. Then the Confession heavily qualified even that assertion by adding that they "are nevertheless the words of men, conditioned by the language, thought-forms and literary fashions which were then current." The qualifications vastly outweighed whatever merit could be salvaged from the original statement.[24] "The one sufficient revelation of God is Jesus Christ," the Confession announced. But that left the Bible to be defined merely as the "prophetic and apostolic testimony in which (one) hears the word of God." The new standard was not deliberately offensive, and evangelicals could assent to much of it, provided that the overall interpretation of those vagaries leaned in an evangelical direction. But as Oswald T. Allis observed, "It is the manifest purpose of the . . . Confession so to change our standards that . . . radical teachings will no longer be in conflict but in harmony with the Standards of the Church and be authorized and approved by them."[25]

As it turned out, the Confession of 1967 rapidly became a document more easily usable against evangelicals than usable by them, and its adoption signaled the beginning of a protracted struggle for survival on the part of those evangelicals who did not consider it right to leave the denomination.

For Mariano Di Gangi, the adoption of the Confession of 1967 meant that even if the evangelicals survived, they had still lost. Di Gangi believed that so long as the Westminster Confession stood, the evangelicals had at least one weapon to fight with and one disciplinary standard against which to arraign liberals. But now liberal Presbyterianism could not be bent back to that standard, and although many evangelicals chose to remain within the church, the church was doomed to be a permanently crooked rod. Saddened by what he saw as the ultimate vanity of evangelical efforts in the denomination and repelled by the possibilities for ethical relativism that the Confession provided, Di Gangi chose to leave.

It was not a decision made blithely. The shades of Henry Augustus Boardman and Donald Grey Barnhouse hung heavy over him as examples of those who had not quit even under excruciating pressure. Moreover, his friends argued, why give up a million-dollar piece of real estate to the liberals to help them further their aims? Retreat into the four-walled fortress of Tenth Church and fight on from there, they counseled. Di Gangi shook his head. "Sooner or later you're going to have to face the matter of corporate responsibility for the actions of the denomination or be tarred with the same brush. You may have to face congregationally the decision I had to face individually."[26]

After preaching a series of sermons outlining his grievances with the Confession of 1967, Di Gangi resigned on June 15, 1967.

Mariano Di Gangi left without any animosity, and he never condemned those who did not follow him out of the denomination. In turn, Tenth Church did not condemn him. In fact, in its twenty-six-page annual report for 1967, the church marked his departure in exactly one bland paragraph, leaving on record the unstated implication that his changes and innovations had been a little too hard on the people for them to have much sympathy for his theological agonizings.[27] Di Gangi bade the church farewell; the church bade him farewell; and that was the end of six years. His only comfort was to remember that such is the thankless fate of all transitional ministries, and it would not be until envy had been laid to sleep by time that people would realize the magisterial skillfulness and aplomb with which Di Gangi had transformed the church and readied it for a modern post-Barnhouse era in evangelicalism and the world.

His was, as he himself later acknowledged, a "buffer ministry." So, as Tenth Church prepared to enter into its longest and most critical period of denominational and doctrinal crisis—a crisis not unlike the ones that had called forth the Gilbert Tennents, the Henry Augustus Boardmans, and the Donald Grey Barnhouses—the church could be thankful that it had had a Mariano Di Gangi to absorb the worst blows of the inevitable transition. It is safe to say that without Di Gangi, the pressure of events within the denomination and within Tenth Church might have squeezed the spiritual and theological life out of the congregation, and made inconceivably harder the task of the pastor who was to follow him.

CHAPTER 5

BOICE

William S. Barker

For almost a year following the resignation of Mariano Di Gangi in June of 1967, the session's pulpit committee searched for a successor as senior pastor. At some point elder C. Everett Koop (who later served as Surgeon General of the United States) was told by fellow physician G. Newton Boice of McKeesport, Pennsylvania, that he had a twenty-nine-year-old son in Washington, D.C., who might be worth considering. "Oh, sure," thought Dr. Koop. But he and elders Roy Chew, Manfred Garibotti, Jay MacMoran, George Moffitt, and Bill Pascoe eventually journeyed to Washington to hear James Montgomery Boice preach on a Sunday evening at the Sixth Presbyterian Church. The elders were immediately impressed with his delivery, his content, and his commitment to the infallibility of the Bible—and, said Koop, "He sounded like Barnhouse." Tenth had found its fifth "B."

The similarity to Barnhouse was not surprising. Newton and Jean Boice had attended Tenth Church for about two years when Jim's father was pursuing orthopedic training at the University of Pennsylvania. During that time, when Jim was a small boy (he was born July 7, 1938), something unusual occurred:

It was at Tenth Church that a special meeting with Dr. Barnhouse took place. "It was about Christmas time," remembers Jean, "and Newt left me and Jimmy out at the door." Once inside, Jean and young Jim were met by Dr. Barnhouse, always an imposing figure. "What, may I ask, are you doing here tonight?" he asked. Jean responded, "Isn't this the night for the Christmas party?" "No, it's next Sunday—you come back next Sunday." Then, Jean remembers, "he picked Jim up, put his hand on his head, and prayed silently. I didn't hear the prayer, but I always felt that the Lord used that prayer in a special way in Jim's life."[1]

It was also Barnhouse who set thirteen-year-old Jim on a course of high-quality education. A frequent visitor to the Boice home when he was speaking in the Pittsburgh area, Barnhouse steered him to Stony Brook, a Christian preparatory school on Long Island. Jim would later recall the story for the school's alumni magazine:

> We had been talking about Stony Brook as we sat around the dinner table one Friday evening. As it turned out, this was the Friday on which the fall term at Stony Brook was beginning. In the course of the conversation he [Barnhouse] asked, "Jimmy, would you like to go to Stony Brook this year?" I said, "Yes." So he answered, "All right." And he got up from the dinner table—we were between main course and dessert—went to the telephone and called Dr. Frank E. Gaebelein, who was the headmaster at the time. I was admitted by phone, and two days later on Sunday I was on Long Island.[2]

Enriched by the academic, dramatic, and athletic opportunities at Stony Brook, James Boice graduated in 1956 and, after prayerful counsel between Dr. Gaebelein and his parents, advanced to Harvard. There he majored in English, was active in Inter-Varsity Christian Fellowship, and attended Boston's historic Park Street Church, then pastored by the evangelical statesman Dr. Harold John Ockenga. In his senior year Boice met Linda McNamara, who was attending the Harvard Graduate School of Education and was also active in Inter-Varsity and at Park Street

Church. The influence of Barnhouse continued for both of them as they discussed his radio messages and books, Linda having attended Tenth Church while an undergraduate at the University of Pennsylvania. When Barnhouse died in the fall of 1960, Jim prayed that he might be granted a double portion of the Spirit God had granted to this preacher-pastor.

From Harvard Jim went to Princeton Seminary, where he had to resolve any doubts he may have had about the doctrine of Scripture:

> I wrestled with the inerrancy of the Bible during my seminary years. It is not that I questioned it. My problem was that my teachers did not believe this, and much of what I was hearing in the classroom was meant to reveal the Bible's errors so that students would not depend on it too deeply. What was a student to do? The professors seemed to have all the facts. How were professors to be challenged when they argued that recent scholarship has shown that the old, simplistic views about the Bible being inerrant are no longer valid and that therefore we should admit that the Bible is filled with errors?
>
> As I worked on this I discovered some interesting things. First, the problems imagined to be in the Bible were hardly new problems. For the most part those problems were known centuries ago, even by such ancient theologians as Augustine and Jerome, who discussed apparent contradictions in their substantial correspondence.
>
> I also discovered that the results of sound scholarship have *not* tended to uncover more and more problems, as my professors were suggesting, still less disclose more and more "errors." Rather they have tended to *resolve* problems and to show that what were once thought to be errors are not errors at all.[3]

Jim was aided at Princeton by Professor Bruce Metzger, who guided his focus on New Testament studies. Linda received her master of religious education degree from Princeton Seminary in June of 1962, and she and Jim were married that summer in her home church, Grace Presbyterian in Montclair, New Jersey. That summer and the next, after Jim's graduation from Princeton Seminary, they lived in Washington, D.C., where Jim served as an editorial assistant to Dr. Carl F. H. Henry, the founding editor of *Christianity Today*. Convinced that he should seek doctoral studies in a European program that would allow him freedom to read, Jim's academic career took them next to the University of Basel in September 1963. There he studied the works of John Calvin, Charles Hodge, B. B. Warfield, and other Reformed theologians while doing his main research in New Testament under Professor Bo Reicke, an expert on the Dead Sea Scrolls, and Oscar Cullmann, an early church history scholar. After producing a dissertation on *Witness and Revelation in the Gospel of John*, Jim was awarded the doctor of theology degree in October 1966.

By December of that year the Boices were settled in Alexandria, Virginia, and Jim was serving once again as an assistant editor at *Christianity Today*. By late 1967 Carl Henry announced his plan to leave *Christianity Today*, and Jim sought the counsel of his former headmaster at Stony Brook, Frank Gaebelein, now retired in suburban Virginia. Gaebelein asked, "Do you plan to stay in Christian journalism?" and Jim replied, "No, I think I am going to pastor a church." That was on a Saturday in November, and on the next day Gaebelein was to preach at Tenth Church. Met at 30th Street Station in Philadelphia by Tenth elder Ralph Lingle, Gaebelein told him, "I think I've found the next pastor of Tenth Church." So it was not only Jim's father who recommended him for this pastorate, but an amazing convergence of providential circumstances and preparation, all pointing toward his becoming a preacher-pastor in a city pulpit, ever since he had preached his first sermon at age 12 in the First Evangelical Free Church of McKeesport, Pennsylvania. On March 17, 1968, Jim preached from Tenth's pulpit, and after the 11:00 a.m. service the congregation voted to extend the call to him as senior pastor. His first regular sermon as pastor was preached on Easter Sunday, April 14. James Montgomery Boice had become pastor of historic Tenth Presbyterian Church before his thirtieth birthday.

EARLY YEARS OF MINISTRY AT TENTH

Youthful vigor and vision were needed at Tenth by 1968. During Mariano Di Gangi's pastorate the doors of the church had been opened to African Americans, but the racial and other controversies of the 1960s, including the denomination's adoption of the new Confession of 1967, had produced some turmoil at Tenth. Membership had declined from a peak of 824 in 1948 to 535 in 1968, and much of the remaining membership was elderly. Dr. Koop remembers being frequently called upon in those days to minister to someone who had fainted at church![4] Elder Fred Garibotti recalls that typically the doors of the church were locked by 12:15 after the Sunday morning service, even during the Barnhouse years. Tenth was primarily a metropolitan preaching post with people coming from as far away as Bucks County, across the river in New Jersey, and even Delaware, but little community life existed within the church.

The Boices moved into the manse at 1827 Delancey Place, a block and a half from the center-city church, and very soon a renewed vitality came to Tenth. Music for congregational worship was improved. Barnhouse had replaced the old pipe organ with an inadequate Hammond in order to increase seating capacity in the balcony. Boice persuaded the trustees to spend the money to install a specially built, one-of-a-kind Allen electronic organ, and Dr. Robert Elmore was enticed from Bethlehem, Pennsylvania, to become organist in support of Tenth's biblical preaching and worship. An evening-service choir was begun, and hymns were sung with energy and enthusiasm.

The pattern for Boice's concept of church life was shaped by his experience in Basel. There a Filipino couple, Raoul and Lily Victorino, had encouraged him to start an English-language service in the Boices' two-room apartment. This service grew out of an Inter-Varsity-style weekly Bible study, similar to the kind that Boice had experienced at Harvard. With five in attendance at the first Sunday service, this weekly gathering for worship eventually moved into a rented Moravian chapel where an organ accompanied singing from Inter-Varsity hymnals. Boice preached from his current doctoral studies in the Scriptures. In due course, fellowship times and prayer meetings were added, so that the essential ingredients of church life were in place. From that time Jim and Linda had both felt that their calling was to a city church with a multicultural outreach. They came to Philadelphia feeling prepared by the Lord for the challenges and opportunities of Tenth Church.

A Bible study and prayer meeting were already well established at Tenth, but the Boices began hosting Thursday-night suppers for a few young couples and some singles in their home. Among these from early on were Norman Koop, Ray Lanning, and Nancy Wise (Hala), a student at Philadelphia College of the Bible (at that time still located in Center City Philadelphia) who resided at the Boices' home from 1972 to 1980 and helped care for their young daughters. This group began to study Puritan literature from the Banner of Truth Trust, fueling Boice's desire to get the Puritan doctrine out to ordinary people. Out of this interest grew the Philadelphia Conference on Reformed Theology, which each spring brought outstanding speakers not only to Philadelphia, but also to two or three other cities on the North American continent. Among the notable speakers over the years were J. I. Packer, Eric Alexander, and Sinclair Ferguson from Great Britain and Roger Nicole, John Gerstner, and R. C. Sproul from America. Sproul, who was teaching at Conwell School of Theology in Philadelphia in 1968–69, met Boice in the kitchen of the manse that year, and would become one of his closest friends and associates. The Westminster Brass, a quintet of two trumpets, a trombone, a French horn, and a tuba, was developed to accompany the PCRT worship sessions and play great church music on other special occasions.

At the beginning of Boice's ministry at Tenth, attendance was 386 on Sunday morning and 270 at the evening service. The budgets for 1969 were $60,000 for the general budget and $40,000 for missions. By the final year of his pastorate, in 2000, attendance averaged 1,200 per Sunday, and the annual budget was

$2.1 million ($1.3 general; $600,000 missions; and $200,000 building).[5] The 150th anniversary of Tenth Church in 1979 marked the progress that had been made in Boice's first decade:

> Tenth is alive. On normal Sundays the church is packed. Of 166 churches in the presbytery of Philadelphia only thirty reported any growth from 1970–1975. Out of the hundred or so churches actually in the city of Philadelphia only ten reported growth, and the growth for all but one or two was negligible. Tenth grew more than any other Presbyterian church in the area. There were 500 members in early 1968. By the summer of 1979 there were 740.[6]

The pattern of ministry that Boice had developed in his Basel experience—straightforward Bible exposition, vital congregational worship with excellent music, meaningful fellowship, and prayer— was being blessed by the Lord with fruitful results.

WIDER RELATIONS WITH EVANGELICALISM

Donald Grey Barnhouse had broadcast his preaching on the radio as early as 1928, but his radio ministry blossomed in 1949 with the founding of The Bible Study Hour under the aegis of The Evangelical Foundation (later Evangelical Ministries Incorporated, or EMI), which also managed *Revelation* (later *Eternity*) magazine. After James Boice arrived as pastor of Tenth Church in 1968, it was only a matter of months before it was recognized that he should become the new voice of The Bible Study Hour. By 1977 the broadcasts were carried on seventy-seven stations with 100 airtimes. In 1978 these messages began to be carried in Asia, and in 1980 Boice's sermons on John (already published in five volumes) were translated into Mandarin and broadcast into China. By 2000 the weekly program was heard on 248 stations in the United States.[7]

Boice's radio ministry, as well as the publication of his sermons as commentaries on books of the Bible that began in 1971 with *Philippians: An Expositional Commentary,* made him well known to fellow evangelicals. When the speakers at a conference on Scripture held at Mount Hermon in the Santa Cruz Mountains of California in January of 1976 expressed a shared concern over the low view of Scripture held by many evangelicals, they decided to launch what became known as the International Council on Biblical Inerrancy (ICBI). Involved in these discussions were John Gerstner, J. I. Packer, R. C. Sproul, Norman Geisler, Jay Grimstead, Greg Bahnsen, J. Barton Payne, and Karen C. Hoyt. This group unanimously decided to ask Boice to serve as chairman of the board, and Karen Hoyt became the executive director. From the beginning, ICBI was committed to staying in existence for no more than ten years, in order to carry out its mission without creating a self-perpetuating bureaucracy. The stated purpose was: "To take a united stand in elucidating, vindicating, and applying the doctrine of biblical inerrancy as an essential element for the authority of Scripture and a necessity for the health of the church of God, and to attempt to win the church back to this historic position."[8]

The process for accomplishing these objectives was a series of academic summit meetings and lay conferences. The first summit produced *The Chicago Statement on Biblical Inerrancy* in 1978, including a short statement defining inerrancy and nineteen articles of affirmation and denial that was signed by 240 of 268 scholars in attendance. Next came the first Congress on the Bible, attended by some 3,000 in San Diego in 1982. A second summit, held in 1986, produced *The Chicago Statement on Biblical Hermeneutics*, with twenty-five articles of affirmation and denial. This was followed by a second Congress on the Bible, which was held in Washington, D.C., in 1987 and focused on the interpretation and application of Scripture.[9]

Boice's connections with such evangelical leaders as Donald Grey Barnhouse, Frank Gaebelein, Harold John Ockenga, and Carl Henry had linked him with the broader evangelical world. Barnhouse was, of course, a Presbyterian and was committed to the doctrinal distinctives of the Reformed faith, although with a dispensational eschatology. As Boice preached through the gospel of John in the 1970s, he became even more strongly convinced of the biblical truth of Reformed soteriology. Since Calvinists often lean on such Pauline passages as Ephesians 1 or Romans 9 in articulating and defending the doctrine of predestination, it is noteworthy that Boice expounded the famous "Five Points" of the Synod of Dort (1618–19) from such passages as John 6 and John 10. He even titled his sermon on John 10:27–29 "Christ the Calvinist."[10]

Boice's commitment to a Reformed position on Christian liberty as opposed to a more restricted evangelical lifestyle is evident in a much later response to an invitation to serve on the Wheaton College Board of Trustees in 1992. Informed that the same lifestyle standards for students would be required of board members, Boice turned down the invitation while at the same time expressing great appreciation for Wheaton as a Christian college:

> My problem comes only at the point of requiring extra-biblical standards of behavior of Christian adults (the status of students is probably ambiguous at this point), which I do think is mistaken and probably non-biblical itself. That is what legalism is, imposing non-biblical standards on another person. One thing I have always been thankful for in terms of my own upbringing is that my parents never insisted on such things for either myself or my sisters with the result that none of us ever felt a need to rebel or even do the questionable things. Personally I have always resisted any steps toward legalism, and in this respect I am one with Tenth Presbyterian Church, which I serve as pastor, and with the Presbyterian Church in America, which is our denomination. I would go further. I would maintain that this resistance is itself biblical obedience since the Bible tells us, "It is for freedom that Christ has set us free. Stand firm, then, and do not let yourselves be burdened again by a yoke of slavery" (Gal. 5:1).[11]

A Reformed understanding of Christian liberty, however, did not mean an antinomian view of sanctification. In the context of the "Lordship controversy" among some evangelicals in the 1970s, Boice made it clear that to know Jesus as Savior meant also to know him as Lord. Saving faith—true biblical faith—involves three elements: knowledge, heart response, and commitment.[12]

Leaving the United Presbyterian Church, USA

A major turning point for Tenth Church came on March 9, 1980, when the congregation voted (362 to 7, with 11 abstaining) to leave the United Presbyterian Church, USA—the mainline Presbyterian denomination to which it had belonged for over 150 years. This decision came after several years of seeking reform within the denomination and after many months of carefully preparing the congregation with regard to the issues involved.

The culminating issue was the adoption by the UPCUSA General Assembly in May 1979 of Overture L, which required that congregations elect women to serve on their sessions. This was a follow-up to the earlier Wynn Kenyon case, in which the eponymous young candidate was denied ordination because he believed ordaining women to the office of teaching or ruling elder to be unbiblical. The denomination had been ordaining women for some years, and Tenth Church, while disagreeing with this practice, had tolerated it in the denomination. But now the denomination was forcing this practice on its congregations. In addition, a cardinal Christian doctrine was being jettisoned by UPCUSA minister Mansfield Kaseman, who denied the deity of Christ yet was accepted early in 1979 by Washington, D.C.'s National Union Presbytery. Another concern was the possible ordination of those who were openly homosexual. Although the 1978 General Assembly prohibited the "ordination of self-acknowledged practicing gay and lesbian persons,"[13] the issue would continue to come before the denomination for the next several years.

The General Assembly had met in Philadelphia in 1977, and several members of Tenth Church had taken the opportunity to attend sessions and see firsthand how the denomination was operating. Prior to the congregational meeting on March 9, 1980, the session sent a five-page letter (see appendix 5) to the members in which the issues were clearly delineated.[14] Reference was made to the change in ordination vows that had taken place with the adoption of the Confession of 1967. Whereas formerly ordinands had been asked, "Do you believe the Scriptures of the Old and New Testaments to be *the Word of God*, the only infallible rule of faith and practice?," the new vows asked, "Do you accept the scriptures of the Old and New Testaments to be, by the Holy Spirit, the unique and authoritative *witness to Jesus Christ* in the church universal, and *God's Word to you?*"[15] As Tenth's elders explained to the congregation:

> The change makes the Scriptures authoritative only in their witness to Christ, not necessarily in other matters, and introduces a subjective element—"in the church universal, and God's Word to you." This is understood by many church officials and others to mean that the Holy Spirit speaks subjectively in today's church, even in ways contrary to what the Bible teaches.
>
> Today Scripture no longer functions as the ultimate authority within the United Presbyterian Church. The authority is the human majority, the authority of the fifty-one-percent vote.[16]

The Westminster Confession of Faith and catechisms had also been diminished in doctrinal authority by the adoption of seven other Reformed confessions in 1969 and a shift in the ordination vows regarding them. Finally, the traditional Presbyterian emphasis on government of the local congregation by its session was being superseded by a hierarchy of presbytery and General Assembly.

The session's letter went on to make reference to the Wynn Kenyon case (*Maxwell v. Presbytery of Pittsburgh*), as well as to the adoption of Overture L, which mandated the ordination of women as ruling elders. This would render seminarians working at Tenth ineligible for ordination in the denomination and would jeopardize Tenth's ability to find a compatible pastor in the denomination if Dr. Boice should ever leave. After a description of the still-pending Mansfield Kaseman case, the letter advised the congregation that, although Tenth's position had previously been to stay in the denomination, "thereby bearing witness to the unity of the church and in order to work for change within," it was now time—being unable to either "actively concur" or "passively submit"—to "peaceably withdraw" from the UPCUSA and "seek alignments more in line with historic Presbyterianism and the dictates of our own consciences as informed by Scripture."[17]

On March 2, 1980—the Sunday preceding the decisive congregational meeting—Boice delivered a "Statement on Leaving the UPCUSA." He offered four reasons why the congregation should make the move recommended by the session. One was religious freedom. The Philadelphia Presbytery, upon learning of the direction Tenth's session was taking, had sent a delegation to have an apparently congenial discussion with the session, which frankly expressed its concerns over denominational trends in both doctrine and polity. The next day the presbytery cited the members of session to show cause why they should not be replaced by an administrative commission and why the pastor's relation to the congregation should not be terminated. Even Professor John Gerstner of Pittsburgh Theological Seminary, who still argued vigorously for staying within the denomination, told Boice over the phone that this was nothing less than ecclesiastical tyranny.

A second reason for leaving was Tenth's future ministry. Boice said: "At the time of the Wynn Kenyon decision there were four young men under care of our session. Each one of those has since been forced into some other denomination. Those under care at the present time have reached a plateau."[18] In addition, there was the session's concern about finding an appropriate successor to their current pastor if he should ever leave. A third reason was rejection of wrongdoing. Here Boice referred to the toleration of unbelief in the Kaseman decision and the admission of the representatives from the Philadelphia Presbytery that it was now impossible to have a heresy trial in the UPCUSA. The fourth reason was the opportunity to work with those of like mind in a fully Reformed and truly Presbyterian denomination.

Although the vote on March 9 was virtually unanimous, the Philadelphia Presbytery entered into litigation over the church building. As Boice wrote to Dr. Bernard Ramm, "They do not need the building, of course. There are three other Presbyterian churches within easy walking distance of us, and two of these others are nearly dying. Upkeep of another building would be a millstone around their neck."[19] Nevertheless, this litigation would drag on for four years. Finally, in 1984 it became clear that a monetary settlement would resolve the issue, and it dawned on Boice that the manse on Delancey Place could be offered in exchange for proprietorship of the historic church building. The manse had been purchased for approximately $55,000. The Philadelphia Presbytery sold it for about $250,000 to a party who refurbished it; it was later sold for over one million dollars. Meanwhile, the church building was obtained for a "jubilee year" lease of one dollar per year for fifty years, to be free and clear if Tenth was still located in Center City Philadelphia at the end of that period.[20]

Tenth Church had no intention of selling the church building and moving to the suburbs, as the presbytery feared. Its firm intention was to stay at its strategic location at 17th and Spruce. In his sermon preached on March 16, a week after the congregational vote to leave the old denomination, Boice said:

> We also have a continuing obligation to the city of Philadelphia, and we must press on here. I have tried to stress this with various reporters who have interviewed me lately. I have said that our concern is to be here in Philadelphia to minister to this neighborhood. That is the basis for our concern with property—not merely to have a building (who really cares what the building is like so long as the ministry goes on?), but to have a building in this neighborhood to which we are committed.

Boice's sermon captured the commitment and progress of his ministry at Tenth at this stage. He expressed his hope "that we might also be effective in planting churches in other parts of our city."[21] And he hinted at some of the preaching he still hoped to do:

> Here are some of the things that we still have to do. We have to go on *teaching the Word of God*. That is what, more than anything else, has characterized the ministry of Tenth Presbyterian Church

for 150 years. For 150 years this pulpit has taught the Word of
God, consistently, in depth, systematically. That work is not yet
done. It has to be done age after age.

   I think of the books of the Bible I still want to teach. Twelve
years ago I began to teach Philippians. After that I taught the Sermon on the Mount. Then I did John for eight years. In the meantime
I taught different things in the evening: Galatians; 1, 2, and 3 John;
1 and 2 Timothy; James. Now I am teaching Genesis and the Minor
Prophets. That is quite a few books. But I think of the books that
have not been taught. Hebrews! Matthew! Isaiah! Romans! We rejoice
that we have the opportunity for such teaching here.

   By the end of his life two decades later, Boice would have
published his sermons on Ephesians, Daniel, Joshua, Nehemiah,
Romans (4 volumes), Psalms (3 volumes), Acts, and Matthew
(2 volumes). And he had begun preaching through Revelation
when he died in 2000.[22]

   In the sermon he preached after leaving the UPCUSA, Dr.
Boice expressed another commitment of his ministry at Tenth:

> We have a second concern: *building up the body of Christ* through
> fellowship, interaction, and mutual support among the members of
> this congregation. We have probably not had an area of Christian
> life that has shown more advance in the last couple years than this
> one. It used to be that nothing much happened here during the week
> except the preparation of the sermon. It was preached on Sunday,
> and then after the morning or evening service everyone went home.
> It does not happen that way anymore. After the services people linger
> on and on. I do not get my lunch until about three o'clock in the
> afternoon anymore. In the evening I hardly get home at all. That is
> marvelous! It is wonderful to see that kind of love and fellowship.[23]

INTO THE NEW DENOMINATION: GROWTH AND URBAN OUTREACH

   In leaving the UPCUSA, Boice and Tenth's session did not
intend to become independent. The biblical connectionalism of

Presbyterian polity was still prized. The question was with which of the small, doctrinally conservative Presbyterian denominations to affiliate. The choices included the Orthodox Presbyterian Church (OPC), the Reformed Presbyterian Church, Evangelical Synod (RPCES), and the Presbyterian Church in America (PCA). Boice's own leanings were toward the RPCES, partly because of his earlier experience with it in the McLean Presbyterian Church in Virginia, and partly because it had the largest presence of the three denominations in the Philadelphia area. For several months, however, he sought and provided for Tenth's session and congregation a full exposure to all three denominations. The PCA had arranged a Consultation on Presbyterian Alternatives in Pittsburgh, at which representatives of the three churches made presentations. The presenters included R. C. Sproul and G. Aiken Taylor of the PCA, Edmund P. Clowney of the OPC, and Francis A. Schaeffer of the RPCES. Schaeffer was the main speaker, urging that "while we indeed maintain and do not minimize our [Presbyterian and Reformed] distinctives, because we believe they are biblical," nevertheless the "real chasm must be between true Bible-believing Christians and others and not at a lesser point."[24]

At the urging of editor Aiken Taylor and associate editor Joel Belz, Boice produced an article entitled "How Can We Choose?" for *The Presbyterian Journal*. In the article he expressed the dilemma for a church such as Tenth in examining the strengths and weaknesses of these smaller, doctrinally sound denominations. He concluded: "We should work toward one national, truly Presbyterian Church with deliberate speed."[25] The momentum was with the most recently formed (1973) PCA, and some feared that if Tenth joined the denomination, it would not have the same incentive to merge as it would if Tenth were to affiliate with one of the older but smaller groups.[26]

A special committee of Tenth's session was formed on July 22 to compare the PCA and the RPCES. On September 23 the committee brought its recommendation that the session encourage the congregation to join the RPCES.[27] The congregation adopted this recommendation on December 5, and a service of induction into the RPCES was held at Tenth on January 25, 1981, with Francis Schaeffer preaching. In 1982 the RPCES joined and was received by the PCA, producing a sound Presbyterian denomination of relatively modest size, but with a rapid growth rate and increasing national visibility.

Freed from conflicts within the old denomination, Tenth's energy could now be channeled into more constructive avenues. Average attendance grew from 916 in 1979 to a peak of 1,232 in 1984. There was a surge of new ministries. Once it was in a denomination that was committed to Scripture, Tenth's bottled-up energy was uncorked in a burst of ministry. As members of the congregation became burdened for various needs in the community, Boice and the session would encourage the development of a new ministry, which might eventually spin off to have its own board and means of support. In 1983—partly out of concern for their two younger daughters' high-school education, but also out of concern for other Christian families trying to raise teens in the city—Linda and Jim Boice founded City Center Academy (CCA), using the Tenth Church facilities and providing a college-preparatory curriculum for an ethnically mixed enrollment of about eighty students by 2000. In 1984 members of Tenth started Harvest, an outreach to Philadelphia's gay community, offering evangelism and counseling to those desiring to leave a homosexual lifestyle. Out of this by 1988 grew Hope, a ministry to those suffering from HIV disease and AIDS. Alpha Pregnancy Services was begun in the early 1980s to provide Christian alternatives to abortion. Under the aegis of the deacons, ACTS (Active Compassion Through Service) was formed as a mercy ministry in 1982. Directed by Dr. David S. Apple from 1988, ACTS provided a weekly Bible study and monthly community dinner for a hundred or more homeless people, tutored inner-city children, visited the elderly, and cared for families suffering from separation and divorce.[28] Much later in Boice's ministry, a group of talented, visionary young doctors came from Atlanta to establish Medical Campus Outreach (MCO)—a discipleship-based, missions-minded outreach to Philadelphia's medical community.

Added to the ministerial staff in the 1980s were Linward A. Crowe, who had served on the session as a ruling elder, and Glenn M. McDowell, who worked with City Light—a ministry to single adults that focused on reaching people in Center City. Also of significance at this stage was the hiring of Cora Hogue in 1982 as a pastoral assistant. Formerly serving as a missionary to students in Florence, Italy, Hogue focused on adult education, counseling, hospitality, and coordinating small groups. Because one of the issues involved in leaving the UPCUSA was the ordination of women, Boice was sometimes accused of being a misogynist. "Nothing could be further from the truth," testified Hogue. Boice's "understanding was that women could not serve as elders or preach from the pulpit. Beyond that, Jim was very supportive of women serving the Lord. It was Jim's idea to have a woman on the pastoral staff and to have a board of deaconesses." From the 1980s on, deaconesses were not ordained, but commissioned, as were missionaries from Tenth.[29]

From the beginning, the Boices had felt a call to city ministry. Linda had loved the city of New York from her youth. In the late 1970s, however, a trip to Pittsburgh with associate ministers Lin Crowe and Glenn McDowell had further inspired Jim to make a commitment to the city of Philadelphia. Held at the Ligonier Study Center, this meeting with the Pittsburgh Offensive, a group of key leaders gathered by John Guest and Reid Carpenter—stressed a commitment to the city of Pittsburgh, to make it a city of God more than a city of steel. Returning to Philadelphia, Boice and his associates formed a similar urban coalition of pastors—white and African American—which at first met monthly in Lin Crowe's home. Tenth elder Elmer Snethen later hosted the meetings, which focused on sharing vision and praying for Philadelphia.

These men made a covenant not to leave their charges in Philadelphia without consulting one another concerning the Lord's leading.[30] This was tested for Boice on at least two occasions with inquiries from Billy Graham. In November of 1980, Graham as chairman of the board of Gordon-Conwell Seminary asked Boice to consider the possibility of becoming president of the seminary. Again in May of 1981 Graham proposed that Boice return to *Christianity Today* as editor. He responded:

> I feel a very strong and God-given call to the ministry of Tenth Presbyterian Church and through it in a broader sense to the city of Philadelphia. As a matter of fact, a number of us have signed a document stating our intention to remain in Philadelphia and work for a greater impact of the gospel upon the city, rejecting whatever promotions or other offers may come our way unless there is overriding evidence that the Lord is leading in another direction, and only then if our brethren concur in that new sense of call. . . . [W]e are just now on the verge of some exciting new ministries and penetration into the overall spiritual life of Philadelphia.[31]

Boice articulated his deepened commitment to the city in a message delivered to a Philadelphia ministries conference in March of 1982. Based on Jeremiah 32 and entitled "This People, This Place," the exposition became known as "Jim's favorite sermon." It expressed principles that Boice uttered as his sentiment on many occasions and in various contexts. The urban pastor's commitment must be to people rather than to programs, to a place of God's calling rather than to promotions that may look more attractive, and for an indefinite period of time until God clearly leads elsewhere.[32] The founding of City Center Academy, with its diverse ethnic student body, helped to give credibility to Tenth in the African-American community. A positive connection was made with several black pastors, including Dr. Benjamin Smith of the large Deliverance Evangelistic Fellowship in North Philadelphia. Smith was a main speaker on the occasion of Boice's twenty-fifth anniversary as pastor at Tenth in 1993, and the Deliverance choir sang at the General Assembly of the Presbyterian Church in America when Tenth hosted that meeting in Philadelphia in 1986—a new experience for many of the commissioners from the still largely Southern denomination.

Façade on Walnut Street

Façade on Spruce Street (1855)

Façade on Spruce Street (1952)

HENRY AUGUSTUS BOARDMAN
(1833–1876)

WILLIAM PRATT BREED
(1856–1889)

JOHN DEWITT
(1876–1883)

MARCUS A. BROWNSON
(1897–1924)

DONALD GREY BARNHOUSE
(1927–1960)

MARIANO DI GANGI (1961–1967)

JAMES MONTGOMERY BOICE
(1968–2000)

PHILIP GRAHAM RYKEN
(2001–)

Sanctuary (with chandelier), after the
Interior renovations in 1893

ROBERT ELMORE AT THE ORGAN

THE CONGREGATION DURING A HYMN SING

ABOVE: JAMES MONTGOMERY BOICE AND
FRANCIS A. SCHAEFFER

RIGHT: THE WESTMINSTER BRASS

ABOVE LEFT: JIM AND LINDA BOICE CROSS SPRUCE STREET WITH STUDENTS
FROM CITY CENTER ACADEMY

ABOVE RIGHT: C. EVERETT KOOP, LONGTIME MEMBER AND ELDER OF TENTH
PRESBYTERIAN CHURCH AND SURGEON GENERAL OF THE UNITED STATES FROM
1981 TO 1989

Plateau, Decline, and Resurgence

The steady growth in average attendance at Tenth up to a peak of 1,232 in 1984 brought with it new challenges. The "Delancey Building" (formerly the home of Dr. Barnhouse and his first wife) adjacent to the church building had been purchased and turned into office and classroom space. The basement of the church was rehabilitated into the "Catacombs" for library, bookstore, and classroom space, and eventually overflow space for worship services with television monitors. To address the challenges of growth, Tenth brought in Dr. Timothy J. Keller as a consultant in September of 1986. Keller was then teaching practical theology at Westminster Seminary in Philadelphia; in 1989 he would become the organizing pastor of Redeemer Presbyterian Church in New York City. In May of 1987 he made his extensive report with twelve recommendations under three headings: vision, coordination, and "care and feeding." A task force of the session then considered this report over the summer and brought a response to a leadership retreat in September. A summary of Keller's recommendations and the task force's response was discussed at Tenth's separate parish meetings in October, and the results were brought back to the session that month.

With the exception of his recommendation to establish separate worshiping congregations, most of Dr. Keller's proposals were viewed positively, but few of them were immediately implemented. Tenth had begun conducting double morning worship services in September of 1986, but overall average attendance began to decline in 1987 and would continue to decline each year through 1994 (with the exception of 1989 and 1991), so that the 1994 average attendance of 964 was about the same as the 1980 average of 960.

What was happening during this gradual decline? For one thing, Boice was tired from the double morning worship services in addition to his preaching in the Sunday-evening service. He also felt that in dividing the congregation for morning worship, the church had sacrificed some of its energy. Another difficulty was administrative support. Several of Keller's recommendations involved the creation of an executive pastor position to relieve Boice of some of his responsibilities in this area, but an effective person for this position had not yet been found by the end of 1988. Having reached his fiftieth birthday in July of that year, Boice told one of his associate ministers, Glenn McDowell, that he felt he had done all he could to enhance the ministry of Tenth Church.[33] The various activities under Evangelical Ministries Incorporated, such as The Bible Study Hour and *Eternity* magazine, were also absorbing a good deal of his time and energy.

But perhaps most telling was a growing difficulty in interpersonal relationships that developed between Boice and his associates and enveloped senior staff members such as Lin Crowe. Crowe had been instrumental in organizing Tenth's parish system and helping in 1983 to establish the Philadelphia Leadership Foundation (PLF)—an outgrowth of the urban pastoral coalition that was housed at Tenth during its first five years. Crowe and Boice were close friends and partners in ministry, but their differences in managing people and pastoral care could not be fully resolved. Responding to a call from PLF's board of directors, Crowe left the staff in 1988 to become the organization's first president. One positive result of this difficulty was the establishment of a liaison committee between the session and the senior pastor to help with accountability and conflict resolution. Some elders believe that this was a turning point in the session's becoming more fully Presbyterian in its function.[34]

It was also in 1988 that the Reverend D. Marion Clark, feeling burned out from a previous pastorate and looking for a job after having moved to Philadelphia, stumbled across Tenth Church while walking in Center City. After picking up literature about City Center Academy and leaving his résumé at the church, he soon received a call from Boice proposing the position of principal at CCA.[35] Clark served in that capacity full-time for four years, then moved to the ministerial staff in 1992 to become the executive pastor, relieving Boice of much of the administrative burden. In September of 1994 Tenth shifted from holding two identical morning worship services to holding its traditional worship service at 11:00 a.m. and adding an early communion service led by Clark.

Equally significant was the session's decision in 1994 to reduce Boice's preaching load further by seeking an additional minister who could preach regularly in the evening service. In September of 1995 Dr. Philip Graham Ryken, a graduate of Wheaton College and Westminster Seminary with a doctorate in historical theology from the University of Oxford, was added to the staff. Ryken proved effective in the pulpit, thus freeing Boice for ministry beyond Tenth, where his gifts were increasingly in demand. Previous additions to the ministerial staff had included Dr. Bruce McDowell in 1988 as associate minister of missions with a focus on the many international students in Philadelphia, and the Rev. Carroll Wynne in 1993 as associate minister of pastoral care, with significant responsibilities for youth ministry and visitation. The effects of these additions were evident as average attendance increased steadily from 964 in 1994 to over 1,300 in 1998 (see Appendix 3).

Boice's own energy was rekindled by the formation of what in 1994 would become the Alliance of Confessing Evangelicals (ACE). During his extensive travels he was exposed to the worship practices of many evangelical churches, and he became concerned over an apparent loss of God-centeredness in the effort to respond to "felt needs" at the human level. Galvanized by Gordon-Conwell professor David F. Wells's 1993 book *No Place for Truth, or Whatever Happened to Evangelical Theology?*, Boice joined forces with Michael Horton's Christians United for Reformation (CURE) in 1996. In April of that year, the Alliance of Confessing Evangelicals attracted 120 evangelicals from Baptist, Anglican, and Lutheran backgrounds, as well as Presbyterian and Reformed, to a conference in Cambridge, Massachusetts. There "The Cambridge Declaration" was produced, reasserting the great "solas" of the Protestant Reformation—*sola Scriptura, solus Christus, sola gratia, sola fide, soli Deo Gloria*—that seemed to be diminished in contemporary evangelicalism.[36]

Sola Scriptura—Scripture alone as the authority for faith and practice—had been Boice's focus during the decade he led the International Council on Biblical Inerrancy. Now his concern included the great "solas" of soteriology—by grace alone, through faith alone. In an Alliance board meeting, Boice responded to J. I. Packer's comment that justification by faith was but the fine print of biblical salvation: "No, it is the bold print!"[37]

But increasingly Boice was concerned with the *soli Deo Gloria*—to God alone be the glory—as manifested in the church's worship. The pattern of worship he maintained at Tenth Church was one that strove to be God-centered, with responsive reading of the psalms, a substantial pastoral prayer, traditional elements such as the Gloria Patri and the Apostles' Creed, successive readings of New Testament passages preceded by a five- to seven-minute exposition (a practice begun at Tenth by Barnhouse, but not unlike that of Ulrich Zwingli and of the Puritans, and highly appropriate when the sermon usually focuses on only a few verses in an extended exposition of a biblical book over months or years), and hymns full of biblical content. In the final year of his life, Boice himself wrote fourteen hymns (including two for children), set to music by Tenth organist and music director Dr. Paul S. Jones, that he hoped would help to fill a void in modern evangelical worship.[38]

At this writing, the Alliance of Confessing Evangelicals continues to sponsor The Bible Study Hour, *Modern Reformation Magazine,* The White Horse Inn radio broadcast, the Philadelphia Conference on Reformation Theology, and other national conferences. The Rev. Richard D. Phillips, who began as executive director for ACE, joined Tenth's ministerial staff in 1999 and aided Dr. Ryken in filling the pulpit, particularly after Boice's death in 2000.

A SUDDEN END

Returning exhausted from the travels of the 2000 PCRT, Boice was diagnosed on Good Friday with an aggressive form of liver cancer. His last weekly sermon at Tenth was preached on Easter Sunday, April 23. At first it was thought that the cancer might respond to chemotherapy, but soon it was determined to be a bile-duct carcinoma, a rare form of cancer originating in the liver.[39] On May 2 Boice informed the Tenth Church staff of the serious-ness of his condition, and requests for prayer were redoubled by e-mail. On Sunday, May 7, he appeared in the pulpit to explain his rapidly deteriorating physical condition before giving the call to worship. After describing his condition, he gave testimony to the combination of the sovereignty and goodness of God—a mysterious juxtaposition of divine attributes that the fallen human mind strug-gles so mightily to comprehend:

> If I were to reflect on what goes on theologically here, there are two things I would stress. One is the sovereignty of God. That's not novel. We have talked about the sovereignty of God here for-ever. God is in charge. When things like this come into our lives, they are not just accidental. It's not as if God somehow forgot what was going on, and something bad slipped by. It's not the answer that Harold Kushner gave in his book, *Why Bad Things Happen to Good People*. God does everything according to His will. We've always said that. But what I've been impressed with mostly is some-thing in addition to that. It's possible, isn't it, to conceive of God as sovereign and yet indifferent?—God's in charge, but He doesn't care. But it's not that. God is not only the one who is in charge; God is also good. Everything He does is good. And what Romans 12:1–2 says is that we have the opportunity by the renewal of our minds—that is, how we think about these things—actually to prove what God's will is. And then it says, "His good, pleasing, and per-fect will." Is that good, pleasing, and perfect to God? Yes, of course, but the point of it is that it's good, pleasing, and perfect to us. If God does something in your life, would you change it? If you'd change it, you'd make it worse. It wouldn't be as good. So that's the way we want to accept it and move forward, and who knows what God will do?[40]

Dr. Boice's last time to be in the sanctuary of Tenth Church was on May 14, when he slipped into the choir loft to hear the children's choir sing a hymn he had written for them. During his final weeks he received the loving care of his wife and daughters. Mercifully spared great or prolonged suffering, he died peacefully at home on June 15, 2000. Thousands attended the memorial service the next week, with countless others listening to the service on a nationwide radio broadcast.

Throughout his ministry at Tenth Church James Boice was committed to high standards of excellence. His family, friends, and colleagues remember him as disciplined and focused. He knew what his gifts were, and he would not allow himself to be distracted from his calling. He had a nearly photographic memory, as anyone sharing the platform with him discovered upon offering to share a hymnal with him. Advised by Carl Henry early in his ministry never to preach a sermon he would not be willing to publish, he spoke from a full manuscript. With a high percentage of Tenth's membership serving as teacher/educators, engineers, nurses, physicians, and other professionals, Boice sought to maintain a high quality of music and general cultural style. Sometimes there was criticism of his leadership style (even from elders who deeply loved and respected him), as one characterized by "telling/selling," rather than "participating/delegating," with "over-control of the decision-making process."[41] Pastoral staff who served with him in later years, however, welcomed the degree of freedom, authority, and support they were given to carry out their ministry at Tenth. On more than one occasion Boice remarked to his colleagues that sometimes in younger years he had taken his own proposals too seriously. Yet he had come to understand that if God wanted something to happen at Tenth, it would happen—according to his divine timetable.

Jim Boice received a good bit of kidding about his usually formal attire. From his days at Stony Brook and Harvard he was accustomed to wearing a coat and tie. While Nancy Wise (Hala) was living in the Boice home, she was quizzed by her Philadelphia College of the Bible classmates (who knew of the formal decorum of Tenth's services) as to whether she had to wear a uniform.[42] Boice and good friend R. C. Sproul were referred to as "Felix" and "Oscar" of movie and television fiction ("The Odd Couple") because, as Sproul put it, "Jim wore those three-piece Brooks Brothers suits. Of course, I wore Brooks Brothers suits too, but somehow I always came across as a fullback."[43] On one occasion, when Boice appeared at a Sunday school picnic in a long-sleeved white shirt and a tie, two sons of elders—Norman Koop and Carl Lingle—stripped him of tie and shirt and set him loose in the middle of the park's lake in a canoe without paddles. But having learned at Harvard how to "gunwale"—that is, to propel the boat by rocking its sides—he got safely to land, though splashed by stones thrown by his friendly pursuers. As the Rev. Norman Koop remarked at the twenty-fifth anniversary of Boice's pastorate at Tenth in 1993, "He is the only Calvinist I know who saved himself and still got himself to the other shore!"[44]

In personal relations Boice tended to be shy, but he was bold and direct in delivering what he believed to be God's clear teaching. His appeal was to the mind, and through the mind to reach the heart. It was God's truth that would set people free. Although through the years some people disagreed with Boice over personal issues, Tenth was spared the kinds of splits that other congregations experienced because they knew he would consistently expound what the Bible said. When offered other positions, he reiterated his commitment to be Tenth's pastor. His service as an experienced minister of a significant city church gave enhanced credibility to his ministries outside of Tenth.

Jim's recreations included running, most often on Mondays. Organist and music director Paul Jones noted: "Dr. Boice wrote a number of the hymns while jogging along the Schuylkill River. The rhythm of his feet hitting the pathway gave meter to his thoughts, which he would formulate and record as soon as he got to his laptop computer. This was a form of recreation for him. 'Let's keep this up,' he wrote. 'It's a good diversion and fun.'"[45] Boice could also enjoy watching the Philadelphia Eagles football team. Serving on one occasion as their chaplain before a game, he was disappointed not to be invited a second time. After receiving his parents' home in Cape May, New Jersey, he frequently resorted to it from Sunday evening until Thursday morning to do his reading and writing. Linda, with her teaching responsibilities at City Center Academy, usually did not accompany him on his extensive travels.

Some of the best times the Boices shared were on family vacations, when they could escape the pressures of ministry to visit some exciting locale or simply have time together as a family on a Florida beach. The ministry itself was always demanding, and according to one of the elders on the liaison committee of the session, Jim's main regret in his last days was the degree of neglect of his family.[46] Eldest daughter Elizabeth married at an early age. Daughters Heather and Jennifer were still at home when they learned rather suddenly over Sunday dinner that the Delancey Place manse—the only home they had ever known—would be exchanged with the presbytery for the church building. For Linda this adjustment was more welcome, since the property at 1827 Delancey Place was a large city townhouse that was not easy to maintain. The Boices' new home at 1935 Pine Street was smaller, more manageable, and still within walking distance of the church. Linda found fulfillment in friendships with women in the church, in teaching a Sunday school class for teenagers, and especially in teaching English at CCA, where as of this writing she continues to serve as head teacher. She was a loyal, hospitable, and gifted partner to her husband, who was able to consult with her on intellectual, spiritual, and practical matters.

Boice's legacy extends far beyond the pews and people of Tenth Presbyterian Church. Sometimes his polished sermons, delivered in his deep and mellow voice, were criticized by members of Tenth as being crafted more for the radio broadcasts of The Bible Study Hour or for eventual publication as commentaries. It is true that most of his sermons, which he characteristically referred to as "studies," ended up as books after passing through radio transmission. But this was his natural style, following the advice of Carl Henry, who also provided him with the model of answering every letter he received. Not all of Boice's publications were Bible commentaries, however. His *Foundations of the Christian Faith,* originally published in four volumes and then reprinted in one volume by InterVarsity Press in 1986, was meant to be a modern version of Calvin's *Institutes*. Similarly, his *Two Cities, Two Loves,* published by InterVarsity Press in 1996 and later republished as *Foundations of God's City,* was intended as a popular restatement of Augustine's *City of God*.[47] As of 2002, most of Boice's more than fifty published titles remained in print, including his multivolume series on John, Genesis, Romans, Psalms, and Matthew.[48] His clear manner of handling the text of Scripture, developed as an English major at Harvard when he learned to deal with primary material rather than secondary sources, produced an abundance of biblical teaching for Christians around the world. Tenth always had a strong missionary zeal, and Boice maintained and strengthened this by his overseas contacts, the distribution of his taped messages, the translations of his writings, and his encouragement of seminaries in France, Africa, and India.[49] Another extension of his Bible teaching was through Bible Study Fellowship International (BSF). During summers from 1981 to 1999, Boice taught numerous Bible study leaders from the widespread (mostly women's) groups of BSF, and his teaching on Exodus and Romans was subsequently studied by women (and men) all over the world.[50]

For Tenth Church Jim Boice's death came as a devastating blow, particularly because of its suddenness. But he departed the earthly scene for that better place when things were on the upswing. After earlier church plants in South Philadelphia and Germantown had not immediately flourished, another attempt in Conshohocken under the Rev. Adam Brice was taking hold, and still another was being planned for a largely African-American community in West Philadelphia under the leadership of the Rev. Lance Lewis. Most encouraging was the congregation's enthusiastic acceptance of the ministry of Dr. Philip Ryken, who at the age of 34, after a thorough search process, was installed as senior minister on March 4, 2001. Ryken's ministry had blended well with that of Boice since 1995. Their minds and style were so much alike that old friend R. C. Sproul confessed in his foreword to *The Doctrines of Grace* (a book that Boice started and Ryken finished) that he "could not detect where Jim's writing ended and Phil's began."[51]

In reviewing Boice's legacy, one is reminded of a story that Sproul told at his friend's memorial service. Sharing the platform at one of the earliest PCRT conferences—perhaps the first one accompanied by the Westminster Brass—with the Tenth Church sanctuary packed and the congregation singing "A Mighty Fortress Is Our God," Jim leaned over to say, "R. C., it doesn't get any better than this." Yet for Jim Boice, it is now far better. And for Tenth Presbyterian Church, it continues to get better as the legacy passed on through Boice's ministry of clear exposition of God's Word and worship to the glory of God is maintained and extended.

CHAPTER 6

A CHURCH FOR THE TWENTY-FIRST CENTURY

Philip Graham Ryken

Tenth Presbyterian Church has a glorious past—glorious in the sense that God has done great things in and through the lives of the people who have worshiped him at the corner of Seventeenth and Spruce.

We praise God for everything he has done. We praise him for raising up the elders who had the vision almost two centuries ago to plant a new Presbyterian church in a growing part of Philadelphia. We praise him for raising up the countless men and women since then who have prayed and labored for God's work at Tenth Presbyterian Church. We praise him for raising up the great preachers whose stories are told in the pages of this book. We praise him for raising up the sinners who have come to faith in Christ and the disciples who have grown in his grace. We praise him for inspiring our growing outreach to people in the city who are lost. We praise him for inspiring the multitude of missionaries who have left Tenth to reach the world for Christ. And we praise him for inspiring the reverent, joyous worship that has

139

been offered in his holy name week after week, down through the decades. We praise God for doing all these things, knowing that "from him and through him and to him are all things. To him be glory forever" (Rom. 11:36 ESV).

But we are not satisfied. Indeed, we cannot be satisfied as long as there is still a city, a nation, a world for us to reach. The God we serve has promised that one day "the earth will be filled with the knowledge of the glory of the LORD as the waters cover the sea" (Hab. 2:14 ESV). By that measure, how could we possibly be content with what we have done? The knowledge of God's glory has not yet saturated our city. And as Charles Spurgeon wrote, "The Christian church was designed from the first to be aggressive. It was not intended to remain stationary at any period, but to advance onward until its boundaries became commensurate with those of the world."[1]

As we consider the vast needs of a lost and dying humanity, we believe that God still has work for us to do. There are times when we are tempted to feel that our efforts are unworthy of the faithful men, women, and children who have gone before us. Nevertheless, we know that God has also called us to serve him—in our own time and place—and we hope that by working together we can do even greater things for Christ and his kingdom. Our fervent prayer is that by the grace of our Lord Jesus Christ, Tenth's best days are yet to come.

A BIBLICAL CHURCH

What kind of church is God calling us to be for the twenty-first century? First and foremost, we are called to be a *biblical* church. This is the foundation for everything we do as a congregation. Whatever God has accomplished at Tenth Presbyterian Church has been accomplished through his Word. It is only by the ministry of God's Word that sinners come to faith in Christ, grow to spiritual maturity, and reach out in compassion.

Shortly after Donald Grey Barnhouse became Tenth's senior minister, he entered the pulpit one Sunday morning and opened the great pulpit Bible to a point near the middle, where he then placed his own Bible and sermon notes. As he looked down he saw one of God's curses against godless nations. It occurred to Barnhouse that he would rather have before him a passage containing a great promise. Immediately Isaiah 55 came to mind: "As the rain and the snow come down from heaven, and do not return to it without watering the earth and making it bud and flourish, so that it yields seed for the sower and bread for the eater, so is my word that goes out from my mouth: It will not return to me empty, but will accomplish what I desire and achieve the purpose for which I sent it" (Isa. 55:10–11 NIV).

So Barnhouse turned to Isaiah 55. To his surprise he discovered that for decades his predecessors had done the same thing. The edges of the pulpit Bible curved inward; the pages were torn and mended. Barnhouse thus commented that the pages "containing the great fifty-fifth chapter of Isaiah and the preceding page with the fifty-third chapter of Isaiah concerning the Lord Jesus Christ as God's Lamb, gave mute evidence that the men who stood in the pulpit of Tenth Church for more than a century were men of the living Word and the written Word."[2] Later he discovered that another section of the Bible was similarly worn: Psalm 119, the long psalm about the Word of God. Evidently his predecessors, finding it difficult to keep their notes on the worn pages of Isaiah, had looked for another passage to remind them of the power of God's Word and their need to build Tenth Church upon it. Together these two passages—Isaiah 55 and Psalm 119—testify to ministries established on the solid foundation of divine revelation.

Dr. Barnhouse told the story of Tenth's pulpit Bible at the twenty-fifth anniversary of his ministry. He concluded:

It is my prayer that no man shall ever stand in this pulpit as long as time shall last who does not desire to have all that he does based upon this Book. For this Book does not *contain* the Word of God, it *is* the Word of God. And though we may preach the Word with all the stammering limitations of our human nature, the grace of God does the miracle of the ministry, and through human lips speaks the divine Word, and the hearts of the people are refreshed. There is no other explanation for the continuing power of a church that is poorly located, that is without endowment, but which still continues to draw men and women to the capacity of its seating arrangements, morning and evening, summer and winter, and which sends its sons and daughters by the score to preach the unsearchable riches of Christ throughout the world.[3]

Dr. Barnhouse's prayer has not gone unanswered. The men who succeeded him—Dr. Di Gangi and Dr. Boice—were unwavering in their commitment to the Bible as the written Word of God. We share their commitment, accepting the Bible as our only infallible authority for life and doctrine. The Bible remains at the center of our life as a congregation. We preach it from our pulpit. We teach it in our classes. We read it in our homes. We study it in our small groups. We teach it to our children. And as God gives us grace, we seek to obey it in our daily lives. We want the Bible to guide and govern everything we do as a church.

The Bible is also at the heart of our witness. In one way or another, all the ministries of Tenth Church communicate biblical truth. This is true not only of our Bible classes and worship services, but also of our outreach to people in need. Whether we are visiting prisoners, tutoring internationals, or feeding the homeless, we combine the ministry of the deed with the ministry of the Word, and in this way people's lives are transformed. We are a biblical church, saturating every aspect of our ministry with Scripture.

An Evangelical Church

Of its very nature, a biblical church is also an *evangelical* church. The term "evangelical" comes from the Greek *evangelion*—the biblical word for "gospel." And what is the gospel? It is simply the good news about Jesus Christ and the salvation he accomplished on the cross and through the empty tomb. The good news is "that Christ died for our sins in accordance with the Scriptures, that he was buried, that he was raised on the third day in accordance with the Scriptures" (1 Cor. 15:3b–4 ESV). And it is only by believing this gospel—this *evangelion*—that we are saved. In the true biblical sense of the word, an "evangelical" is someone who believes in Jesus Christ as crucified Savior and risen Lord.

The term "evangelical" also has meaning in church history. The term was first used in Germany to describe Christians who embraced the doctrines of the Protestant Reformation. In the eighteenth and nineteenth centuries it was used in Britain and America to refer to conservative Christians who believed in the inerrancy and infallibility of Scripture, the substitutionary atoning death of Jesus Christ, and the necessity of being born again by the Holy Spirit.[4] More recently the term has come to have an even more specific sense. Evangelicalism is the Christian movement that sought to find a middle ground between liberalism and fundamentalism and that rose to prominence in America during the 1950s. Like the fundamentalists, evangelicals defended the doctrines of God, Christ, Scripture, and salvation against liberal attacks. Unlike the fundamentalists, however, they sought to remain engaged with the surrounding culture, working to bring it under the transforming influence of Jesus Christ.

Throughout much of the twentieth century, Tenth served as a flagship church for the evangelical movement. Whether it was Barnhouse's war on liberalism or Boice's battle for the Bible, Tenth played a leading role in the conflicts that defined evangelicalism in America. The church saw as part of its mission the defense and advancement of evangelical orthodoxy in ways that would serve as an example and inspiration to other churches.

Tenth continues to identify itself as an evangelical church. We mean this, first of all, in the biblical sense of the word: we believe in the gospel of Jesus Christ. We must believe it, because no one is in greater need of its grace than we are. As members of

Tenth Church, we continue to be what we have always been: sinners saved by grace. We also know that we are not the only ones who need the gospel, so we are evangelistically minded. The grace of God compels us to reach out in deeds of mercy, to share our faith in Christ, to invite others to join us for worship, and to live in a way that proclaims the glory of God in every area of life.

Beyond this, we also aspire to provide leadership for the wider evangelical community. Sadly, there are signs that evangelicalism is losing its way. This was one of Dr. Boice's major concerns in the last years of his ministry. Boice believed that like the liberal church of an earlier generation, the evangelical church was adopting the world's wisdom, theology, agenda, and methods.[5] Nowhere did he articulate this more clearly than in the 1996 Cambridge Declaration, which begins by saying, "Evangelical churches today are increasingly dominated by the spirit of this age rather than by the Spirit of Christ. As evangelicals, we call ourselves to repent of this sin and to recover the historical Christian faith." Boice saw that evangelicals were becoming increasingly man-centered in their worship and witness. They were denying the sufficiency of Scripture for evangelism, guidance, spiritual growth, and social change.[6] And they were abandoning the doctrine of justification by faith alone, partly out of a desire to join forces with Roman Catholics.

The evangelical church continues to struggle with these issues. But there are new struggles as well—issues that were on the horizon at the end of Boice's ministry, but that Tenth had yet to fully engage. Within the evangelical community there is a trend toward post-conservative evangelicalism. Among the threats posed by this movement to evangelical orthodoxy are the following:

- *A new doctrine of God.* Some evangelical scholars advocate a theology known as the "openness of God," or "open theism." This is an attempt to resolve the mystery of divine sovereignty and human responsibility by denying that God has full knowledge of the future. The new evangelical deity is a risk-taker whose will is sometimes thwarted and whose plans often change in response to human actions.[7] But he is not the God of the Bible, who says, "I am God, and there is none like me, declaring the end from the beginning and from ancient times things not yet done, saying, 'My counsel shall stand, and I will accomplish all my purpose'" (Isa. 46:9c–10 ESV).

- *A new doctrine of Christ.* Here the trend is toward religious relativism. Today many people believe that all religions are equally true, that they all provide equally valid perspectives on ultimate reality. In the church this takes the form of denying that Jesus is the only way to God. The Bible says, "'And there is salvation in no one else, for there is no other name under heaven given among men by which we must be saved'" (Acts 4:12 ESV). Yet some scholars who claim to be evangelicals now claim that explicit personal faith in Jesus Christ is unnecessary for salvation. Under the influence of other world religions, they conclude that God must also offer forgiveness through non-Christian faiths. Jesus Christ is one possible expression of salvation, but not its exclusive means.[8]

- *A new doctrine of salvation.* Evangelicals are forgetting and in some cases denying vital Reformation teaching on the doctrine of justification by grace through faith. As part of a "new perspective" on Paul and the law, some post-conservative evangelicals dismiss the necessity or even the possibility of receiving Christ's righteousness by faith alone. In their view, what the New Testament terms "the righteousness of God" (e.g. Rom. 1:17) refers to God's justice in the plan of salvation, but not to anything that can or may be imputed to sinners. These theologians also reinterpret New Testament theology, claiming that the apostle Paul was not (as the Reformers taught) trying to combat the works-righteousness of the Jews after all because first-century Judaism was already a religion of grace! But this is to misunderstand both the New Testament's and the Reformers' teaching on salvation. The biblical view is that God imputes or credits his righteousness to believers in Christ, so that when we stand before him we possess the perfect righteousness of Jesus Christ. We are not justified by anything we do for ourselves, but only by what Christ has done for us.[9] By contrast, many post-conservative evangelicals downplay the centrality of justification for the New Testament gospel, with some redefining it more in terms of membership in the Christian community than in terms of personal righteousness before a holy God.

If Tenth is to remain an evangelical church in both the biblical and historical senses of the word, it will need to confront these challenges—and whatever others may come. This means something more than simply repeating the same old evangelical slogans. It means presenting a coherent critique of post-conservative theology. It also means offering a vigorous defense of the full omniscience of the sovereign God, the true uniqueness of Jesus Christ as the only Savior, and the gracious imputation of his righteousness as the only basis for our standing before God. Although the evangelical church seems to be losing its way, all is not lost, and we continue to call evangelicals back to the biblical doctrines of their faith.

A REFORMATIONAL CHURCH

Tenth is also a *reformational* church. Our theology and ministry continue to be shaped by the great doctrines of the Reformation in the sixteenth century. By the end of the Middle Ages, the Roman Catholic Church had fallen into doctrinal as well as moral decay. Reformers such as Martin Luther, John Calvin, and John Knox sought to recover essential biblical truths about salvation in Christ. Their Reformation is part of our heritage, as it is for all Protestant churches, and while we do not wish to glamorize the Reformers themselves, we believe that the truths they

recovered are biblical, and that therefore they have abiding significance for the church.

Reformation theology can be summarized in terms of five
theological principles, sometimes known as the "solas" (or *soli*, to
use the proper Latin form for the plural) of the Reformation:[10]

Sola Scriptura. The foundational principle for Reformation
theology is *sola Scriptura*, or "Scripture alone." The importance
of this principle should be obvious from everything we have said
about being a biblical church. *Sola Scriptura* simply means that
the Bible alone is our only ultimate authority. The Roman
Catholic Church taught (and continues to teach) that church tradition has equal authority with the Bible. As Presbyterians, we
acknowledge that the church has true spiritual authority. But we
believe that the Bible alone—not the church, not a confession,
and certainly not our own private judgment—is our ultimate
authority for faith and practice. Other authorities must all submit to Scripture, and to the extent that they depart from biblical
teaching, they are to be resisted.

Solus Christus. The next reformational principle is *solus
Christus*, or "Christ alone." Every church says that it is committed to Christ. The problem in the Middle Ages (and also today)
was that people were adding other things to Christ as the basis
for their salvation. The good news of the gospel is that Jesus Christ
has done everything that needs to be done to save us, keeping
God's law to make us righteous before God and dying in our place
to atone for our sins. Our hope is the same as that of the apostle
Paul, who wanted to gain Christ "and be found in him, not having a righteousness of my own that comes from the law, but that
which comes through faith in Christ, the righteousness from God
that depends on faith" (Phil. 3:9 ESV). Salvation is not our work,
or even Christ's work plus our work, but Christ's work alone.

Sola gratia. The salvation we have in Christ is given to us *sola
gratia*, or "by grace alone." As sinful human beings, we have no
claim on God's mercy. As a matter of strict justice, the only thing
God owes us is wrath against our sin. So if he does save us, it is

only because of his sovereign mercy, which he shows to some but not to all. This doctrine is in sharp contrast to the belief of many people today—including many evangelicals—that human beings are basically good, that God owes everyone a chance to be saved, and that salvation ultimately depends on our own good decision to follow God. But human beings are not basically good, and apart from God's saving grace, no one would ever be saved. In our lost and fallen condition, we are not capable of earning, seeking, or even cooperating with God's grace. The initiative in salvation always comes from God as his Spirit convicts us of sin, causes us to understand the gospel, calls us to faith in Christ, and gives us new spiritual life. Since all of this happens by grace alone, there is no human method or technique we can use to save ourselves or anyone else. Conversion is a gracious and supernatural gift from God.

Sola fide. Here we come to what is perhaps the best known of all the Reformation slogans—what John Calvin called "the main hinge on which salvation turns:"[11] *sola fide*, or "faith alone." The Reformers used this phrase as a convenient way to summarize their teaching about salvation. How does God save sinners? The full answer is that we are justified by grace alone, through faith alone, in Christ alone. Or to put it more simply, we are justified by faith alone. Justification is God's holy declaration that a person is righteous in his sight. Since we are sinners, we cannot be justified on the basis of our own righteousness; we can be declared righteous only on the basis of what Jesus has done. And the way his righteousness becomes ours is by faith: "This righteousness from God comes through faith in Jesus Christ to all who believe" (Rom. 3:22 NIV). We are not justified by anything we can do, but by believing in what Christ has done. Righteousness is a gift from God. Even our faith is a gift from God, because it is only by his grace that we are able to believe the gospel. As the Scripture also says, "For by grace you have been saved through faith. And this is not your own doing; it is the gift of God, not a result of works, so that no one may boast" (Eph. 2:8–9 ESV).

Soli Deo Gloria. The fifth great doctrine of the Reformation—and the goal of all the others—is *soli Deo Gloria,* or "to God alone be the glory." This doctrine rightly acknowledges that the supreme purpose for everything is for God alone to receive all the honor and praise. Our salvation is all from God, so that he and he alone will receive all the praise. According to the opening answer of the Westminster Shorter Catechism, in words so often quoted from the Tenth pulpit, "Man's chief end is to glorify God and to enjoy him forever." Rather than claiming any credit for ourselves, our deepest desire is to see God glorified in everything we do. To him be the glory forever!

These five great doctrines continue to nourish our faith. As Dr. Boice wrote, "Without these five confessional statements—Scripture alone, Christ alone, grace alone, faith alone, and glory to God alone—we do not have a true church, and certainly not one that will survive for very long. For how can any church be a true and faithful church if it does not stand for Scripture alone, is not committed to a biblical gospel, and does not exist for God's glory? A church without these convictions has ceased to be a true church, whatever else it may be."[12] So we continue to hold these convictions. We celebrate them every spring at the Philadelphia Conference on Reformation Theology (PCRT). But more than that, we try to live by them throughout the year. We honor the principle of *sola Scriptura* by making God's Word the foundation for our worship, teaching, and witness. We honor the principle of salvation by grace alone, through faith alone, in Christ alone by denying any merit of our own and putting complete trust in the finished work of Jesus Christ. And we honor the principle of *soli Deo Gloria* by making the glory of God our ultimate aim in all we do.

There is one further principle for reformation that we seek to honor, and that is *semper reformanda*—"always reforming." Reformation is not a bygone era in church history, but a biblical imperative. We are not content with our progress in ministry but, like the Reformers, seek a continual reformation by the life-transforming power of God's Spirit.

A Presbyterian Church

Tenth is a biblical, evangelical, and reformational church. And of course it is, as it has always been, a *Presbyterian* church. By this we mean at least three things. First, we mean that we believe that Presbyterianism—or rule by elders—is the most truly biblical form of church government. In the New Testament, we find that the apostles appointed elders (or pastors, or bishops—the terms are used interchangeably; see Acts 20:17–30) in all the churches, and that together these elders provided spiritual leadership for the people of God.

For nearly 200 years, Tenth has benefited from the leadership of strong elders. In considering the history of a church, people naturally think first of a congregation's pastors. Indeed, the pages of this book are dominated by the stories of some of the outstanding men who have preached from Tenth's pulpit. But good ministers do not lead congregations by themselves; they work in partnership with other men whom God has called to govern the church. It was elders who had the vision to plant Tenth Church, helped guide the congregation to the choice of each new minister, provided spiritual care for every generation of church members, and prayed for God's blessing on the church's ministry. The spiritual vitality of Tenth Church today is their legacy.

The second thing we mean when we say that Tenth is a Presbyterian church is that we belong to the Presbyterian Church in America (PCA). It is not always easy to be associated with a denomination. As a congregation, Tenth has experienced the pain of trying to minister within a denomination (the United Presbyterian Church U.S.A.) that had drifted away from its biblical moorings. But we also know that Scripture requires us to stay connected with other Christians as a visible demonstration of our unity in Christ. Thus we belong to a national church that is Presbyterian in its government and theology. Together with other PCA churches, we share a commitment to the Confession of Faith and catechisms written by the Westminster Assembly in London (1643–49). Like us, these churches want to reach our nation and our world with the gospel. To this end, our denominational agencies include Mission to the World (MTW), which sends missionaries all over the globe, and Mission to North America (MNA), which sponsors church-planting across our own country and in Canada.

There is something else that we mean when we describe ourselves as a Presbyterian church. Truly Presbyterian theology is always Calvinistic (some Baptists, Congregationalists, and Episcopalians are also Calvinists). That is to say, it promotes the distinctive doctrines of grace often associated with the theology of John Calvin and most clearly articulated by the Synod of Dort (1618–19). These doctrines are usually identified as *T*otal depravity, *U*nconditional election, *L*imited atonement, *I*rresistible grace, and the *P*erseverance of the saints. The first letters of these phrases form the acronym TULIP, which is another way these doctrines are identified. They are also known as "the Five Points of Calvinism."[13] But what do these doctrines teach?

Total depravity. This doctrine does not mean—as it is sometimes thought—that we are all as bad as we can possibly be. Nor does it mean that we are wholly evil in everything we do. Rather, it means that nothing we do is ever completely good. Sin pervades every part of our physical, intellectual, and emotional makeup, so that nothing we are or do is completely free from sin. In this sinful state we have no inclination to seek God, and therefore *cannot* seek him, or even respond to the gospel when it is presented to us. As the Scripture says, we are "dead in . . . trespasses and sins" (Eph. 2:1 ESV). We cannot even see our need for Christ until God first gives us spiritual understanding.

Unconditional election. If we are totally depraved, then salvation must be a work that God accomplishes and applies without any assistance on our part. Left to ourselves, we will never seek him, so he must reach out and save us (if, in fact, we are to be saved). And this is what God does. The first step is his choice to save us, which is what the word *election* refers to. The salvation of any individual Christian is determined by the prior decision of God, who "chose us in [Christ] before the foundation of the world"

(Eph. 1:4 ESV). "Unconditional" indicates that God made this decision apart from anything good that he might have foreseen in us. If election were based on anything that sinners might be or do, then salvation would ultimately depend on human merit. But in order to prove that salvation is all of grace, election is a loving act of God's totally sovereign will.

Limited atonement. The doctrine of limited atonement does not mean that somehow the death of Christ did not accomplish everything it was supposed to accomplish (thus, the word "limited" is somewhat misleading; it is more accurate to call the doctrine "definite atonement" or "particular redemption"). Rather, it means that the atonement had a specific object in view—namely, the salvation of those whom the Father had given to the Son before the foundation of the world—and that it was effective in saving those persons. By dying on the cross, Christ did not merely make salvation possible, but actually achieved it. He made real satisfaction for the sins of his people, offering himself as their perfect substitute. His death truly atoned for their sins, but not for the sins of those who never come to him in faith. In keeping with God's plan, the cross has saving efficacy only for the elect.

Irresistible grace. Somehow the benefits of Christ's atoning work must be applied to the elect. This is the work of God the Holy Spirit, whose inward operation enables sinners to repent and believe in Christ. In addition to the outward call of the gospel, which by God's command is made to everyone, the Holy Spirit issues an inward call to salvation. This inward calling is made only to the elect and inevitably draws them to faith in Christ. Because God is sovereign in their salvation, it is not possible for them permanently or effectively to reject his effectual calling. God's grace is irresistible and invincible; the Spirit never fails to accomplish his saving purpose in the minds, hearts, and wills of God's chosen people.

The perseverance of the saints. This doctrine has two parts. First, it teaches that God perseveres with his people, remaining faithful to the very end. As the Scripture says, "he who began a good work in you will bring it to completion at the day of Jesus

Christ" (Phil. 1:6 ESV). The perseverance of the saints depends on the perseverance of their Savior. Second, the doctrine of the perseverance of the saints teaches that because God perseveres with us, we also persevere. The saints are simply God's people, who are considered holy through the work of his Son. Perseverance means that God's true saints will never fall away, but will persevere to the very end and inherit eternal life. For those whom God "predestined he also called, and those whom he called he also justified, and those whom he justified he also glorified" (Rom. 8:30 ESV). As this verse implies, the perseverance of the saints is really the *preservation* of the saints, for our perseverance depends on God's preserving grace. It is God's faithfulness, rather than our own, that will bring us to glory.

Together these five Presbyterian doctrines preserve the sovereignty of God's grace. Rather than emphasizing what human beings can do to choose God or remain faithful to him, we believe that from beginning to end salvation is all of God, and all of his grace. God really does *save* sinners! We are dead in our sins, and therefore could do nothing to save ourselves, but God has done and will continue to do everything necessary for our salvation: choosing, redeeming, calling, and preserving. Thus the one point of Calvinism that together the Five Points aim to demonstrate is that every aspect of salvation is the absolutely gracious work of our totally sovereign God.

A CITY CHURCH

At this point our list of adjectives takes what may seem like a surprising turn: Tenth is also an *urban* church. What makes this surprising is that so many evangelical congregations have abandoned the city and its problems. As Harvie Conn documented in his book *The American City and the Evangelical Church*, during the twentieth century evangelicals "moved to survive by forming a subculture that would protect itself against the perceived monstrous power of the city and its secularizing effect on the church. ... Evangelicalism among whites was moving away from its original stance of urban engagement and more and more toward a socially passive Christianity. A functional Christian social ethic was dimming, quiet in the suburbs to which evangelicals increasingly withdrew."[14]

Rather than withdrawing from the city, Tenth has made a commitment to stay. As one of our neighboring churches in Center City Philadelphia likes to say, we are "in the city for good." We have made this choice for a number of reasons. One is that this is where God has put us, and we would not dare to move unless God himself told us to do so. Tenth's members have an unusually strong sense of place, closely identifying with the city as our church home. As we look at the community around us, we believe that we have been called to serve—as Dr. Boice loved to say—this people, in this place.

Another reason we stay here is that the city is a place of great spiritual need, full of poverty, greed, homelessness, crime, corruption, violence, and alienation. All of these problems are the result of human depravity. In other words, they are the very kinds of problems that compelled Christ to come into the world to do his saving work. So if we claim to follow Christ, how can we fail to do our part to address them?

Then there is the strategic significance of the city to consider. Back in the nineteenth century Dwight L. Moody said, "Waters run downhill, and the highest hills in America are the great cities. If we can stir them we shall stir the whole country."[15] This is still true today. The city is the place where the nation's culture is formed and from which its values are disseminated. Cities such as Philadelphia also have worldwide significance. The global village is fast becoming a global metropolis, with more than 80 percent of the world's population expected to live in urban areas before the end of the twenty-first century. These urban areas are connected by a global communication network and by the ceaseless flow of worldwide immigration. Each city is a microcosm of the world, with people of all different classes and cultures living in close proximity. If we reach the heart of the city, we can reach the world.

But reaching the city is difficult. This is because there are really two cities in the world: the City of God and the city of man.[16] In Augustine's famous words, the human race is "distributed into two parts, the one consisting of those who live according to man, the other of those who live according to God. And these we also mystically call the two cities, or the two communities of men, of which the one is predestined to reign eternally with God, and the other to suffer eternal punishment with the devil."[17] The city of man is what human beings construct in their own strength, according to their own plans, in rebellion against God. By contrast, the City of God is the spiritual community of the elect that God is building into an eternal kingdom.

These two spiritual cities are locked in a ceaseless struggle, and it is in urban centers that the battle lines are most sharply drawn. The city is the place where humanity's grandest achievements are on display; it is also the place where our depravity is most densely concentrated. Thus, the best and worst of everything in the human heart are found in the city. Because the city has power and influence, it is where the forces of darkness gather, but it is also where the light shines most brightly and has the greatest opportunity to spread.

In this crucible of conflict, God is building his eternal city, and one day it will triumph. Although history began in a garden, it will end in a city—the New Jerusalem. And while it is true that this city's builder and architect is God (Heb. 11:10), it is also true that God uses his people to help do the building. As we live for Christ, God uses our work and witness to establish a new spiritual community. The opportunities to have this redemptive influence are greatest in urban areas, where our goal is not simply the conversion of individuals to faith in Christ, but cultural transformation as the gospel penetrates whole segments of society. We want to renew the city through Christian community development and by serving Christ faithfully in all our vocations. But to do this redemptive work, we have to make a personal and congregational investment in urban ministry. Like the Israelites in Babylon, we have been told by God: "Seek the peace and prosperity of the city to which I have carried you into exile. Pray to the LORD for it, because if it prospers, you too will prosper" (Jer. 29:7 NIV).

At Tenth we take seriously our call to serve the city. This has been especially true in recent decades, when our distinctively urban ministries have grown. God has put us in Philadelphia to pray for its peace and pursue its prosperity. As we survey our congregational history, we praise God that he has allowed us to keep our church building in Center City. Our decision to stay in Philadelphia is not temporary; it is a permanent, congregation-wide commitment. Although the city can be a place of special difficulty, it is also a place of extraordinary opportunity. Many of our members have made the choice to live in Philadelphia. Others also work here. But even those who live elsewhere have a heart for the city and try to serve it any way they can.

A CHURCH WITH A MISSION

Thus far we have mainly been describing what Tenth believes. But what is our mission? What is God calling us to do, not only now, but also in the coming decades?

To answer these questions, we need to recognize that we are living in increasingly post-Christian times, when biblical Christianity no longer exercises a prevailing influence on the mind and heart of our culture. While the problems of American culture have been analyzed in many ways, two of its distinguishing characteristics are relativism and narcissism.[18]

Relativism is radical skepticism, the rejection of absolute truth. It is the view that reality itself varies according to one's perspective. No one knows anything with objective certainty; it all depends on one's point of view. There are no exclusive truth claims. This is part of what people mean by "postmodernism," and it represents a global shift in the way people think about truth and meaning. When it comes to theology, relativism means that no religion can claim to be superior to any other. Each faith is true in its own way—a valid perspective on ultimate reality. Therefore, if Christianity is true at all, it is only relatively true.

Narcissism is radical individualism, or infatuation with the self. In ancient Greek mythology, Narcissus was the beautiful youth who fell in love with his own reflection. As he sat beside the pool, gazing longingly at his own image, he was transformed into a flower. There has long been a narcissistic tendency in American culture, but we have now entered an era of radical selfishness when people demand absolute individual autonomy, and when self-fulfillment is actually considered a virtue. People feel justified in doing whatever seems to be in their self-interest, without showing much compassion or giving much consideration to their neighbors, co-workers, employees, spouses, or children. We live in a culture of takers, not givers.

Considered together, the relativistic mind and narcissistic heart explain a good deal of what is wrong with America today. People who do not know what is true (or wonder whether anything is true at all) are unable to do what is right and good. Intellectual skepticism quickly leads to moral relativism. And because people who live for themselves are unable to establish loving communities, many Americans end up feeling alienated and abandoned.

In response to these cultural trends, many Christian leaders say that we need to find a new way of doing church. Their approach is pragmatic: do what works. Some are busy marketing Christianity to the masses, turning Christ into a commodity. Others are trying their hand at entertainment, seeking to make their worship services appeal to a secular audience. Christian theology has been reduced to the lowest common denominator. There is an overall "dumbing down" of worship and doctrine. This is all done, of course, in the name of relevance. When churches make relevance their primary goal, however, they are vulnerable to the twin perils of postmodernism: relativism and narcissism. They succumb to relativism because they are willing to sacrifice biblical principles for popular success. And they are guilty of narcissism because they crave the acceptance of secular society. What will happen in the end is that the church will become indistinguishable from the surrounding culture. A church that accommodates to post-Christian culture soon becomes a post-Christian church.

The only way to avoid this failure is by following the biblical pattern for the church. We will not carry the gospel forward by living in the past or looking to our present culture, but only by listening to what God tells us in his Word. At Tenth, we are committed to pursuing seven objectives as a church. These objectives may seem very basic, but they are biblical, and in our experience they have God's blessing. Furthermore, in God's infinite wisdom, they turn out to be exactly what a relativistic, narcissistic culture needs. Here are our objectives:

1. *To uphold a tradition of strong expository preaching by gifted men of God.* This will hardly come as a surprise to anyone who knows Tenth's history. We have been blessed with an extraordinary series of preachers who devoted their lives to the careful exposition of Scripture. Every church has preaching of some sort or other, but what is distinctive about Tenth is our commitment to systematic Bible exposition. Whether it was Barnhouse's long series through Romans or Boice's sermons on everything from Genesis to Revelation, we have slowly worked our way through large sections of Scripture in our Sunday services.

By expository preaching we simply mean preaching that teaches the Scriptures. Expository preaching carefully and thoroughly communicates what the Bible actually says. It involves explanation and proclamation, with exhortation. Each week the minister preaches a particular Bible passage in a way that explores its context, explains its meaning, expounds its doctrine in connection to Christ, and then applies it to the spiritual needs of those who listen. In the main, such preaching is neither topical nor experiential, but it is always practical and evangelistic. This is because expository preaching teaches God's Word, which is "useful for teaching, rebuking, correcting and training in righteousness" (according to 2 Tim. 3:16; hence the preaching is practical) and which contains the gospel on every page (thus the sermons are evangelistic).

We follow this method of preaching because it is biblical, but it also proves to be the perfect remedy for relativism. In a relativistic culture, God is no longer permitted to speak his authoritative word. This is why we are now suffering what the brilliant French critic Jacques Ellul called "the humiliation of the word."[19] The church's proper response is to continue teaching objective truth from God's eternal Word. At a time when truth-claims are under increasing suspicion, what people most need to hear is "the whole counsel of God" (Acts 20:27 ESV). So we continue to follow the simple command that Paul gave to Timothy: "Preach the word" (2 Tim. 4:2 ESV).

2. *To worship God in a worthy manner through thoughtful words, fervent prayers, and excellent music.* The opening words of this statement are significant: *to worship God*. This is the proper place to begin. In a narcissistic culture, even worship can become a form of self-gratification. People no longer attend services to bless God, but to benefit themselves. There is a subtle change of audience. God is no longer sovereign—the congregation is. According to Kent Hughes, who serves as senior pastor of the College Church in Wheaton, Illinois:

> The unspoken but increasingly common assumption of today's Christendom is that worship is primarily for us—to meet our needs. Such worship services are entertainment focused, and the worshipers are uncommitted spectators who are silently grading the performance. . . . Anything and everything that is suspected of making the marginal attender uncomfortable is removed from the service. . . . This philosophy instills a tragic self-centeredness. That is, everything is judged by how it affects man. This terribly corrupts one's theology.[20]

The way to correct this problem is by putting God back at the center. Once the right theology of worship is restored, the right practice of worship will follow. And a good place to begin our theology of worship is with Paul's words to the Colossians: "Let the word of Christ dwell in you richly as you teach and admonish one another with all wisdom, and as you sing psalms, hymns and spiritual songs with gratitude in your hearts to God. And whatever you do, whether in word or deed, do it all in the name of the Lord Jesus, giving thanks to God the Father through him" (Col. 3:16–17 NIV). These verses establish the pattern for Word-communicating, God-glorifying worship—worship that springs from loving hearts that are eternally grateful for salvation in Christ.

True worship is Word-communicating. The main elements of our corporate worship services—praying and singing, reading and preaching the Bible, confessing our faith, giving our tithes and offerings, celebrating the sacraments of baptism and the Lord's Supper—are all mandated by Scripture. Furthermore, they are all suffused with Scripture. From the opening words of the call to worship through the last phrase of the benediction, we want our worship services to be saturated with Scripture. As the Rev. Dr. J. Ligon Duncan loves to tell his congregation at the First Presbyterian Church in Jackson, Mississippi: "Read the Bible; Preach the Bible; Pray the Bible; Sing the Bible." Our prayers, our readings, our sacraments, and our testimonies echo the words and phrases of the Bible. Even our hymns give musical expression to biblical truth. One of the best ways to learn theology—and tune it to God's praise—is to sing the great hymns of the faith.

True worship is also God-glorifying. Our worship is theocentric, not egocentric, and this is the remedy for our inherent narcissism. We do not worship because we love ourselves, but because we love God. As we gather with his people for worship, we take the attention off ourselves and put it back on him. Rather than seeking to gratify ourselves, we desire to glorify him. This is implicit in the word "worship," which comes from the old Anglo-Saxon term "worth-ship." And this is exactly what we do when we worship: we give God our very best, honoring him for the supremacy of his grace and thus acknowledging his genuine and

infinite worth. The commitment to do our best has special significance for musicians, who are called to sing, play, and compose
according to the highest standards of musical excellence: "Sing
joyfully to the LORD, you righteous. . . . Sing to him a new song;
play skillfully, and shout for joy" (Ps. 33:1a, 3 NIV).

   *3. To integrate every member of the congregation into Bible stud-
ies and other groups where individual needs can be met and each can
minister to others.* We want to be a caring church as well as a teaching and worshiping church. Today America is facing a crisis of
community, when nearly all our cultural institutions are under
attack, especially the family. People feel disconnected. They find it
increasingly difficult to foster and nurture meaningful relationships at home, at work, and sometimes even at church. Given the
prevailing narcissism of these post-Christian times, this is not surprising. When people are in love with themselves, they do not have
much love left for anyone else.
   The church is supposed to be different. It is the alternative
society in which we are known and loved, and in which we know
and love others. One way the Bible shows how connected we are
in Christ is by comparing the church to a body: "You are the body
of Christ, and each one of you is a part of it" (1 Cor. 12:27 NIV).
As we are united to Christ by faith, we are also united to one
another in love.[21]
   Belonging to the body has profound implications for our life
as a church. If each of us is part of the same body, then we all
belong to one another. We need the body and the body needs us.
There is no spiritual life outside the body of Christ, in which we
have mutually interdependent relationships that bridge all the
other barriers that threaten to separate us, including the barriers of gender, age, language, ethnicity, disability, and class. At
Tenth we prize our growing diversity as a sign of our fundamental unity in Christ. And in the same way that every body part has
its own vital function, each of us has something essential to contribute. There is no appendix in the body of Christ! The body can
grow only "as each part does its work" (Eph. 4:16 NIV). And to

enable us to do our part, God has given each of us one or more
spiritual gifts that we are called to use for his glory.

How can we stay connected to one another? Perhaps the best
way is by getting involved in small groups for prayer, Bible study,
fellowship, and ministry. The center of our congregational life is
corporate worship. Yet many essential aspects of our life as a
church cannot take place in that context. We also need to be
together during the week. This is in keeping with the pattern we
find in the New Testament, when believers often met together in
people's homes. The church is a spiritual family. In order to function as a healthy family, we need to meet with one another in
smaller, more intimate gatherings, including some that are closer
in size to a nuclear family. Many different kinds of groups help to
meet this need, but the most complete is the small-group Bible
study. Such a group is an ideal place not only for teaching, but
also for praying, sharing, and caring.

Church history shows that the gospel advances only when
people are committed to prayer. As a congregation, we need to
remain in prayer if we are to have any hope of seeing God's blessing. A significant part of this intense spiritual work takes place
in our small groups, where we help one another intercede for the
church and its ministry. Something else significant happens when
we pray. As group members share their personal prayer requests,
they start to care for one another. Then, as they have the opportunity, they begin to serve one another in practical ways. Therefore, as an extension of corporate worship, a healthy small group
can provide virtually all the spiritual care that anyone needs. This
is why we strongly encourage every member of Tenth Church to
participate in a ministry or small-group Bible study (or both!).
In a large church, the small group is the best place for personal
needs to be met and for each person to minister to others.

4. *To supply loving pastoral care for each member of the church
family.* Good small groups are on the front lines of spiritual care.
But they must be supported by the care of the church's pastors,
elders, and deacons. Providing good pastoral care is a perennial

challenge, especially for a sizable church that draws its congregation from a large metropolitan area. Yet we believe that it is a challenge we must meet if we are to remain faithful to our calling.

As we have seen, a Presbyterian church is under the spiritual oversight of a brotherhood of elders. There are two kinds of elders: ruling elders and teaching elders, who are usually called "pastors" (see 1 Tim. 5:17). Together these men serve as a team of shepherds to provide loving pastoral care for every member of the church family.

Tenth Presbyterian Church is organized into geographic parishes, plus a special parish for Tenth International Fellowship. Some of our ruling elders serve as *parish* elders. As the name implies, these men have spiritual oversight over the people in their parish. The other ruling elders serve as *session* elders. These men chair the church's committees and commissions (such as Church Planting, Family Life, Growth and Maturity, Missions, Music, and Nominating). But whatever their specific assignments, all our elders work together to provide spiritual leadership and pastoral care for the church.

By definition, an elder is a mature, gifted man who is called by God to serve as a shepherd in the church. The Bible provides clearly defined minimum standards for the gifts and godliness that the office requires (1 Tim. 3:1–7; Titus 1:6–9). Once he has been elected and ordained, an elder must continue to watch his life and his doctrine closely (see 1 Tim. 4:16). Unless he is growing in godliness and in his understanding of what the Scriptures teach, he will be unable to lead the church or offer good spiritual care to others.

What, specifically, does an elder *do?* Elders watch over the church's worship and preaching. They defend the church's doctrine, protecting the Bible and its theology from doubters and detractors. They offer loving spiritual care. They teach and visit the members of the church to encourage and exhort them; to correct, counsel, and comfort them; and to pray for them. The elders help church members identify and exercise their spiritual gifts. They resolve conflicts and settle disputes. They give spiritual advice for difficult life decisions. They comfort the sick, the dying, and the bereaved. They help church members deal with the unique challenges of childhood, adolescence, singleness, or marriage. And when necessary, the elders correct sin by exercising firm, loving pastoral discipline, following the biblical guidelines for bringing people to repentance and safeguarding the purity of the church.

As we consider these duties, it is important to understand that elders have God-given spiritual authority. This authority is not absolute; remember, the Bible is our only ultimate authority. Nevertheless, their authority is real. Since the days of the apostles, elders have been given the responsibility to govern the church in the name of Jesus Christ. For this reason they deserve our honor, encouragement, and obedience.

Today many people chafe against any form of authority. By definition, relativists and narcissists are anti-authoritarian. Relativists object to God's intellectual authority; they deny that God has the right to tell them what to think. Narcissists resent God's moral authority; they deny that God has the right to tell them what to do. Here again, the biblical pattern for the church provides the best corrective. Elders exercise moral and spiritual authority on Christ's behalf. Provided that these men are good and godly, this is for our spiritual benefit. As the Scripture says: "Obey your leaders and submit to their authority. They keep watch over you as men who must give an account. Obey them so that their work will be a joy, not a burden, for that would be of no advantage to you" (Heb. 13:17 NIV).

5. *To provide an effective Christian education program to inform, train, and disciple all members of the congregation.* Discipleship is an important theme in the gospels. Although Jesus had many followers, he invested the largest portion of his time in the small group of men and women who were known as his disciples. And as he discipled them, one of the things that he emphasized most clearly was the *cost* of discipleship. If people decided to follow him, he said, it would cost them everything they had.

This is not a sacrifice that most people are willing to make, especially in these post-Christian times. Our narcissism keeps getting in the way. Even in the church, most people want to know what's in it for them. People who think this way will never give themselves away for Jesus Christ. Instead, they will continue to view costly discipleship as something that is only for advanced Christians. But Jesus said, "If *anyone* would come after me, let him deny himself and take up his cross daily and follow me" (Luke 9:23 ESV; emphasis added).

Jesus was not speaking about a literal death, of course. He was talking about the kind of daily self-denial—death to self—that enables people to live for him. Paul made this clear when he wrote: "I appeal to you therefore, brothers, by the mercies of God, to present your bodies as a living sacrifice, holy and acceptable to God, which is your spiritual worship. Do not be conformed to this world, but be transformed by the renewal of your mind" (Rom. 12:1–2a ESV). Here again, the costliness of following God is emphasized. We are called to give ourselves to God for sacrifice. But it is a *living* sacrifice—a life offered in perpetual service to God.

Such costly discipleship goes against everything a post-Christian culture stands for. So how can we learn to live this way? According to Paul, the first step is the renewal of our minds, which is why we need good Christian education in the church. God's method of training us to follow Christ starts with developing a Christian mind—what James Boice called "mind renewal for a mindless age."[22] This is not merely an intellectual exercise. Ideas have consequences, and God changes our minds with the purpose of changing our hearts. Our thoughts influence our affections, so that we start to feel what we believe. Then we start to say what we think and do what we think. As Dr. Boice so often said, it is by thinking biblically that we learn to act biblically. So Christian discipleship is not a self-help program for improving our spiritual performance; the transforming change comes from God, through his Word.

At Tenth Presbyterian Church, our primary training comes from the preaching of God's Word Sunday by Sunday. We also receive training in small groups, and in special seminars and conferences held throughout the church year. But the backbone of our training program is the Bible school that meets on Sunday mornings. For adults there are classes in Bible, theology, church history, missions, evangelism, and practical areas of Christian living, such as marriage and church membership. For children there are classes for every age and grade level from age two through high school. The children's Bible school uses its own curriculum, which was first written by Dr. Barnhouse and later revised by Dr. and Mrs. Boice. The Tenth curriculum teaches the Bible and its doctrine in a systematic way. There is also a graded program for memory work, with hundreds of children memorizing Bible verses and learning catechism questions and answers. Our goal is to train a new generation of disciples by giving our children the intellectual framework for a Christian view of the world. We also teach them how to worship, believing that even from a young age, children belong in public worship with their parents. In order to assist them, we prepare a weekly children's worship bulletin and each Sunday the minister gives the elementary school students a short preview of the sermon and the music director teaches them one of the morning hymns.

Tenth provides advanced training for men and women who hope to serve in full-time Christian ministry. The church has a growing internship program for seminary students and others who wish to gain practical experience in vocational ministry. We want to train pastors, missionaries, and other full-time Christian workers so that they in turn can disciple others. In years to come, we hope to add internships for college students, minorities, and internationals, preparing a new wave of Christian leaders to lay down their lives for Jesus.

6. *To advance the missionary work of the church in the local community and throughout the world.* The church of Jesus Christ has always had a global vision. The supreme expression of this vision is the Great Commission that Jesus gave his disciples when he returned to glory: "Go therefore and make disciples of all

nations, baptizing them in the name of the Father and of the Son and of the Holy Spirit, teaching them to observe all that I have commanded you" (Matt. 28:19–20a ESV).

This commission—the commandment of Christ that gives us our mission—is still in effect. It is first of all local. Missionary work is not something that some*one* else does some*where* else; it is what God has called us to do wherever we go. Wherever we are, we have been sent here. For Tenth this means supporting missionary work in and around Philadelphia, especially among high school and college students, artists, medical professionals, and businesspeople. But perhaps our most significant local mission is to plant new churches. This has become a renewed focus in recent years, as thriving congregations have been established in Conshohocken (Christ the King) and Overbrook (Christ Liberation Fellowship). We have also partnered with other churches in our presbytery to establish new congregations in the Northeast and near the Art Museum.

Planting such churches is part of our long-term strategy for saturating Philadelphia with the gospel. New churches are generally more effective than established churches at reaching the unchurched, especially in emergent communities that lack a strong Christian presence. In coming years we hope to plant new churches in other parts of the city, especially within Philadelphia's burgeoning ethnic communities. If the church is not advancing by planting new congregations, it is usually in decline. Therefore, in partnership with other churches, we pray that God will enable us to plant new churches all over Philadelphia.

Our mission is not merely local, however; it is also global. The worldwide need for the gospel is vast. There are still approximately 10,000 unreached people groups in the world—cultural communities that have no significant Christian presence. Thousands of these people groups have no portion of the Bible in their own language. And there are still some 3 billion people who have never had the gospel presented to them in any form. They cannot be reached through friendship evangelism because none of their friends knows the gospel. And even among the nations that have been reached with the gospel, there are many who still need to be discipled in the way that the Great Commission demands. Thus there is still an urgent need for personal, long-term, cross-cultural missionary work that establishes new churches in new places. This is especially true in the world's darkest places, where missionaries must be willing to face persecution. But this is what true discipleship always requires: laying down our lives for Jesus. We believe that many parts of the world will not be penetrated with the gospel until Christians are willing to go suffer and die for the sake of the gospel.

For these and many other reasons, Tenth remains committed to supporting missionary work around the globe. We support the church in other parts of the world through praying, giving, and sending. One focus of our giving is indigenous work, which we support in the hope that eventually it will become self-sustaining. We believe that only the local church is able to do the complete work of evangelism and discipleship in its own community. Thus we want to help start and sustain gospel-spreading churches, especially in urban areas, among unreached people groups, and where there is significant outreach to young people. We also want to publish good books, build solid buildings, and train gifted workers. And we want to show mercy, especially through our annual Easter Sacrificial Offering, which is sent overseas in the name of Christ to address acute physical needs brought about by war, earthquakes, famine, disease, the exploitation of women and children, and other calamities.

Tenth is also a sending church. Our prayer is that each year God will call some of our own members to go somewhere else with the gospel. Nearly all our career foreign missionaries worshiped at Tenth Church during some period of their lives, and many are still members of the church today. We also send out short-term missionary teams for the purposes of lending whatever practical and spiritual help we can offer and expanding our vision for what God is doing around the world.

Our worldwide witness is motivated by the belief—over against those who want to relativize Christianity—that Jesus Christ is the one and only way to God. We believe that what Jesus said is true: his gospel "will be proclaimed throughout the whole world as a testimony to all nations, and then the end will come" (Matt. 24:14 ESV). And until the end does come, our mission is to spread the message of salvation to all peoples, in all places, so that God will receive all the praise.

7. *To serve the church and its community through ministries of mercy.* We have already seen that Tenth has a special calling to serve the city of Philadelphia. This is part of our mission—what Jesus has sent us here to do. But one aspect of this mission deserves special emphasis: sharing God's mercy by performing good works of practical Christian love. Our gospel outreach is not complete unless we add deeds of mercy to our words of grace.

In a narcissistic culture, people find it hard to show mercy. Whatever mercy we do show tends to be superficial. We are willing to pay lip service to the poor, and perhaps even to send a donation, but not to get personally involved. We are too busy looking out for ourselves. This is why our nation is suffering a crisis in compassion. Sadly, this is even true in the church, where many Christians are too selfish to serve.

But mercy is not an option. In Matthew 25 Jesus described six acts of charity that are vital signs of living faith: feeding the hungry, satisfying the thirsty, welcoming the stranger, clothing the naked, caring for the sick, and visiting the prisoner. Furthermore, he said that people who do these things will be welcomed into God's eternal kingdom. Their faith will be proven genuine by their love. But by failing to do these things, people who do not show mercy reveal that they never had true love for Christ. So mercy is one true test of our faith. The credibility of our Christianity, both as a church and as individual Christians, is determined by how we treat the people nobody wants, nobody loves, and nobody touches.

Charity begins at home. When Jesus spoke about showing mercy "to one of the least of these my brothers" (Matt. 25:40 ESV), he was referring most specifically to his own beloved people, who have been adopted into God's family. Our first priority is to provide for our brothers and sisters in Christ, not just within our own families and churches, but anywhere in the world where Christians are in need. The Scripture says: "So then, as we have opportunity, let us do good to everyone, and especially to those who are of the household of faith" (Gal. 6:10 ESV).

Although charity begins at home, it certainly doesn't stop there. Our compassion extends to our city, where many basic human needs still go unmet. Homeless people are sleeping in the streets; children are living at risk; inmates are locked up in prison; immigrants are struggling to adjust to an alien culture. Meeting such needs requires us to make a personal investment. There are times when we can help by giving money, but our most valuable contribution is to spend time sharing the love of Christ with people in need. To provide real help, we need to know what people truly need. This takes time. But unless we get personally involved, the underlying issues of urban problems are almost never addressed. And this is what ought to distinguish the church from the world: a willingness to show mercy in ways that can lead to fundamental change.

There are many reasons for us to show mercy. There are the needs themselves, which compel us to show compassion. There is also the opportunity for witness. Helping to meet people's practical needs often provides a context for addressing their deeper spiritual needs. When words of truth are accompanied by works of mercy, the volume gets turned up on the gospel. But our strongest motivation is love for Jesus, who said, "Truly, I say to you, as you did it to one of the least of these my brothers, you did it to me" (Matt. 25:40 ESV). And the reason we do it for Jesus is that he did it first for us. We were hungry and thirsty, and he gave us the bread and water of life. We were strangers, and he made us God's friends. We were naked, and he clothed us with his righteousness. We were sick, and he healed us. We were imprisoned by our sin, and he came—not just to visit us, but to set us free. And now Jesus wants us to do something for him: show mercy to people in need.

Mercy ministry is the special responsibility of deacons. At Tenth Presbyterian Church we ordain deacons and commission deaconesses to prepare our sanctuary for worship, welcome visitors, and care for the material needs of God's people within each parish. As they have done since the days of the early church, deacons demonstrate the sacrificial love of Christ by meeting practical needs. The PCA's *Book of Church Order* (9–1,2) describes the office as one of "sympathy and service," in which deacons are given the privilege to "minister to those who are in need, to the sick, to the friendless, and to any who may be in distress." To fulfill this office, deacons must be of "spiritual character, honest repute, exemplary lives, brotherly spirit, warm sympathies, and sound judgment." Their servant ministry is a reflection of the ministry of Jesus Christ, who "did not count equality with God a thing to be grasped, but made himself nothing, taking the form of a servant" (Phil. 2:6–7 ESV).

Our compassion extends beyond our own congregation through the urban mercy ministry known as Active Compassion Through Service (ACTS). We also form ministry partnerships with other Christian agencies in Philadelphia, including some that were started at Tenth Church. Our past and present outreach includes feeding the homeless, helping AIDS patients, welcoming internationals, providing medical care for the poor, loving the sexually broken, caring for unwed mothers, teaching inner-city children, facilitating racial reconciliation, visiting the elderly, assisting the disabled, helping the jobless, communicating with the deaf, discipling prison inmates and their families, and encouraging parents and children who suffer the alienating effects of separation and divorce. We are ready to do more in years to come, starting new ministries to respond to new areas of urban need. From our base in Center City, we dream about doing more community development in Philadelphia's neediest neighborhoods.

AN INVITATION TO THE FUTURE

Expository preaching. Vibrant worship. Small groups. Pastoral care. Christian education. World missions. Mercy ministry. This is the mission God has given to us as we serve him in our city. We believe that this mission is thoroughly biblical. We also believe that it is totally relevant for post-Christian times.

What is our response to relativism? We teach the Bible, making God's Word plain in an evangelical, doctrinal, and practical way. The standard of biblical authority is preserved and protected by the elders who shepherd our flock. In our missions and evangelism, we present Jesus Christ as the only way to God. Maintaining these priorities helps us promote God's unchanging truth in changing times.

At the same time, the biblical pattern for the church helps preserve us from becoming self-centered or narcissistic. God-centered worship shifts our attention away from what we want to what God wants, so that our goal becomes pleasing him with our praise. Within our fellowship we use our gifts to care for others rather than to serve ourselves. And then in gratitude to God for his great love, we extend the mercy of Christ to those who are outside the church. In these post-Christian times, Tenth is a countercultural community that stands for God and his truth, expressed in love.

We do not do all these things equally well all the time. Of course we don't. Like any other church, we struggle with sin, both individually and corporately. The only reason we are able to do anything for Christ at all is that he has shown us his grace. But by his divine grace, we aim to carry out our mission as well as we can: preaching the Bible, worshiping the Triune God, loving one another, shepherding God's flock, making disciples, advancing the gospel around the world, and showing mercy to our city.

If you are a member of Tenth Church, then this is your mission. Please pray that God will use you to do his work more and more effectively. But even if you are not a member of Tenth Church, will you please pray for us? Satan is trying to destroy us every day—really, he is. So if we are to carry out our mission, we need friends to pray that God will "restore, confirm, strengthen, and establish" us, as he has promised to do (1 Peter 5:10 ESV).

Only God knows what the future holds for Tenth Presbyterian Church. We have some idea where we have been. We also know what God has done for us, and this gives us confidence that God will bless us as we follow him. The one thing we know for certain is that Jesus Christ will come again. Our firm belief and fervent hope is that he is coming soon. And our prayer is that when he does, he will find a faithful church at the corner of Seventeenth and Spruce Streets in Philadelphia, still issuing this wonderful invitation:

> To all who are spiritually weary and seek rest;
> to all who mourn and long for comfort;
> to all who struggle and desire victory;
> to all who sin and need a Savior;
> to all who are strangers and want fellowship;
> to all who hunger and thirst after righteousness;
> and to whoever will come—
> this church opens wide her doors
> and offers her welcome
> in the name of the Lord Jesus Christ.[23]

CORNERSTONE DOCUMENT (1828)

The cornerstone of the Tenth Presbyterian Church was laid July 14, 1828, in the City of Philadelphia by Ashbel Green, a minister of the gospel of said city, John Quincy Adams being President of the United States, John Andrew Shultz Governor of the State of Pennsylvania, and Joseph Watson Mayor of Philadelphia.

The enterprise of building this house for the public worship of Almighty God was conceived, undertaken and the funds for the erection of the same were principally furnished by the following gentlemen, who acted as a building committee, viz.: John Stille, Furman Leaming, James Kerr, Solomon Allen, George Ralston, William Brown. In the erection of this edifice the architect was William Strickland; the carpenter and builder, James Leslie; the bricklayers, A. and E. Robbins. When the stone was laid the inhabitants of the United States were enjoying perfect peace and zealously engaged in promoting agricultural, mechanical and industrial improvements, associations and enterprises. Steamboat navigation was much in use. Of our canals and railroads, some were completed and many more were planned and commenced. For the promotion of good morals and Christian piety infant Sunday schools and Bible classes had been instituted; the Bible and tract societies formed; missions, both domestic and foreign, commenced and successfully prosecuted.

The Presbyterian Church in the United States, under the care of the General Assembly, consisted of 16 synods, 90 presbyteries, 1,285 ministers, 1,968 congregations and 146,308 communicants.

The house of which this is the cornerstone is ever to be considered as dedicated to the worship of the one only living and true God, Father, Son and Holy Ghost. In it no doctrine ought ever to be taught, no worship ever attempted, not consistent with a belief of the unity and personality of the Godhead, the natural and deep depravity of man, the atonement and intercession of the Lord Jesus Christ, the indispensable necessity of the renewing and sanctifying influences of the Holy Spirit in life, sincere obedience to all the commands of God, and a future state of endless rewards and punishments. And may many souls be won to God in this his temple on earth that shall be translated to the glorious worship and eternal bliss of the "house not made with hands, eternal in the heavens."

SENIOR MINISTERS OF TENTH PRESBYTERIAN CHURCH

Thomas A. McAuley, D.D., LL.D	1829–1833	(4 years)
Henry Augustus Boardman, D.D.*	1833–1876	(43 years)
William Pratt Breed, D.D.*	1856–1889	(33 years)
John R. DeWitt, D.D.	1876–1883	(7 years)
William Brenton Greene Jr., D.D.	1883–1892	(9 years)
James D. Paxton, D.D.	1891–1896	(5 years)
Marcus A. Brownson, D.D.*	1897–1924	(27 years)
John D. McNeil, D.D.	1924–1926	(2 years)
Donald Grey Barnhouse, D.D., Th.D.*	1927–1960	(33 years)
Mariano Di Gangi, D.D.	1961–1967	(6 years)
James Montgomery Boice, D. Theol.*	1968–2000	(32 years)
Philip Graham Ryken, D. Phil.	2001–	

*The Five "B's"

MEMBERSHIP TRENDS

Tenth Presbyterian Church

1829	founding
1833	292
1858	450
1893	merger with the West Spruce Street Church

West Spruce Street (Tenth) Church

1856	founding	1966	602
1867	923	1968	535
1915	487	1978	734
1927	347	1984	913
1929	468	1988	1125
1948	824	1994	1028
1950	765	2002	1508
1961	694		

LETTER TO WELCOME NEW MEMBERS (c. 1879)

Beloved in the Lord:

This is to inform you that, by vote of our Session, you were admitted, on the _____ day of _____, upon (Confession of Faith, Letter, etc.) to membership in the West Spruce Street Presbyterian Church and affectionately declared to be entitled to all its privileges.

Suffer us now to remind you that according to your profession you have been brought, as you humbly trust, by the Spirit of God to feel your misery, guilt, depravity and helplessness as a sinner and to desire and purpose to consecrate yourself wholly to the service and glory of the Lord, looking to the merit of Christ as your only righteousness, to assistance of the Spirit as your only strength and to the ways of piety as your only comfort.

You have covenanted to walk with the people of God here, in a church relation, agreeably to the acknowledged doctrines and order of the Presbyterian body.

You have promised to study earnestly the peace, purity, and edification of the church and to walk with its members in love, meekness and faithfulness.

And now, Beloved in the Lord:

Remember that you can never more be as you once were. You have entered into relations you can never renounce and have come under obligations from which you can never escape.

The eyes of the world are upon you. Walk worthy of your high calling. Let your light so shine before men that they may see your good works and glorify your Father which is in heaven. Be faithful unto death, and he will give you a crown of life. Our heart's desire and prayer to God is that as the blessing of God was upon the Egyptian's house and all he had for Joseph's sake, the blessing of the same Jehovah may be upon our spiritual house for your sake; that your fervent prayers, your heavenly spirit, your untiring zeal, your holy example, may prove a rich enhancement of our spiritual treasures.

Among the duties we shall hopefully look for at your hands are the following:

First, if you have not already done so, the selection of a pew or part of a pew that you may call your own, in order that you may feel more at home in our house of worship and also that you may take part with your brethren in the Lord in bearing the necessary expenses of the public worship of God.

Second, we shall hope to be cheered with your presence with all possible regularity at our Sabbath services and also at our more social religious gatherings on Wednesday and Friday evenings, and at our monthly concert of the consideration of Christian progress in and prayer for the conversion of the world to him who bought us with his blood. We are persuaded that you will find attendance upon these services promotive of Christian fellowship and growth in grace.

Third, we trust also that you will practice and enjoy the duty of contributing with regularity and liberality, as God may prosper you in worldly things, to our various objects of Christian beneficence, remembering that "God loveth the cheerful giver."

Fourth, we also earnestly invite your attention to our Sabbath School, our Dorcas and Missionary Society, our Industrial

School and our Woman's Missionary Society, soliciting your personal cooperation and reminding you of the words of him who said, "Inasmuch as ye have done it unto one of the least of these, my brethren, ye have done it unto me."

The Lord bless you and keep you; the Lord make his face to shine upon you and be gracious unto you; the Lord lift up his countenance upon you and give you peace. In the name of the Lord Jesus Christ, our Redeemer. Amen.

A P P E N D I X 5

Letter from Session to Congregation (February 1980)

Presbyterianism

For one hundred and fifty years Tenth Presbyterian Church, Philadelphia, has functioned as a local congregation of the largest Presbyterian denomination in the United States, now called the United Presbyterian Church in the U.S.A. For much of this time it has done so with enthusiasm, for it has believed that Presbyterianism comes closest to that system of belief and government outlined in the pages of the New Testament. The basic elements of that system are:

1. The centrality of Scripture as the inerrant, infallible, ultimate authority of the church,
2. The *Westminster Confession of Faith* and the *Larger* and *Shorter Catechisms* as containing that system of doctrine taught in Scripture, and
3. The authority of the congregation, led by the Session, as the basic unit of church government.

181

Today each of those elements has been lost, and the United Presbyterian Church in the U.S.A. has become Presbyterian in name only.

1. The most serious loss is the abandonment of biblical authority. This has happened over a long period of time, as those who do not believe the Bible to be the authoritative Word of God have been admitted first to the seminaries as teachers, then to the pulpits, and eventually to the denominational hierarchy. But the situation has become acute since the adoption of the *Confession of 1967* (in 1969) with its accompanying changes in the vows taken by church officers for ordination or installation. The old vows asked: "Do you believe the Scriptures of the Old and New Testaments to be, the *Word of God*, the only infallible rule of faith and practice?" The new vows ask: "Do you accept the scriptures of the Old and New Testaments to be, by the Holy Spirit, the unique and authoritative *witness to Jesus Christ* in the church universal, and *God's word to you?*" The change makes the Scriptures authoritative only in their witness to Christ, not necessarily in other matters, and introduces a subjective element— "in the church universal, and God's Word to you." This is understood by many church officials and others to mean that the Holy Spirit speaks subjectively in today's church, even in ways contrary to what the Bible teaches.

Today Scripture no longer functions as the ultimate authority within the United Presbyterian Church. The authority is the human majority, the authority of the fifty-one-percent vote.

2. Adoption of the *Confession of 1967* also undermined the Westminster Standards which define the theology Presbyterians formerly believed to be biblical. It has done this in two ways. First, it demoted the *Westminster Confession of Faith* and the *Shorter Catechism* to being merely two among nine confessions which United Presbyterians now refer to (the *Larger Catechism* has been dropped). Second, it changed the ordination and installation vows so that today one merely promises to be "instructed" by the con-

fessions rather than "sincerely receive and adopt" the Westminster standards, as was required previously.

These changes are not inconsequential. In practice they mean that it is virtually impossible to purify the denomination's pastoral or administrative leadership. No one can be removed for denying the basic tenets of the Christian faith, because no one is officially required to believe them. Unfortunately, the only thing one can be removed for is refusing to follow each particular of the denomination's *Constitution* or *Book of Order*, for the vows of ordination and installation now require one to "endorse" these while being asked merely to "accept" the Scriptures and be "instructed" by the confessions.

3. In the early days of the development of the Presbyterian Church in the United States governmental authority was centered in the congregation, led by its Session. This is why our system of government is called Presbyterianism. It is a system of rule by elders, which is what the word "presbyter" or "elder" (*presbyteros*) refers to. Presbyterianism is distinguished from congregationalism which is pure democracy, each person having an equal vote, and from episcopacy which is ruled by bishops. Over the years, however, the hierarchy of the church has built up power at the expense of the local congregation. Presbyteries have become stronger than local congregations, the General Assembly stronger than the presbyteries. According to current practices, the local church cannot even choose its own minister or buy or sell its own property without its presbytery's consent.

THE DENOMINATION TODAY

Today each of the essential tenets of Presbyterianism has been lost by the United Presbyterian Church. The authority of Scripture has been replaced by the authority of the fifty-one-percent vote. The Westminster Standards have been replaced by our current, amendable Constitution. The authority of the local congregation, through its Session, has been replaced by a system of church courts which place ultimate power in the hands of the hierarchy. The United Presbyterian Church in the U.S.A. has become a secular institution so far as its official documents and structures are concerned. To be sure, there are many believing people within it. Again, its practice has in the past often been better than its policy. But it has still become secular! Officially it has become very much like those against whom Paul warned Timothy—those "having a form of godliness but denying its power" (2 Tim. 3:5). Since the Bible tells us to test the spirits (1 John 4:1, 2), it is time to ask whether Tenth Presbyterian Church should continue within the United Presbyterian denomination.

STAYING OR LEAVING

The Session has recognized that there is a great difference between the questions "When *may* one leave a denomination?" and "When *must* one leave a denomination?" Obviously, one may leave at any time providing he or she is convinced that God is so leading. In a pluralistic church situation, such as we have in the United States, there is no one true denomination. There is not even one true Presbyterian denomination. Therefore, we have never condemned those who have left our fellowship for other denominations. We believe that God has led some to depart, thereby bearing witness to the need for purity within the church. We believe he has led some to stay, thereby bearing witness to the need for a visible unity among all true believers (even though some may err very badly in doctrine or morals). Tenth Presbyterian Church has elected to stay, thereby bearing witness to the unity of the church and in order to work for change within. Our text has been Revelation 3:2: "Strengthen what remains and is about to die."

But when must one leave? And is now the time? We maintain that an individual or local church must leave for only one of two reasons: 1. when the denomination requires an individual or local congregation to do something the individual or local congregation judges to be unbiblical, or 2. when the denomination becomes apostate.

These are matters to be handled with great care. Since separation from a parent body is a serious matter, an individual or church must always carefully examine the issue on which the denomination is mandating action believed to be unbiblical. They must carefully re-examine the Scriptures in light of the challenge of the larger church. It is always possible that they may have missed something. In the matter of apostasy, the individual or church must be careful that the matter involved is actually a denial of a cardinal truth of Christianity and that at the highest or most official level of the denomination. It must involve matters like the deity of Christ, the vicarious atonement, the necessity for the new birth and other similar doctrines.

In the last few years each of these conditions has suddenly come upon us. It is true that they are not yet fully resolved, which gives some small amount of time to think, discuss and pray concerning them. But they are nearly resolved. The matter is urgent.

1. The condition of being required to do something which we judge to be unbiblical has come in the matter of Overture L, mandating the ordination of women to the office of ruling elder. This is not an issue which we have sought out. In itself it is not even a major issue. It is not one over which we or any other congregation should willingly leave the United Presbyterian Church. On the contrary, although women have had the right to be ordained to this office for many years and although the action of the Permanent Judicial Commission in the case of the young ordinand Wynn Kenyon (*Maxwell versus the Presbytery of Pittsburgh*) prejudiced the status of all who think like Kenyon and yet take ordination or installation vows—we are told that those who think like Kenyon cannot properly promise to "endorse" the Form of Government—we nevertheless believed it right to stay and work for any possible alleviation. Overture L has changed that. Now ordination of women to the session is required, and since this takes place through election by the congregation, the members

of the congregation and not just ministers and other church officers are likewise affected. We are all being told through the highest and most official action of our church that we must comply
in the requirement. If we do not (because we cannot "actively
concur" or "passively submit"), we must "peaceably withdraw"
(*1758 Plan of Reunion, Old Side–New Side*).

Are we and those who have gone before us in this church
as well as the majority of other Presbyterian churches in four
hundred or more years of our history wrong on this matter? It
is always a possibility that we may be. We are human and prone
to error. But we have not been persuaded that this is the case,
nor has our denomination really tried to persuade either ourselves or others scripturally. We have merely been told that this
is the law of the church and that we must conform to it. We
believe:

a. That Scripture is superior in authority to that of church
   councils (*Westminster Confession of Faith*, XXXI, 3).
b. That church councils err whenever they attempt to force
   those under them to conform to anything either contrary
   to Scripture or not clearly required by Scripture (*Westminster Confession of Faith*, XX, 2).
c. That the Bible teaches the equality of women and men,
   both being made in God's image (Gen. 1:26, 27), both being
   equally objects of God's redeeming grace in Christ Jesus
   (Gal. 3:28).
d. That the Bible also teaches the need for subordination of
   a wife to a husband within the home and of women as
   well as other men to duly appointed male leaders within
   the church (1 Cor. 11:2–16, 14:33–35; 1 Tim. 2:11–15).
e. That the texts commonly used to deny the need for subordination of a wife to a husband within the home and of
   the women to male leaders within the church (Eph. 5:21;
   Gal. 3:28) do not do so; Ephesians 5:21 is followed by
   examples of the submission here enjoined, wives to hus-

bands being among them, and Galatians 3:28 speaks of unity in Christ only, not these relationships.

f. That the restrictions on women functioning in the chief positions of authority within the home and the church are not cultural, Paul clearly deriving it from the orders of creation (1 Tim. 2:13–14).

g. That to go against what we perceive to be the clear teaching of Scripture, regardless of the pressures of any denomination or secular culture, is neither safe nor wise.

We emphasize that our stance is based solely on what we believe to be Scripture's teaching. The current Moderator of the United Presbyterian Church, the Reverend Howard L. Rice, recognizes this, though he himself does not share our viewpoint. "Women's ordination is the issue that's on the surface, but that's not the issue," he has said. It is "differences over the authority of the Bible" (*The Presbyterian Journal,* Nov. 21, 1979, p. 6).

The issue here is not merely *where* we stand but *why* we stand where we do. We stand where we do because of Scripture. We cannot do otherwise. We cannot ordain women to the office of teaching or ruling elder because we believe that God does not permit it.

It is possible that, although our views are contrary to the current position of the denomination on this matter and we should properly be disciplined by the denomination or (to avoid that) withdraw, the denomination may not discipline us or force us to withdraw. Presbytery may ignore our stance in the interests of the greater harmony of the church. This would be welcome for the immediate future, but it does not help us in the long run. Even now our seminarians are ineligible to be candidates for the ministry within the United Presbyterian Church of the U.S.A. If they are to serve, it must be with us unofficially (as assistants to the pastor but not as ministers) or else in some other denomination. Again, ministers who hold our convictions in the matter of women's ordination cannot change churches within the denomination. This means that if something happens to our present pastor, we will be unable to find another of like convictions able to transfer to our church. Even assuming that our current pastor will be able to remain with us for many years, we face increasing dilution of the pool of strong ministers of attrition and even greater difficulty in finding a pastor later. We believe that in the future it will be almost impossible to find faithful, Bible-believing men to fill Tenth's pulpit.

2. The second condition under which one must leave a denomination, apostasy, is now developing within the United Presbyterian Church. Early in 1979, the National Union Presbytery (Washington, D.C.) received for installation as a minister within the church a man who officially denied the deity of Jesus Christ during his examination. His name is Mansfield Kaseman. He was asked, "Do you believe Jesus Christ to be the Son of God?" He answered "No!" Further examination left no doubt as to what he meant; he was denying Jesus' full divinity. Yet in spite of this, the presbytery voted to approve him by a vote of approximately two to one. This case was appealed to synod, and synod upheld presbytery, not on the issue of Kaseman's theology but on the grounds that presbytery has the legal right to examine, install and ordain. The case is currently under appeal from synod to the Permanent Judicial Commission. It is shocking that although the case has not yet been finally resolved at the highest level, National Union Presbytery has nevertheless proceeded with the installation.

Few would be foolish enough to think that Kaseman is the only person in our denomination who disbelieves in the deity of Christ. But his situation is different from others' in that he is a pastor and his is a public and official denial. His installation, in the face of that denial, is an official declaration by the National Union Presbytery that it is possible to be a Christian and even a minister while refusing to believe in Jesus as God's unique Son. If upheld by the Permanent Judicial Commission, how can that be anything other than apostasy at the highest possible level of our denomination?

CONCLUSION

We would stress that the issue of mandating the ordination of women to the office of teaching and ruling elder and the acceptability of a denial of the deity of Christ within our church are not yet fully resolved. The Permanent Judicial Commission has not yet ruled on the Kaseman case, and there may yet be some relief in the case of ordination. But we are not hopeful. For years Tenth Presbyterian Church, through its leadership, has worked for reform within the United Presbyterian Church. We have worked with others to introduce overtures to the General Assembly. We have helped to produce documents which expressed our concern: "A Declaration and Call" (1973), "A Call to Reformation" (1975), "Ordination and Subordination" (1976), "October 11, Motion" (1979). These have increased in intensity. Yet we have discerned no disposition in the church to legitimate, let alone endorse, our position. On the contrary, the trend has consistently been the other way, and numerous ministers and churches who share convictions similar to ours have either withdrawn from the denomination or have been removed by presbytery action.

What is there to hold us within a denomination no longer distinctly Presbyterian or even conciliatory toward those believers who disagree with it in matters such as those we delineated? We urge the congregation to consider whether it is not now time for us to "peaceably withdraw" from the fellowship of the United Presbyterian Church in the U.S.A. and seek alignments more in line with historic Presbyterianism and the dictates of our own consciences as informed by Scripture.

APPENDIX 6

MEMBERSHIP BOOKLET (2004)

We are happy to welcome you into the membership of Tenth Presbyterian Church. You have been received on the basis of your faith in God the Father, maker of heaven and earth, and in Jesus Christ as your Lord and Savior, and in the Holy Spirit as the One who can enable you to be his faithful disciple to your life's end.

What are your obligations as a member? In coming into our fellowship, you promise "to make diligent use of the means of grace, to share faithfully in the worship and service of the church, to give of your substance as the Lord may prosper you, and to give your whole heart to the service of Christ and his kingdom throughout the world."

1. *To make diligent use of the means of grace.* The Christians of apostolic times "continued steadfastly in the apostles' doctrine and fellowship, and in breaking of bread, and in prayers" (Acts 2:42).

The grace of God ordinarily comes to us as we hear his Word, as we partake of the sacrament of the Lord's Supper, and as we engage in prayer, with the attitude of faith. To neglect these means of grace is to starve the spirit and stunt the soul. To use them diligently is to "grow in grace, and in the knowledge of our Lord and Savior Jesus Christ" (2 Pet. 3:18).

190

2. *To share faithfully in the worship of the church.* We are told in God's Word not to forsake "the assembling of ourselves together" for the public worship of God (Heb. 10:25).

Allowing for illness, or works of necessity and mercy, Christians ought to support the morning and evening services on the Lord's Day, as well as activities that occur throughout the week whenever possible. Where even "two or three" are gathered together in Christ's name, he is present (Matt. 18:20). Since he is present, we should not be absent. Our response should be, "I was glad when they said unto me, Let us go into the house of the LORD" (Ps. 122:1).

3. *To share faithfully in the service of the church.* Some members have the privilege of serving as elders, deacons, trustees, ushers, and teachers in the Bible school. But all of us can serve by being good missionaries or evangelists for Christ—inviting others to public worship, greeting worshipers in a friendly way, and witnessing to Christ day by day.

If you know of someone who is interested in church membership or who wishes to inquire further about the Christian faith, you can serve by introducing that person to your pastors.

Remember the apostle's saying, "And whatsoever ye do in word or deed, do all in the name of the Lord Jesus, giving thanks to God and the Father by him" (Col. 3:17).

4. *To give of your substance as the Lord may prosper you.* We are taught in God's Word to support the Lord's work by giving regularly, proportionately and joyfully: "Upon the first day of the week let every one of you lay by him in store, as God hath prospered him" (1 Cor. 16:2) . . . "for God loveth a cheerful giver" (2 Cor. 9:7).

Tenth Church has two main budgets: a missionary budget and a general budget for the maintenance of a Christian witness here in center city Philadelphia. We ask you to indicate what you trust God to enable you to give through the church in each of these categories, using a pledge card. We also ask you to contribute regularly through a set of envelopes. Count your blessings, consider the need, and give with gratitude in your heart.

5. *To give your whole heart to the service of Christ and his kingdom throughout the world*. The Christian life is lived in obedience to Christ the King. His will is the law of our lives. Our purpose in living is to serve him as loyal and loving subjects. God forbid that we should bring disrepute upon his banner by the inconsistency of our conduct. May we ever be zealous for the crown rights of our Redeemer, wholeheartedly committed to him who loved us and gave himself for us.

"Walk worthy of God, who hath called you unto his kingdom and glory" (1 Thess. 2:12).

We have commented on the sacred obligations of membership. But what of its blessed privileges?

Church members are invited to share in the Lord's Supper and have the right to present their covenant children to God in baptism. They are entitled to the oversight and care of the session. They have the opportunity to learn more of Christian doctrine and ethics in our Bible school.

You will have a place in this fellowship of God's family and the benefits of pastoral care. Christ appoints pastors so that his people may hear the inspired Scriptures faithfully preached from the pulpit and souls in need may receive encouragement. Your pastors are always willing to pray for you in times of sickness and sorrow and to counsel you in confidence when you are faced with problems and decisions.

MUSIC AT TENTH: A SHORT HISTORY

Paul S. Jones

Fine church music has been closely linked with the pulpit ministry at Tenth Church for many years. When visitors speak of the church, two things are usually mentioned: the powerful expository teaching ministry and the excellent music. Such impressions are based on a tradition of great church music stretching back to the early days of Tenth Church, and of the strong preaching that has always been central to its ministry.

Shortly after the founding of Tenth Church in 1829, during the era when Henry Boardman was senior minister and then pastor emeritus, music played an important role in the worship service, and Tenth had a similarly important role in providing musical leadership for the Presbyterian Church in the United States. While there have been decades when the significance of music within Tenth declined, overall it has remained a strong force. There has also been a substantial amount of hymn-related activity associated with the church, including (in addition to singing and playing) compiling, editing, hymnology, authoring texts, and composing tunes.

193

Boardman and His Hymnal (1833–76)

Henry Boardman compiled a hymnal entitled *Hymns of Praise*, which was prepared as a supplement to the standard *Psalms and Hymns* used by the Presbyterian Church.[1] The new hymnal added more than 500 Greek, Latin, German, and other hymns that had been translated into English since the publication of *Psalms and Hymns*. In the preface Boardman made it clear what he believed to be the true purpose of hymn-singing:

> Let it suffice to say here, that the fundamental idea which underlies this Collection, is that the singing of Hymns is an office of WORSHIP. This does not import that every Hymn must be throughout a direct address to the Deity. For there are songs of Zion eminently fitted to nourish devotional feeling, and breathing the very spirit of praise, which could not bear this test. . . . Still, the *principle* is a sound one: and the neglect of it has turned many Hymn-Books into repositories of mere descriptive and hortatory poems, which lack the first element of WORSHIP.

Boardman also articulated the purpose of the new hymnal, with Tenth Church obviously in mind: "In the preparation of this volume, the Compiler has had a special eye to the wants of his own pulpit and people. He is not without the hope that it may prove an acceptable offering to some other congregations, and to private Christians. It is now humbly commended to His blessing, who is at once the Object and the Inspirer of all true Worship, and who has said, 'WHOSO OFFERETH PRAISE GLORIFIETH ME.'" Boardman made certain that a healthy selection of hymns for family worship and private devotion were added as well, and the hymns were printed in their original form, with all stanzas fully intact.

A paid choir existed at Tenth at least as early as 1857, and there were pipe organs in both the Tenth Presbyterian Church and the West Spruce Street Presbyterian Church (whose building became the site of the unified Tenth Presbyterian Church in

1893). By 1858 the session determined that it had sufficient funds "to procure a first-class instrument." The organ's installation was completed the next year by Jardine and Son of New York and was "universally admitted by disinterested and competent judges to be at least equal to any instrument heretofore erected in this city." George Jardine personally superintended the installation at a total cost of $3,800. Building a large instrument required considerable alterations in the gallery, which could also accommodate a large number of singers. Twenty years later the organ was altered with a new hydraulic blower, revoicing, the addition of some stops, cleaning, and repair, so that it was again "one of the very finest instruments in our city or state."[2]

BREED THROUGH BROWNSON (1856–1924)

During Boardman's tenure, another important figure in the history of Presbyterian hymnody grew up in the congregation. Louis Fitzgerald Benson (1855–1930) has been described as "the foremost hymnologist that America has produced."[3] His father, Gustavus S. Benson, a successful businessman and trustee of Princeton Theological Seminary, was a long-serving elder of Tenth Church and is memorialized in one of the large plaques at the front of the present sanctuary. Louis abandoned a legal career at age 32 for seminary, and later left the pastoral ministry to become a hymnologist. He amassed an enormous collection of old hymnals, sheet hymns, and other information on the history of hymns. His personal library of 9,000 volumes is one of the world's greatest collections of hymnological literature (now The Benson Collection at the Speer Library, Princeton Seminary, where he lectured from 1903).[4]

Among Benson's most important books were *The English Hymn: Its Development and Use in Worship* (1915) and *The Hymnody of the Christian Church* (1927). Benson also contributed to the second edition of John Julian's *Dictionary of Hymnology* and was responsible for locating accurate and previously lost information on many hymns in their original forms. In addition, he edited at least seven hymnals, including *The Hymnal* (1933) of the Presbyterian Church that was used at Tenth throughout the Barnhouse and Di Gangi pastorates. Benson's historical research became the basis for large parts of *The Hymnal*, in which at least eight hymns appear that he translated or revised.[5]

Little is known about the performance of music at Tenth before 1857, other than that there was a pipe organ in the loft. The music program at Tenth has never dwarfed the pulpit ministry, as has happened in many other churches. It has long been understood that the music ministry is the "handmaiden" of the pulpit ministry. In 1876 Pastor William Breed asserted that the singing gallery had not been yielded up to "the musical artist, according to whose creed the chief end of the church is the organ loft and the chief end of the performers there is to display their accomplishments, sing their own praises, and gratify a cultivated musical taste."[6] The Lord has blessed Tenth with talented musical artists and a cultivated musical taste, even among its congregants, but there is no boasting, except in the great God from whom, through whom, and to whom are all things (Rom. 11:36).

In 1894 the pipe organ from the old Tenth Church building on Walnut Street was installed in the chapel (now known as Reception Hall) of the building on West Spruce Street. Later a choir was formed to sing in the chapel during Wednesday evening services. As of 1908, the salary for the choir was set at $2,450 (the minister was then paid $5,000); the pianist and the leader of the music for the Sunday school and the prayer meeting were also paid for their services. In 1914 the board of trustees decided to rebuild what was by then the "old organ" in the sanctuary. Philadelphia's C. S. Haskell rebuilt the instrument for a little more than $4,000. Tenth's music ministry took a major step forward in the 1925 budget, which added organ cleaning, Easter music, Christmas music, special music, the Princeton Chorus, and Service Song Books to the regular list of priorities. By 1929 the organ was again in need of repair, and Owen J. W. Burgess and Son were contracted to service the instrument.

Many talented musicians played and sang at Tenth during these years. Ellis Clark Hammann served as organist and choirmaster from 1901 to 1907. Hammann was succeeded by Stanley Addicks, and then by Gilbert R. Combs, who played at the church from 1908 to 1915. John Woods Jr. played for the sabbath school and Wednesday-evening prayer meeting until 1911. At least by 1910 there was a paid quartet of soloists (choristers) who served as section leaders for the choir. The music program seems to have progressed largely without incident, except for an occasion when "the attention of the session was called to the fact that our Sabbath School Anniversary May 1st (1910), the singers of our choir left the church before the last two hymns were sung. The Clerk was directed to notify the choir that the session was grieved at this action, and trusts it may not be repeated."[7]

In 1918 the church treasurer was authorized to purchase 100 copies of the *New Collection of War Hymns* at a price of $5. Beginning her twenty years of service to Tenth in October of 1919, Elizabeth Porter Earle was hired as soloist for $550 per annum. Some years later, something happened that would change the course of music at Tenth for several decades. The congregation expressed the desire to have a precentor instead of a choir to lead congregational singing. So in September 1922 the choir was disbanded, with Mrs. Earle retained as precentor.

MUSIC UNDER BARNHOUSE (1927–1960)

The music committee hired Ella E. Day as organist in 1927 at a salary of $800 per year, with one month for vacation. Miss Day played for Dr. Barnhouse's installation and served as organist during his early years at Tenth. She played classical organ music for preludes and postludes each Sunday, including works by Guilmant, Bach, Borowski, Dubois, Gounod, Wagner, and Bizet. Traditional hymns from *The Hymnal* were sung in services, but not necessarily all the stanzas. Mrs. Earle, who had formerly served as a chorister and precentor, was the staff soloist from 1931 to 1939, and she sang the offertory at all morning and evening services.

In 1928 Barnhouse was authorized to purchase 300 new hymnals for the evening service and to donate the old ones to a needy church. It is unclear whether he did this, however, because 400 copies of "Greatest Hymns" were purchased in 1932 for evening use. Other music went on in the church as well, including a Bible school Christmas program from 1938 forward. For the fiscal year ending March 31, 1936, the salaries of the organist, soloist, music supplies, and instrument maintenance totaled $2,110 (the total church budget that year was $22,611).

Each year the music committee (a committee of session) would recommend to the session whether Miss Day and Mrs. Earle's contracts should be renewed. In 1936 the committee was authorized to continue its services on a monthly basis, "pending further developments." This was because Dr. Barnhouse wanted to engage a full-time minister of music "to develop this phase of the church work in all its departments, including the Sunday services." Barnhouse first tried to lure Carleton Booth to move to Philadelphia from Providence, Rhode Island. When this failed, the church eventually hired Douglas Davies, whose arrival meant the end of Mrs. Earle's long service to the church. Mr. Davies served from 1939 to 1941 and was ordained during his second year at Tenth. He placed a "Song Service" at the beginning of evening worship, which started at 7:45 p.m. in those days. He also served as soloist, singing sacred classical works and expanding the hymn repertoire of the congregation.

There was a marked increase in the use of other male soloists as well. Apparently, after more than twenty years of hearing the same soprano, the congregation was ready to hear some men sing! Mel Dibble succeeded Mr. Davies, and served as music director and soloist from late 1941 into 1945. Lily Orr began her lengthy tenure as organist in September of 1943, playing the prelude, hymns, and postlude each week, and accompanying the various soloists who sang the offertory, as had her predecessor.

Donald Grey Barnhouse Jr. was listed next as staff soloist, serving from 1945 to 1949. He had begun to sing prior to this, while still a student at Harvard, and was also the leader of the evening Song Services. For a period of three months while the elder Barnhouse was preaching in California (January to March 1947), the famous Scottish minister J. Sidlow Baxter filled the pulpit. On Thursday evenings he gave a Bible lecture and the young Dr. Barnhouse would sing one of Baxter's original musical compositions.

With Dr. Barnhouse Sr. at the height of his popularity, Tenth was characterized even more exclusively as a "preaching" church. Music became more an indentured servant than a handmaiden. According to previous accounts, Barnhouse rid the church of its pipe organ, drained the music budget, and banished any idea of having a choir.[8] But this is not the full story. In truth, Barnhouse loved the pipe organ—which was used regularly during his early years at Tenth—but it had fallen into such disrepair that the session voted to disassemble it. Removing the organ did not go over well with everyone in the congregation, and efforts were made to raise enough money to make the necessary repairs. But they were never made, perhaps because the organ was—as the trustees put it—"entirely out of use." In 1940 the church began using a Hammond organ that Walter H. Dilworth had purchased from Wanamaker's Department Store for $5,000. In 1946 the pipe organ was removed from the premises altogether.

The congregation made its first attempt to purchase a new pipe organ in 1952, when Robert Grasberger chaired a committee "to induce other members of the church to pledge enough money to reach the $25,000 required to purchase the organ as per provisions of a former resolution." The resolution read as follows: "That the meeting now in session hereby instruct the Board of Trustees to proceed with the purchase and installation of a pipe organ for a sum not to exceed $45,000, if and when signed pledges to the amount of $25,000 have been received." In April the congregation called for an appraisal of the four-manual Casavant organ put up for sale by the First Presbyterian Church in

Philadelphia. The congregation also wanted to know whether the Moeller Company, which had made the original bid for the reactivation and installation of the pipe organ, was still willing to do the work for $35,000. If so, the church was prepared to offer not more than $5,500 for the organ. By February 1953 pledges totaled more than $20,000, so the congregation made a formal bid. Unfortunately, by then the First Presbyterian Church had already sold the organ to someone else. Seeing no alternatives, the Trustees returned the moneys they had raised.

Pursuing a pipe organ was in keeping with Dr. Barnhouse's musical interests. Barnhouse was a renaissance man who wanted a more prominent music program and regularly exhorted evangelicals "to rise above artistic philistinism."[9] He prized the arts, loved singing hymns, and played the piano for personal enjoyment. He also encouraged his family to experience music by taking piano lessons, attending operas and performances of the Philadelphia Orchestra, singing hymns as a family, and hosting Jorge Bolet (the soon-to-be-famous pianist who was then a student at the Curtis Institute). Barnhouse also tried to encourage his church to appreciate excellent music. After one trip abroad he suggested acquiring the pipe organ from the Erlen Theatre in Philadelphia, but the people of Tenth resisted. In the past he had convinced them to put their money into missions rather than into any "frills," and they balked at the expense. This was one of the few times that the congregation said "no" to Barnhouse. His motivation was not primarily musical, but evangelistic, and he viewed music as a means to gather an audience. He wanted his good friend Robert Elmore to come to Tenth as organist and concert director, but Elmore declined because the church had no real organ for him to play.[10]

Some have said that the decline of the music program could be explained by Barnhouse's neglect, but there is little evidence of this. In fact, there was real consistency in having a paid organist and soloist performing sacred classical church music throughout his pastorate. Still, one wonders why the music budget did not increase for more than 30 years. But as Elmore noted in his 1980 annual report, it was Barnhouse who taught him that Jesus Christ "sings" with us according to Hebrews chapter 2. And when Barnhouse wrote about church music in the bulletin, his desire was to teach the proper perspective on worship for a church musician:

> Church music can be anything from reverent worship of God to carnal exhibitionism, and in musical quality may be anything from a joyful noise to an artistic musical presentation. It goes without saying that a good voice is better than a bad one for church music, provided the hearts are equally yielded to the Lord. If the hearts are not yielded, the curse on unspiritual music is stated very definitely in the Bible. It is hateful to the Lord. Of many a cantata and many an Easter day it might well be written, "I hate, I despise your feast days . . . take thou away from me the noise of thy songs" (Amos 5:21, 23).
>
> These thoughts were emphasized recently in the choir room of a certain church. The pastor had typewritten a letter addressed "To the Members of the Choir." . . . He wrote in part: "You can be a great asset to the worship hour when you realize your first duty is not to sing but to worship. . . . Let this hour be a holy hour and let your example be wholesome and helpful. Cease everything that would distract from the purpose of the hour, which is to worship God in the beauty of holiness."[11]

Although records are sketchy from 1952 to 1957, Gordon Curtis was listed as Minister of Music, a unique title in the history of Tenth. If Barnhouse had banished any thought of a choir, it surely was not evident when Mr. Curtis started a choir to sing the morning offertory each week and to rehearse on Thursday evenings following prayer meeting. This choir tackled many great, traditional anthems, including works by Stainer, Mozart, Bortniansky, Bach, Goss, and Grieg. The choir began to sing in both morning and evening worship in September of 1959, but ceased to exist after Mr. Curtis's departure at the end of the year. Rodney McWherter was the staff soloist during this time. Upon Mr. McWherter's leaving near the end of November 1958, many different soloists were engaged—a new pattern for the church. A quartet of singers was

prominent by 1960, and by 1962 a quartet and octet were sometimes heard as remnants of the earlier choir.

THE DI GANGI YEARS (1961–67)

During Mariano Di Gangi's six-year term as senior minister, the music program changed from what it had been under
his predecessor. Di Gangi was troubled by the atrophied state of
the music ministry and initiated several things to enliven it. The
music program was seriously underfunded, as is evidenced by
the fact that in 1961 more was spent on advertising than on the
entire music program (salaries, instrument maintenance, and
music supplies included). This pattern held true through 1964.

One thing Di Gangi desired was to get, once again, a grand
pipe organ for the church. To help get around entrenched crit-
ics, he proposed to call it the "Donald Grey Barnhouse Memorial
Organ." Funds were collected into 1965, and a special appeal was
regularly printed in the bulletin, but the congregation apparently
did not agree with the need or urgency of this project. As of the
end of 1965, $3,800 existed in this account, but a year later only
$677 more had been given. The congregational thinking was that
there was no need for an elaborate music program, so in 1967
these funds were disbursed to other endeavors, notably the building fund and renovations to Fellowship Hall.

While Di Gangi never got his pipe organ, he made other
inroads to establishing a positive attitude toward church music.
In 1964 he had the following statement printed at the beginning
of each bulletin: "Let the Organ Prelude be your call to worship.
Prepare for the service by meditation on the words of today's
hymns, and by prayer for the pastors, your fellow worshippers,
and the world." Previously Di Gangi had added "Organ Inter-
lude/Silent Prayer" to the order of service before the sermon and
again following the reading of the Scripture text. He brought in
a string quartet from The Curtis Institute for Good Friday services. On several occasions, he invited touring choral groups to

sing, including the Student Nurses' Choir of the Presbyterian Hospital, the Philadelphia College of Bible Chorale, the Columbia Bible College Choir, and the Gordon College Chorale. These choirs sang multiple anthems in either morning or evening services, with a sermon or meditation offered by Di Gangi. He also re-implemented a Song Service to begin Sunday evening worship services—three hymns each week. To supplement the existing hymnal, he introduced a new one: *Inspiring Hymns*, which featured more gospel-style hymnody. The use of this second hymnal gradually increased until it was used almost exclusively in the evening service.

In 1965 Miriam Zito (later Mrs. Zito-Hermosa), mezzo-soprano, began serving as staff soloist and evening music director. Walter Emery joined her as a staff soloist in 1967. During this period, the bulletin advertised concerts, such as one given by Daniel Majeske (Cleveland Orchestra) and William Dawson (a Curtis Institute student). The Campus and Career Club started a choir in February 1965 and rehearsed John Stainer's oratorio *The Crucifixion*. As of Di Gangi's resignation in 1967, there were no soloists on staff, but Zito was once again the evening music director. November of that year marked Nancy Nicks's first appearance as soloist, and by the time James Boice arrived, Miss Nicks was the soloist for all regular services, morning and evening.

A NEW ERA IN MUSIC (1968–85)

When James Montgomery Boice became senior minister, he purposed to revolutionize the music program. He began initiating changes at the end of 1968, when Lily Orr retired after twenty-five years of service spanning three pastorates (the longest serving Tenth staff musician). On March 2, 1969, Dr. Robert Hall Elmore became organist, with Joel Krott serving as assistant organist. Nancy Nicks and Miriam Zito were named "morning soloist" and "evening soloist," respectively. In 1968 the entire budget line for music had been $2,724. For 1969 this increased to $20,498, paid for by significant donations toward the launch of an enhanced music ministry.

Under Boice's leadership, and with help from elder Robert Grasberger, the session had hired one of America's most prominent organists and church composers. Grasberger had known Elmore from their college days at the University of Pennsylvania and was aware of his availability following a thirteen-year tenure in Bethlehem, Pennsylvania. Elmore was not a stranger, having played for the wedding of Donald and Margaret Barnhouse, and having reviewed recordings for *Eternity* magazine, of which Barnhouse was editor. As a young man, Elmore had studied piano, organ, and composition for eight years with the famous organist and composer Pietro Yon. He earned the Licentiate degree from London's Royal Academy of Music in three subjects: organ, concert piano, and piano accompaniment—an achievement unprecedented in the institution's history. He also held two honorary doctorates for his outstanding contributions to church music. Prior to service at Tenth, Elmore had held posts at Central Baptist Church, Wayne, Pennsylvania (1925–33); Arch Street Methodist, Philadelphia (1933–38); Holy Trinity Episcopal on Rittenhouse Square, Philadelphia (1939–55); and Central Moravian Church, Bethlehem, Pennsylvania (1955–68). He brought a rich performing background as well as an intimate familiarity with Moravian church music.

One of Elmore's conditions in coming to Tenth was that the church invest in a good organ, which it did with the purchase of a four-manual Allen at the cost of $64,000. The new Allen organ was paid off within three years. Many organists questioned Elmore's decision to come to Tenth because of its woefully inadequate music program for an artist of his stature, and in particular his decision to endorse an electronic instrument. Yet Elmore was aware that this was the means of birthing a serious church music program at Tenth, particularly in light of the congregation's views about spending money on music. As the largest electronic instrument in the world at that time, the new Allen organ was designed to Elmore's specifications and touted by the company as "the Elmore organ." It was installed in June of 1970 in the choir loft at the back of the sanctuary, with speakers in the former organ chambers and antiphonal speakers in the pulpit area cleverly hidden beneath the apse. A series of three dedicatory concerts was given, featuring Elmore playing Bach, Reubke, Bingham, Duruflé, and Elmore.

Boice and Elmore brought immediate and long-lasting changes to Tenth's music ministry. From Elmore's first Sunday (which coincided with Dr. Boice's first day on the air with "The Bible Study Hour"), the bulletin was noticeably different, having all the preludes and postludes listed. The first Sunday, Elmore played Bach for the morning and Mendelssohn for the evening. And so it began—organ music of Franck, Messiaen, Karg-Elert, Buxtehude, and many other masters brilliantly executed and regularly heard at Seventeenth and Spruce. Elmore expanded the soloists' repertoire to include Schubert, Sowerby, Handel, and Bach. His second Sunday celebrated the introduction of *The Trinity Hymnal* to Tenth Church. On the fourth Sunday, the bulletin included a lengthy explanation, written by Elmore, of the organ service music for the week. By Good Friday/Easter, all texts (solo and choral) appeared in the bulletin, with no deletions. On May 11, 1969, there was a performance (in the evening service) of the Fauré *Requiem* by the Philadelphia Academy of Music Chorus with Krott on the organ, and then Boice preached. Musical prominence of this kind was groundbreaking for Tenth Church. By 1973 the music ministry was considered significant enough to merit a page in the annual report. Here Elmore thanked the regular and occasional choir members and stated his gratitude for contributions toward music at Tenth from both inside and outside the church. He then wrote, "But above all we ask for your prayers, that our ministry may be not only artistically valid but filled with and energized by the Holy Spirit."

It was Elmore who founded the choir in 1969 and engaged paid soloists as section leaders. Among these were John Corbin, tenor, Marjorie Camp, soprano (later replaced by Carol Corbin), and Albert Smith, baritone, as well as Mimi Zito-Hermosa, mezzo-soprano, and, later, Nancy (Nicks) Bucklin. Soloists would sing in the morning while the choir participated in the evening, a unique arrangement among church choirs. This permitted area singers who were members elsewhere to participate in Elmore's choir, which numbered 40 singers by 1973 and 60 by 1976. The choir rehearsed initially on Thursday evenings at 6:00 p.m., but soon began the tradition of rehearsing on Monday evenings (rare for a church choir) and Sunday evenings before the worship service, a practice that continues to the present day.

On Christmas Eve 1969, Elmore had brass and percussion join him as his cantata *Wondrous, Divine Child* was sung by the choir and soloists with Donald Barnhouse Jr. as narrator. Christmas Eve 1970 marked the first service of lessons and carols with five choral anthems. Boice preached at these services until 1974, when he expanded them to include eight anthems and more Scripture readings but omitted the sermon. For Boice, the Christmas Eve candlelight and carol service was one of the most significant services of the year. He loved Christmas and chose Christmas carols for worship throughout December, whereas his predecessors had selected them only for the Sunday preceding Christmas Day. Elmore almost always began the Christmas Eve service with either Holst's "Christmas Day" or Vaughan Williams' "Fantasia on Christmas Carols," and a chorus from Elmore's cantata *The Incarnate Word* was often included.

The Tenth Choir presented four concerts annually, in addition to the special service each Christmas Eve. Sunday afternoon programs at 5:00 were a means of outreach to the unchurched community, which might come to hear a choral masterwork such as Handel's *Samson*, Mendelssohn's *Elijah*, Brahms' *A German Requiem*, Liszt's *Thirteenth Psalm*, Debussy's *The Prodigal Son*, or Rossini's *Stabat Mater*. Following the performance, there was a buffet supper and then the evening worship service. And there were performances of many of Elmore's own compositions as well, his cantata *Psalm of Redemption* being a particular favorite. By 1970 there was a junior choir, and April 1971 witnessed Tenth's first Latin text sung by the choir, with an English translation provided in the bulletin.

Elmore frequently engaged brass and percussion players from The Philadelphia Orchestra to play with him for special services, as well as members of the Concerto Soloists Chamber Orchestra and students from The Curtis Institute. Elmore had the respect of these players as the organist for The Philadelphia Orchestra under Eugene Ormandy. He brought string soloists to Tenth as well as brass players and, in later years, flute and classical guitar. Preludes to both morning and evening services were 15 minutes in length.

Elmore always had at least one assistant organist working with him, many of whom went on to considerable posts of their own. Among these assistants at Tenth were Joel Krott (1969–71), Norman D. Mackenzie (1971–81), and Jeffrey J. Shuman (1981–90). Elmore was noted for his hymn improvisations and modulations, paying particular attention to the text of the hymns. His rendition of "Onward, Christian Soldiers" gained popularity for his treatment of its march-like character, complete with flourishes and multiple key changes. Elmore contributed numerous articles, reviews, and essays for journals and magazines, including *Eternity* magazine, in which he reviewed recordings monthly from 1958 through 1965, and in which he repeatedly urged excellence in sacred music. Many of his essays dealt with the relationship between theology and music, with such titles as "Art for the Lord's Sake" and "The Place of Music in the Christian Life."[12]

For the children's choir, Elmore wrote an anthem at the request of director Millie Stockdale. His music was widely published, especially choral anthems, cantatas, and music for organ and brass. His *It Began at Breakfast* was the first American opera to be televised. In 1979 the Tenth Choir performed his *Psalm of a Pilgrim People* for the church's 150th anniversary. Leopold Stokowski (The Philadelphia Orchestra) and Frank Black (NBC Symphony) were among the major conductors who programmed Elmore's orchestral and choral compositions. A number of his pieces are still performed regularly, and many of the organ works have been recorded by his prodigious student, Robert Plimpton.

In conjunction with the birth of the Philadelphia Conference on Reformed Theology (PCRT) in 1974, the Westminster Brass assumed a prominent place in the music ministry. By 1987 it was a resident performing ensemble at Tenth Church, enlivening morning worship once each month (September through June) and playing for special services on Christmas Eve and Easter, as well as at PCRT and other events. The five long-standing members of the Westminster Brass include James Hala (director), Dr. Kenneth Laudermilch, Dr. Dan McCartney, Thomas Elliott, and Dr. Timothy Witmer.

Dr. Stuart Sacks, who served on the Tenth staff as assistant to the minister from 1975, founded the Tenth Chamber Orchestra that same year. The Chamber Orchestra was comprised largely of college students from area music schools. Two of its stated purposes were to provide an outlet of ministry for talented young people and to bring unsaved musicians into the church to hear the gospel ("edification of Christians and evangelization of the lost"). Several musicians came to know the Lord through participation in this ensemble, which played at special events such as PCRT and about three times annually during worship services. Mark Laycock conducted the ensemble from 1978 until 1985 and, in addition to Mozart, Handel, and Haydn symphonies and concertos, enjoyed programming late-nineteenth-century and twentieth-century composers such as Debussy, Strauss, Stravinsky, Copland, Prokofiev, and Delibes. Laycock increased the group's appearances to five times annually. During Laycock's time, numerous Tenth musicians were involved, as well as players from outside the church. Although unpaid, the musicians came out in good number. The only reported conflict was that some would not return because the congregation talked throughout their prelude music!

From 1983 to 1986, a Bible study comprised of artists from various disciplines met weekly. This eclectic group of individuals, which was organized by Mark Laycock and Marshall Taylor, forged strong relationships and contributed to the strength of the arts community at Tenth. They alternated topics by week, had guest speakers on Christianity and music, and studied chapters from the Bible.

ELMORE'S WORTHY SUCCESSORS (1985–2000)

Robert Elmore died suddenly on the afternoon of Sunday, September 22, 1985 after playing the morning worship service. Within a short time Dr. Boice called his old friends Marlan and Kathy Allen, who immediately uprooted from Chicago and moved to Philadelphia to fill the need. Bringing over 30 years' experience as a church musician in New York, California, and Illinois, Allen began serving as interim organist the Sunday after Elmore died. He accepted the session's appointment as organist and music director at the end of the year and, with the church's subsequent switch to two morning services, had increased responsibilities.

Allen made a point of not having paid section leaders in the choir, which he felt allowed a better tonal blend and promoted a better *esprit de corps*. In 1987 he had fifteen new vocalists sing solos in the morning services. He did a fine job of maintaining the overall quality of the music program, although the choir's repertoire changed. The big choral works and concerts did not continue, but Allen used the choir more during regular services. At the end of his first complete year, he outlined some of the changes: "1. We have moved to a totally volunteer choir, with no more paid section leaders and additional paid 'ringers.' 2. We have introduced seasonal 'mini-concerts' of 10–15 minutes duration within the evening service, scheduled on Communion Sundays, and have retained the Sunday afternoon 5:00 p.m. Annual Spring Music Festival. 3. The choir is singing two anthems instead of one each Sunday [evening], the texts being Scripture, almost exclusively. 4. Four 'single occasion' choirs have rehearsed and presented anthems in Sunday morning services." In addition, a greater variety of vocal and instrumental soloists participated in morning offertories to, as Allen put it, "encourage the talents of our own proficient singers and instrumentalists."

During his five years at Tenth, Allen expanded the music program by adding a men's choir and considerably increasing the choral library. The men's choir began in 1988 with about fifteen members and sang one Sunday morning each month. It rehearsed in the Tower Choir Room (which also served as the music office) following the second morning service. Allen also had portions of the organ expanded, digitized, and renovated; this was paid for by a single anonymous gift. In 1988 the organ console was rebuilt and redesigned, and the instrument converted to solid-state electronics. Allen also restarted informal hymn sings on the newly rebuilt and donated Bechstein grand piano as the prelude to evening worship. The Westminster Brass took a more significant role during his tenure as well, particularly from 1987, when the quintet began playing at Tenth monthly.

Allen brought Daniel Doody (Howe) (1987–89) and then Douglas Wimer (1989–90) on as his assistants. Mr. Doody was assistant organist and directed, briefly, a motet choir. The children's choir during these years was directed by Georgia Hogeland and accompanied by Karen Sharrar. In 1988 Gloria Hague became the director. The children's choir, numbering about 15 members, rehearsed between the morning services in the Tower Music Room and sang six times a year. Mr. Allen left Tenth after Easter 1990 and went on to serve at St. John's Episcopal Church in Huntingdon Valley.

Tenth's next master musician was Robert Carwithen, professor of organ at Westminster Choir College for more than 45 years and organist-choirmaster of First Presbyterian Church, Germantown, for over 25 years (1960–86). Carwithen had been a student of Alexander McCurdy at the Curtis Institute as well as of Mme. Marie Madeleine Duruflé-Chevalier, André Isoir, and Xavier Darasse in France. He had been the Wanamaker organist for three years (1960–62), and he had served as organist-choirmaster at Wayne Presbyterian Church (1986–88) and then at First Presbyterian Church, Philadelphia (1988–90).

During his seven-year tenure at Tenth, which began in December of 1990, Carwithen strengthened the adult choir. He brought with him not only years of church choir experience, but also years as conductor of the Westminster Symphonic Choir, where he prepared choruses for legendary conductors Leopold Stokowski, Eugene Ormandy, and Leonard Bernstein, among others. Under Carwithen the Tenth choir grew again to more than 50 members. Carwithen reinstated Elmore's tradition of performing major choral works annually by conducting performances of *Creation, Messiah,* Mendelssohn's *Mass in G Minor* and *Lobegesang,* and the Rutter *Requiem.* He involved a large number of musicians in the music ministry and especially encouraged college-age musicians to participate. Carwithen was known for his exciting reharmonizations and energetic hymn-playing, which Dr. Boice especially appreciated. In 1997 Carwithen and Boice transformed the spring choral service into an integrated evening service of musical psalms, with Boice preaching.

Carwithen named choirs according to their roles, with some overlapping members. Among these choirs were the Evening Choir, the Morning Choir, the Oratorio Choir, and the Choraliers (a small ensemble of nine to twelve people that sang in the morning or evening until 1995). Carwithen arranged numerous anthems for the Tenth men's choir. With Boice he instituted an evening prelude of classical/sacred music called *Soli Deo Gloria,* which featured excellent Christian musicians playing and singing for God's glory from the front of the sanctuary. This was partially to compensate for the reduction of evening choir anthems from two to one per service to make way for Dr. Philip Ryken's weekly "Window on the World." Hymn sings were a regular part of this evening prelude, carrying on a tradition from earlier years.

The children's choir (from at least 1992–95) was directed by Gwen Griffith and accompanied by Evelyn Larter. The children sang about six times annually in morning worship services. From 1996 to 1998, Deborah Rojas was its director. Evelyn Larter served in a variety of musical capacities during Carwithen's years at Tenth and following. She organized music for the Lenten services, directed music for City Light, and served as substitute organist for worship services and weddings. Doug Wimer continued as an assistant for a while, but Carwithen generally preferred to conduct from the keyboard. He also took several aspiring church musicians under his wing to fulfill their undergraduate internship requirements.

NEW DIRECTIONS IN MUSIC MINISTRY

In the autumn of 1997, Carwithen asked Paul Jones to be his associate and then stepped aside at the end of the year, announcing his desire for Jones to become his successor. Jones was born in Canada and came to Pennsylvania for undergraduate study in Bible and music. In addition to theological training, he received degrees in piano performance, studying with Samuel Hsu, Martin Canin, Edward Auer, and Menahem Pressler. His doctorate in choral conducting from Indiana University included a thesis on the theology of J. S. Bach as displayed in his Leipzig cantatas. Jones also studied voice, composition, organ, and chamber music.

After serving a four-month period as interim while a search was conducted, Jones was called by the session as organist and music director beginning the first Sunday in April 1998. At age 28, he was the youngest music director in Tenth's history—a new direction for the church, since his three immediate predecessors had all been veteran church musicians. Boice made a point of reminding the session of the fact that he himself, like Barnhouse before him and Philip Ryken after him, had been called to Tenth Church at a similarly young age. Jones had previously served at Chambers-Wylie Memorial Presbyterian Church, Philadelphia (1989–92), The Blue Church (Lownes Free Church), Springfield, Pennsylvania (1993–95), and Arlington Methodist Church, Bloomington, Indiana (1992–93 and 1995–97).

Since 1998, the music ministry has expanded in several ways. The staff has increased considerably, the budget has doubled, and the role of the music director has been enlarged. Dr. Jones regularly attends pastoral staff meetings and retreats and speaks about hymnody each week to the children attending Bible school. He has given sessions on music and worship to various groups in the church, including parishes, adult classes, Tenth College Union, the Pastoral Ministry Roundtable, and new members' classes. He speaks regularly at conferences for pastors, musicians, and educators on the role of church music and musicians and has written articles, book chapters, and radio programs on similar topics.

About 125 musicians now make up the church's musical roster (Tenth's choir, soloists, and instrumentalists). All three choirs have grown (Tenth to 75 members, men's to 50, children's to 80), and 1999 saw the rebirth of a chamber orchestra—the Tenth Chamber Players. This group is composed primarily of Tenth members and college students from area music programs who attend Tenth Church, and it plays for morning worship services bimonthly. Themed hymn services, presented monthly, have replaced hymn sings during the evening prelude. An annual Reformation hymn festival began in the year 2000, as Boice and Jones together had planned. This was the occasion for the first use of their hymnal, *Hymns for a Modern Reformation*. The festival was structured around the five "solas" of the Reformation, and successive years have focused on one "sola" in rotation.

Each year the spring choral service includes choral masterworks, as it did with Elmore and Carwithen, but with full orchestral accompaniment. These services are fully integrated worship services in which choral music, hymns, and sermon align on one topic. Programs in recent years have centered on Scripture-based settings of the *Gloria, Magnificat, Sanctus,* and *Te Deum.* The Fauré *Requiem* was performed at a Hope concert on May 1, 2001, in memory of James Montgomery Boice. The choir still primarily sings at evening services, as it has since Elmore founded it, although it now has an expanded role in communion services and sings once monthly in morning worship.

Other new ventures include the Tenth Concert Series, launched in 2002 as an outreach into the cultural community of Philadelphia. The same year a music program Web site (www.tenth.org/music) was posted. New instruments have been purchased, including percussion instruments and four pianos. At this writing, a harpsichord and pipe organ are part of current planning. Tenth Choir members participated in a choral missions trip in 2002 to Odessa, Ukraine. A Sunday-evening "singing school" (Schola Cantoram) for children ages 4 through 12 began in September 2003 to provide solid musical education for young people from Tenth and elsewhere. The Tenth Singers, a chamber-sized vocal ensemble, was founded the same month.

As one of the few conservative, evangelical churches in the United States with a traditional, classical approach to sacred music, Tenth wants to help other churches, musicians, and ministries offer music of the highest order to our Creator. Many churches are embracing a return to great church music but have limited experience in doing so. The contemporary music movement affords little in the way of musical and theological substance, particularly in the biblical demand for beauty; yet churches with Reformation heritage have more than 500 years of excellent church music on which to draw. Elmore put it well in his annual report for 1983:

> Our purpose is to show forth the praise and glory of God with music of variety and beauty, both instrumental and vocal. For some reason, in this country there is a tradition that if a church is evangelical and the truth is preached, it is coupled with inferior music; liberal churches often have better music. This is not the case at Tenth. The gospel is preached with power from one end of the auditorium. It is sung and played with power from the other end. The greatest music ever written does not begin to exhaust the greatness of our God. But it is the least we can do while here on earth.

It is incumbent upon those who have been blessed with a wonderful musical heritage—both from the Reformation and from our own congregational history—to share it with others. Dr. Boice noted that periods of real Christian reformation have always witnessed great hymnody and music accompanying the biblical preaching. This is our desire and prayer for the music ministry at Tenth: to be part of a reformation within Christian worship, alongside the clear teaching of the Word, to the praise and glory of God alone.

A P P E N D I X

CITY CENTER ACADEMY

Lux Urbi

Royalties from the sale of this book will be awarded to City Center Academy (CCA), the urban Christian high school started at, located in, and supported by Tenth Presbyterian Church. CCA is a co-educational, non-profit independent school whose purpose is to offer a superior college-preparatory education for grades nine through twelve at an investment most city families can afford. The school's mission is to train urban teens to think biblically and excel academically.

The Board of Trustees and faculty of City Center Academy are committed to a Christian, as opposed to a merely secular, world-and-life view, and consider the Judeo-Christian value system as the necessary and desirable undergirding for the best in education. CCA presents Jesus Christ as Redeemer and Lord. It seeks to integrate faith with learning, believing that all truth is God's truth and that "the knowledge of the Holy One is understanding" (Prov. 9:10).

City Center Academy began as a small Christian high school through the vision of James and Linda Boice of Tenth Presbyterian Church. Tenth has long encouraged Christians to live and work in the city. The Boices realized that a major obstacle to a continuing ministry in the city was parents' concerns about the education of their children. Some adequate education exists at the grade school level, either in the better public schools or in scattered Christian day schools. But many urban public schools fail at the high school level, and most private high schools are either too far out of the city or too expensive. CCA was started to meet this unique need. The school began in 1983 with eight students. Since then, it has graduated 185 students. The current enrollment is roughly 80 students, representing a variety of ethnic and cultural backgrounds. Young people from China, Eritrea, Indonesia, Korea, Liberia, Sudan, and Vietnam learn with African-American, Hispanic, and Caucasian students in an atmosphere of true diversity.

The school's curriculum, governed primarily by the requirements of college preparation, is built around the following core subjects: English (four years), history (four years), mathematics (three or four years), science (three or four years), languages (four years), and Bible (four years). The extracurricular program is built into the school day. Once a week, students participate in choir, drama, mime, liturgical dance, or publications. There is also a weekly prayer meeting for students as well as opportunities to participate in student government. CCA's competitive sports program includes basketball and track and field. Many students also participate in community service and missions activities through their local churches.

By providing quality pre-college education, City Center Academy prepares urban young people for colleges that are anxious to enroll them. They are thus able to pursue meaningful careers. If these young people drop out of high school, there is very little left for them but low-paying, unskilled jobs, or perhaps even a life of crime. But over 90% of CCA graduates are accepted into colleges and universities across the country, where they are further prepared to become productive citizens. CCA alumni have attended Drexel University, Fordham University, Hampton University, Howard University, Northeastern University, Pennsylvania State University, Rutgers University, Spelman College, Temple University, The American Center for Technical Arts and Sciences, the University of Pittsburgh, and other fine institutions of higher education.

City Center Academy continues to enjoy a unique relationship with Tenth Presbyterian Church. The school's bylaws require two-thirds of the Board of Directors to be elders of Tenth Church. Many CCA faculty and some students also worship at the church. While the church and its members support the school in various ways, City Center Academy is also dependent upon the financial support of a growing body of donors to meet its annual budget. This support enables tuition charges to be kept as low as possible, so that no qualified student needs to be turned away. For more information about the school's programs and needs, please contact the Headmaster by telephone (215-731-1930), Internet (www.citycenteracademy.org), or regular mail (City Center Academy / 315 S. 17th Street / Philadelphia, PA 19103).

NOTES

Chapter 1 Roots

1. Ernest Trice Thompson, *Presbyterians in the South: 1607–1861* (Richmond: John Knox Press, 1963), 20–21.

2. "Francis Makemie to Increase Mather, July 22, 1684," in Boyd Schlenther, ed., *The Life and Writings of Francis Makemie* (Philadelphia: Presbyterian Historical Society, 1971), 249.

3. Thompson, *Presbyterians in the South*, 22; Schlenther, *Life and Writings of Francis Makemie*, 20.

4. Harry Emerson Wildes, *William Penn* (New York: Macmillan, 1974), 223.

5. Francis Makemie, *An Answer to George Keith's Libel Against a Catechism* (Boston: n.p., 1694), 7.

6. Makemie, *An Answer*, 8, 18.

7. W. C. Ford, ed., *Diary of Cotton Mather* (New York: Frederick Ungar, 1911), vol. 1, 599.

8. Charles P. Keith, *Chronicles of Pennsylvania* (Philadelphia: Patterson and White, 1917), 335–36.

9. "Letterbook and Minutes" of the Presbytery of Philadelphia, 1698–1743 (Presbyterian Historical Society Collection).

10. Morgan Edwards, *Materials Toward a "History of the American Baptists"* (Philadelphia: n.p., 1770), 106.

11. John F. Watson, *Annals of Philadelphia*, revised by Willis P. Hazard (Philadelphia: Leary and Stuart, 1909), vol. 1, 447.

12. Edwards, 109.

13. Ibid.

14. Alexander Mackie, "The Presbyterian Churches of Philadelphia," in Luther Eisenstadt, ed., *Historic Philadelphia* (Philadelphia: American Philosophical Society, 1953), 217.

218

15. "Jedidiah Andrews to Thomas Prince, October 14, 1720," in Hazard's *Register of Pennsylvania*, vol. 15, 200.

16. Guy S. Klett, *Presbyterians in Colonial Pennsylvania* (Philadelphia: University of Pennsylvania Press, 1937), 18–20; Alfred Nevin, *History of the Presbytery of Philadelphia* (Philadelphia: W. S. Fortescue, 1888), 112; Sydney E. Ahlstrom, *A Religious History of the American People* (New Haven: Yale University Press, 1972), 275.

17. "Francis Makemie to Benjamin Colman, March 28, 1707," in Schlenther, *Life and Writings of Francis Makemie*, 252–53.

18. Guy S. Klett, *Minutes of the Presbyterian Church in America, 1706–1788* (Philadelphia: Presbyterian Historical Society, 1976), 29.

19. Theodore H. Tappert and John W. Doberstein, eds., *The Journals of Henry Melchior Muhlenburg* (Philadelphia: The Muhlenburg Press, 1942), vol. 1, 260.

20. Benjamin Franklin, *The Autobiography*, ed. L. Jesse Lemisch (New York: New American Library, 1961), 93–94.

21. Keith, *Chronicles of Pennsylvania*, 624.

22. "Jedidiah Andrews to Benjamin Colman, April 7, 1729" (Presbyterian Historical Society Collection).

23. Archibald Alexander, *The Log College* (London: The Banner of Truth Trust, 1968), 20. Original edition 1851.

24. George Whitefield appears to be the only one who thought to record a description of the Log College (Alexander, *The Log College*, 12).

25. Klett, *Minutes of the Presbyterian Church*, 157.

26. Arnold A. Dallimore, *George Whitefield* (London: The Banner of Truth Trust, 1970), 432–33; Stuart C. Henry, *George Whitefield: Wayfaring Witness* (New York: Abingdon Press, 1957), 51–52.

27. Dallimore, *George Whitefield*, 434.

28. Alexander, *The Log College*, 29.

29. Gilbert Tennent, "The Danger of an Unconverted Ministry" (1741), in Alan Heimert and Perry Miller, eds., *The Great Awakening* (New York: Bobbs-Merrill Company, 1967), 81, 74, 87.

30. Edwin S. Gaustad, *The Great Awakening in New England* (Chicago: Quadrangle Books, 1968), 36. The quote is from John Hancock.

31. Klett, *Minutes of the Presbyterian Church*, 174; Joseph Tracy, *The Great Awakening* (London: The Banner of Truth Trust, 1976), 70.

32. Klett, *Minutes of the Presbyterian Church*, 211.

33. Watson, *Annals of Philadelphia*, vol. 1, 538.

34. John Thomson, "The Government of the Church of Christ" (1741), in Heimert and Miller, *The Great Awakening*, 125.

35. A. Mervyn Davies, *Presbyterian Heritage* (Richmond: John Knox, 1965), 95.

36. Melvin H. Buxbaum, *Benjamin Franklin and the Zealous Presbyterians* (Harrisburg: Pennsylvania State University Press, 1975), 3.

37. Klett, *Presbyterians in Colonial Pennsylvania*, 248.

38. Ibid., 252.

39. Buxbaum, *Benjamin Franklin*, 196–99.

40. *A Looking Glass for Presbyterians* (Philadelphia: n.p., 1764), 4.

41. Elisha P. Douglass, *Rebels and Democrats: The Struggle for Equal Political Rights and Majority Rule During the American Revolution* (Chicago: Quadrangle Books, 1965), 224.

42. *The Quaker Unmasked or Plain Truth* (Philadelphia: n.p., 1764), 7, 9.

43. Klett, *Presbyterians in Colonial Pennsylvania*, 266.

44. "A Looking Glass, Number II, Copy of a Circular Letter, March 30, 1764," in John R. Dunbar, ed., *The Paxton Papers* (The Hague: Martinus Nighoff, 1957), 311, 321.

45. "Petition of the First Presbyterian Church to the Synod of New York and Philadelphia, November 12, 1771" (Presbyterian Historical Society Collection).

46. Eisenstadt, *Historic Philadelphia*, 228.

47. Klett, *Minutes of the Presbyterian Church*, 503–6.

48. Robert H. Wilson, *Freedom of Worship: Meeting Houses, Churches, and Synagogues of Early Philadelphia* (Philadelphia: Old Philadelphia Churches Historical Association, 1976), 26.

49. Carl Bridenbaugh, *Mitre and Sceptre: The Transatlantic Faiths, Ideas, Personalities and Politics, 1689–1775* (New York: Oxford University Press, 1962), 257.

50. Mark Noll, *Christians in the American Revolution* (Grand Rapids: Eerdmans, 1977), 51–52.

51. D. Earl Daniel, "The Presbyterian Insurrection," *Liberty Magazine* 51, no. 2 (American Philosophical Society Pamphlet, No. 331).

52. Klett, *Minutes of the Presbyterian Church*, 545.

53. Lefferts A. Loetscher, *A Brief History of the Presbyterians* (Philadelphia: The Westminster Press, 1958), 63.

54. J. T. Headley, *The Chaplains and Clergy of the Revolution* (New York: Charles Scribner, 1864), 101.

55. Hugh Oliphant Gibbons, *A History of Old Pine Street* (Philadelphia: John C. Winston Co., 1905), 145, 146.

56. Ibid., 149.

57. Klett, *Minutes of the Presbyterian Church*, 628.

58. Walter L. Lingle, *Presbyterians: Their History and Beliefs* (Richmond: John Knox Press, 1960), 79.

59. Nevin, *History of the Presbytery of Philadelphia*, 306–18.

60. Ibid., 324.

61. Watson, *Annals of Philadelphia*, vol. 1, 310.

Chapter 2 The First Three "B's"

1. Sydney E. Ahlstrom, *A Religious History of the American People* (New Haven: Yale University Press, 1972), 434–35.

2. Charles G. Finney, *Memoirs of Charles G. Finney* (Old Tappan, N.J.: Fleming H. Revell, n.d.), 58–60. Original edition 1876.

3. "The One Hundredth Anniversary of The Tenth Presbyterian Church in Philadelphia" (pamphlet, 1929), viii.

4. Alfred Nevin, *History of the Presbytery of Philadelphia* (Philadelphia: W. S. Fortescue & Company, 1888), 217.

5. Stuart Blumin, "Residential and Occupational Mobility in Antebellum Philadelphia," in Edward Pessen, ed., *Three Centuries of Social Mobility in America* (Lexington: D. C. Heath & Co., 1974), 88.

6. Robert F. Looney, *Old Philadelphia in Early Photographs 1839–1914* (New York: Dover Publications, 1976), 134–51.

7. Nevin, *History of the Presbytery of Philadelphia*, 234.

8. Henry A. Boardman, *Two Sermons Preached on the Twenty-fifth and Fortieth Anniversaries of the Author's Pastorate* (Philadelphia: Inquirer Book and Job Print, 1873), 11.

9. Ibid.

10. Ibid., 31.

11. Nevin, *History of the Presbytery of Philadelphia*, 237.

12. "Boardman to the Members of the Tenth Presbyterian Church, December 26, 1868" (Tenth Presbyterian Church archives).

13. Boardman, *Two Sermons*, 17.

14. Ibid., 165.

15. Henry A. Boardman, *The Bible in the Counting House: A Course of Lectures to Merchants* (Philadelphia: Lippincott, Grambo & Co., 1853), 18–19.

16. Ibid., 228.

17. Ibid., 102–3.

18. Ibid., 90, 129.

19. Boardman, *Two Sermons*, 37–38.

20. Henry A. Boardman, *The Low Value Set upon Human Life in the United States: A Discourse Delivered on Thanksgiving-Day, November 24, 1853* (Philadelphia: Joseph M. Wilson, 1853), 14–15.

21. Henry A. Boardman, *The American Union: A Discourse* (Philadelphia: Lippincott, Grambo & Co., 1851), 32, 38.

22. James H. Moorhead, *American Apocalypse: Yankee Protestants and the Civil War 1860–1869* (New Haven: Yale University Press, 1978), 37.

23. Henry A. Boardman, *A Sermon on the Death of George M. Ramsaur* (Philadelphia: Hayes & Zell, 1856), 13.

24. Henry A. Boardman, *The Sovereignty of God the Sure and Only Stay of the Christian Patriot in Our National Troubles* (Philadelphia: William S. and Alfred Martien, 1862), 7.

25. Henry A. Boardman, *God's Providence in Accidents* (Philadelphia: Parry and McMillan, 1855), 9–10.

26. "Historical Sketch of the West Spruce Street Presbyterian Church, to be read at the laying of the cornerstone of the same, April 26, 1855" (Tenth Presbyterian Church archives).

27. Boardman, *Two Sermons*, 170.

28. "Historical Sketch," 2.

29. "Circular to the Members of the Tenth Presbyterian Church and Congregation" (Tenth Presbyterian Church archives).

30. "Franklin Fire Insurance Co. Survey, October 20, 1855, Policy no. (779) 23414" (Tenth Presbyterian Church archives).

31. William P. Breed, *A Discourse Upon the History of the West Spruce Street Presbyterian Church Delivered Sabbath Morning, June 5, 1876* (Philadelphia: Inquirer Book and Job Print, 1876), 8–9.

32. "The One Hundredth Anniversary of the Tenth Presbyterian Church in Philadelphia," xvi.

33. Breed, *A Discourse*, 5.

34. Ibid., 10.

35. Ibid., 11–12.

36. *The Directory of The West Spruce Street Presbyterian Church in Philadelphia* (Philadelphia: A. G. DeArmond, 1871); *The Directory of the Tenth Presbyterian Church* (Philadelphia: n.p., 1885).

37. W. P. White and W. H. Scott, *The Presbyterian Church in Philadelphia* (Philadelphia: Allen, Lane & Scott, 1895), 109; *The Philadelphia Times*, April 22, 1894.

38. "Draft Minute of Church and Congregation of the West Spruce Street Presbyterian Church, March 2, 1887" (Tenth Presbyterian Church archives).

39. For more information about Dr. Paxton, see Mary Elizabeth Kinnier, *Our Goodly Heritage: A History of the First Presbyterian Church of Lynchburg, Virginia, 1815–1940* (Lynchburg, VA: J.P. Bell, n.d.).

40. "Memorial Minute on the Life and Work of the Rev. Marcus A. Brownson, D.D.," Minutes of the Presbytery of Philadelphia, March 6, 1939.

41. Marcus A. Brownson, "The Ideal for Our Church," *The Presbyterian* (April 1, 1937), 11.

42. White and Scott, *The Presbyterian Church in Philadelphia*, 108.

43. *Directory of the Tenth Presbyterian Church* (Philadelphia: Hathaway & Brothers, 1902); *Directory of the Tenth Presbyterian Church* (Philadelphia: Phoenix Printing Co., 1910).

44. Harry P. Ford, *A History of the Harriet Holland Memorial Presbyterian Church* (Philadelphia: Castle & Heliman, 1899), 31–35.

45. "The One Hundredth Anniversary of the Tenth Presbyterian Church in Philadelphia," xxvii.

46. *Directory of the Tenth (West Spruce Street) Presbyterian Church* (Philadelphia: Hathaway & Brothers, November 1895).

47. Brownson to "My Beloved Parishioners," January 1, 1904 (Tenth Presbyterian Church archives).

48. "Memorial Minute on the Life and Work of the Rev. Marcus A. Brownson, D.D."

Chapter 3 Barnhouse

1. Interview with Margaret Bell Barnhouse, Spring 1978; "Tenth Presbyterian Church: For 33 Years Its Pastor," *Eternity* 12 (March 1961): 24–25.

2. Paul A. Hopkins, "What Made the Man?," *Eternity* 12 (March 1961): 16–17.

3. Sidney E. Ahlstrom, *A Religious History of the American People* (New Haven: Yale University Press, 1972), 746.

4. Interview with Margaret Bell Barnhouse, Spring 1978; Hopkins, "What Made the Man?," 18, 35.

5. Russell T. Hitt, "Barnhouse of Philadelphia," *Eternity* 26 (April 1975): 17.

6. Paul A. Carter, *The Spiritual Crisis of the Gilded Age* (DeKalb, Ill.: Northern Illinois University Press, 1971), 18.

7. Ahlstrom, *A Religious History of the American People*, 815–16.

8. The Text of the Auburn Affirmation is included in N. B. Stonehouse, *J. Gresham Machen: A Biographical Memoir* (Philadelphia: Westminster Theological Seminary, 1977), 365. Original edition 1954.

9. "Tenth Presbyterian Church: For 33 Years Its Pastor," 24.

10. "Tenth Presbyterian Church Statement of March 21, 1922" and "Report of Treasurer to Board of Trustees, June 30, 1922" (Tenth Presbyterian Church archives).

11. "Report of Treasurer to Board of Trustees, September 30, 1923"; "Report of Treasurer to Board of Trustees, December 31, 1924"; "Memorandum of the Treasurer, 1925"; "Statement of Maintenance Receipts and Disbursements, March 31, 1926" (Tenth Presbyterian Church archives).

12. "Tenth Presbyterian Church: For 33 Years Its Pastor," 24.

13. Ibid.; "Report of the Treasurer and Special Committee on Finance: Estimated Cost of Operation, Per Plan of Mr. Barnhouse, March 18, 1927" and "Statement of Maintenance Receipts and Disbursements, March 31, 1928" (Tenth Presbyterian Church archives).

14. *Philadelphia Bulletin*, January 8, 1932.

15. "To the Ministers and Elders of Philadelphia Presbytery, A Statement by the Christian Business Men's League of Philadelphia" (Manuscript Collection of the Presbyterian Historical Society, Philadelphia).

16. *Philadelphia Public Ledger,* September 30, 1930.

17. *Philadelphia Inquirer,* November 7, 1930; *Philadelphia Public Ledger,* July 21, 1931.

18. Hopkins, "What Made the Man?," 36; *Philadelphia Public Ledger,* March 8, 1932.

19. "Remarks Made by Dr. Donald Grey Barnhouse at Stated Meeting of the Presbytery of Philadelphia, January 6, 1936" (Tenth Presbyterian Church archives).

20. "Statement by Dr. Barnhouse Concerning the Course of Events Leading up to the Preaching of Dr. Machen in Tenth Church Pulpit on June 21, 1936" (Tenth Presbyterian Church archives).

21. Letter to Carl McIntire, February 6, 1937.

22. Donald Grey Barnhouse to Miss Alice Pendlebury, October 30, 1935.

23. Donald Grey Barnhouse, "To the Church at Philadelphia: The concluding part of a message delivered before the Philadelphia Fundamentalists, September 26, 1946" (Tenth Presbyterian Church archives).

24. Donald Grey Barnhouse, "How Great Is Your God?," WIP Broadcast, September 22, 1935.

25. Donald Grey Barnhouse Jr., "In Memoriam," transcript of the Bible Study Hour memorial broadcast, November 20, 1960 (Philadelphia: The Bible Study Hour, 1960), 11.

26. Walter Storey, "Dr. Barnhouse—Radio Pastor," *Center City Philadelphian,* February 1960, 6.

27. Barnhouse's telephone conversations with Roland Armes were transcribed, December 18, 1936, and were part of a more lengthy disagreement that resulted in Armes's resignation from the session (Tenth Presbyterian Church archives).

28. "Tenth Presbyterian Church: For 33 Years Its Pastor," 25.

29. *Directory of the Tenth Presbyterian Church* (Philadelphia: n.p., January 1950).

30. "Tenth Presbyterian Church: For 33 Years Its Pastor," 24.

31. Robert J. Lamont, "In Memoriam," transcript of the Bible Study Hour memorial broadcast, November 20, 1960, 6–7.

32. Hopkins, "What Made the Man?," 38.

33. *Philadelphia Evening Bulletin,* November 12, 1954.

34. Donald Grey Barnhouse, "Statement to the Presbytery of Philadelphia, November 9, 1954" (Manuscript Collection of the Presbyterian Historical Society, Philadelphia).

35. Interview with Margaret Bell Barnhouse, Spring 1978.

36. From a formal letter sent to all Tenth Church missionaries by Barnhouse's assistant, Robert F. Scott, announcing Barnhouse's death, November 11, 1960 (Tenth Presbyterian Church archives).

37. Ralph L. Keiper, "In Memoriam," transcript of the Bible Study Hour memorial broadcast, November 20, 1960, 2–3.

38. Donald Grey Barnhouse, "Death Shall Not Separate Us," *Eternity* 12 (March 1961): 46.

Chapter 4 City Church Again

1. "Brief Statement of Faith of Mr. Di Gangi" (Tenth Presbyterian Church archives).

2. Interview with Mariano Di Gangi, Spring 1978.

3. "Circular Letter of the Bible Study Hour, 1961" (Tenth Presbyterian Church archives).

4. Interview with Mariano Di Gangi, Spring 1978.

5. Ibid.

6. Ibid.

7. "Annual Reports to the Congregational and Corporation Meetings for the year 1961" (Tenth Presbyterian Church archives), 3, 4; Herschel Engebretson, "City Church," *The Sunday School Times*, May 25, 1963.

8. Interview with Mariano Di Gangi, Spring 1978.

9. Ibid.

10. "Annual Reports," 1961.

11. "Annual Reports for 1964, Congregational and Corporation Meetings, February 25, 1965" (Tenth Presbyterian Church archives).

12. Interview with Mariano Di Gangi, Spring 1978.

13. These names appear in the "Annual Reports" for 1964–1966.

14. Interview with Margaret Bell Barnhouse, Spring 1978.

15. Engebretson, "City Church," 5.

16. Mark Hanna, "The Challenge of Reaching Internationals for Christ" (Colorado Springs: International Students, Inc., n.d.), 1–2.

17. "Annual Reports to the Congregational and Corporation Meetings for the year 1962"; "Annual Reports for 1966 presented to the Congregational and Corporation Meetings, February 23, 1967"; "Strategy Committee Report, Presbytery of Philadelphia, Special Report on Tenth Church, April, 1967" (Tenth Presbyterian Church archives).

18. "Annual Reports for 1966"; "Annual Reports for 1967 presented to the Congregational and Corporation Meetings, March 21, 1968"; "Annual Reports for 1965, Congregational and Corporation Meetings, March 3, 1966" (Tenth Presbyterian Church archives).

19. Mariano Di Gangi, "Where Is Tenth Church?," *Tenth Tidings*, May 1963 (Tenth Presbyterian Church archives).

20. Interview with Mariano Di Gangi, Spring 1978.

21. Ibid.

22. Ibid.

23. Sydney E. Ahlstrom, *A Religious History of the American People* (New Haven: Yale University Press, 1972), 1082.

24. Edmund P. Clowney, "The Broken Bands: Constitutional Revolution in American Presbyterianism," in John H. Skilton, ed., *Scripture and Confession: A Book about Confessions Old and New* (Nutley, N.J.: P&R, 1973), 165.

25. This point is discussed by Harold Lindsell, *The Battle for the Bible* (Grand Rapids: Zondervan, 1976), 151.

26. Interview with Mariano Di Gangi, Spring 1978.

27. "Annual Reports for 1967."

Chapter 5 Boice

1. Linda M. Boice, "A Life in Ministry," in Philip G. Ryken, ed., *The Life of Dr. James Montgomery Boice, 1938–2000* (Philadelphia: Tenth Presbyterian Church, 2001), 4.

2. Quoted from Stony Brook (December 1970), 11, in Philip G. Ryken, J. Ligon Duncan III, and Derek Thomas, eds., *Give Praise to God: A Vision for Reforming Worship, Celebrating the Legacy of James Montgomery Boice* (Phillipsburg, N. J.: P&R, 2003), 3.

3. James Montgomery Boice, *Whatever Happened to the Gospel of Grace? Recovering Doctrines That Shook the World* (Wheaton, Ill.: Crossway, 2001), 69–70.

4. Interview with Dr. C. Everett Koop, December 12, 2002.

5. George K. McFarland, "The Boice Years at Tenth," in *The Life of Boice*, 12.

6. Timothy Clark Lemmer, "Introduction," in James Montgomery Boice, ed., *Making God's Word Plain: One Hundred and Fifty Years in the History of Tenth Presbyterian Church of Philadelphia* (Philadelphia: Tenth Presbyterian Church, 1979), book jacket and pp. 5–6.

7. C. Everett Koop, "The Bible Study Hour," in *The Life of Boice*, 20–23; *Philadelphia Inquirer* obituary, June 17, 2000, E10.

8. Karen C. Hoyt, "International Council on Biblical Inerrancy," in *The Life of Boice*, 28.

9. The two Chicago Statements may be found in the appendixes to James Montgomery Boice, *Standing on the Rock: The Importance of Biblical Inerrancy* (Wheaton, Ill.: Tyndale, 1984), 125–57.

10. James Montgomery Boice, *The Gospel of John; Volume 3: Those Who Received Him, John 9–12* (Grand Rapids: Baker, 1999), 777–82.

11. Letter of James M. Boice to Gunther H. Knoedler, November 7, 1992 (Tenth Presbyterian Church archives). Boice's letter had some influence on Wheaton's 2003 decision to replace its Statement of Responsibilities with a new

Community Covenant that espoused what Boice would have regarded as a more thoroughly biblical understanding of Christian liberty.

12. Boice, *Making God's Word Plain,* 112–16.

13. See *Presbyterians and Human Sexuality, 1991: The 203rd General Assembly Response . . . Including a Minority Report,* 87, #7.

14. See Appendix 5.

15. Emphases added.

16. "Letter from the Session to the Congregation of Tenth Presbyterian Church, Philadelphia" (February 1980), 1 (Tenth Presbyterian Church archives).

17. "Letter from the Session," 3, 5. For the full text of the letter, see Appendix 5. See also Boice to Members of Tenth Presbyterian Church, April 9, 1980.

18. James Montgomery Boice, "Two Sermons on Leaving the United Presbyterian Church: 1. Why We Should Leave," *Tenth: An Evangelical Quarterly* (January 1981), 20.

19. James Montgomery Boice to Bernard L. Ramm, June 3, 1980 (Tenth Presbyterian Church archives). See also *Eternity* vol. 31 (May 1980): 10.

20. Interviews with Clive Stockdale, Linda Boice, Linward Crowe, Glenn McDowell, Jay MacMoran, and Elmer Snethen, November 15–17, 2002.

21. Boice, "Two Sermons on Leaving the United Presbyterian Church: 2. Pressing On," *Tenth: An Evangelical Quarterly* (January 1981), 28–29.

22. For a complete bibliography of Dr. Boice's books, see "Books Published by James Montgomery Boice," in *The Life of Boice,* 46.

23. Boice, "Two Sermons on Leaving," 28.

24. Francis A. Schaeffer, "Lessons for Today and Tomorrow," in *Tenth: An Evangelical Quarterly* (January, 1981), 8–9.

25. James Montgomery Boice, "How Can We Choose?," *The Presbyterian Journal* (May 28, 1980), 8–9; Boice to Joseph F. Ryan Jr., June 20, 1980, and Joel Belz to Boice, May 16, 1980 (Tenth Presbyterian Church archives).

26. Belz to Boice, May 16, 1980, and Boice to Steven E. Smallman, June 5, 1980 (Tenth Presbyterian Church archives).

27. "Session Report to the Congregation on a Comparison of the PCA and the RPCES" (Tenth Presbyterian Church archives).

28. James Montgomery Boice and Philip Graham Ryken, *The Doctrines of Grace: Rediscovering the Evangelical Gospel* (Wheaton, Ill.: Crossway, 2002), 203–6.

29. Interview with Cora Hogue, December 27, 2002; interview with Erna Goulding, December 14, 2002.

30. Interviews with Linward Crowe and Glenn McDowell, November 15 and 16, 2002.

31. James Montgomery Boice to Billy Graham, May 28, 1981; Boice to Graham, December 15, 1980 (Tenth Presbyterian Church archives).

32. Tapes of Boice's sermons can be obtained from the Alliance of Confessing Evangelicals (www.AllianceNet.org). See also James Montgomery Boice, *Two Cities, Two Loves: Christian Responsibility in a Crumbling Culture* (Downers Grove, Ill.: InterVarsity, 1996), chap. 8, especially pp. 166–76.

33. Interview with Glenn McDowell, November 16, 2002.

34. Interview with Jay and Jane MacMoran and Elmer and Sherry Snethen, November 17, 2002.

35. Interview with D. Marion Clark, November 26, 2002.

36. Michael S. Horton, "Alliance of Confessing Evangelicals," in *The Life of Boice*, 36–39.

37. Interview with R. C. Sproul, December 5, 2002.

38. James Montgomery Boice and Paul Steven Jones, *Hymns for a Modern Reformation* (Philadelphia: Tenth Presbyterian Church and the Alliance of Confessing Evangelicals, 2000).

39. Interview with Dr. C. Everett Koop, December 12, 2000.

40. James Montgomery Boice, "Final Address at Tenth Presbyterian Church," in *The Life of Boice*, 44–45.

41. Tim Keller to James M. Boice, May 28, 1987, re "Consultant's Report" (Tenth Presbyterian Church archives).

42. Interview with Nancy Wise Hala, November 23, 2002.

43. Interview with R. C. Sproul, December 5, 2002.

44. Interview with Norman Koop, December 16, 2002.

45. Paul S. Jones, "The Hymns for a Modern Reformation," in *The Life of Boice*, 42; "Foreword," *Hymns for a Modern Reformation*, 5.

46. Interviews with Linda Boice, November 15 and December 3, 2002; with Nancy Wise Hala, November 23, 2002; with Elmer and Sherry Snethen, November 17, 2002; and with Erna Goulding, December 14, 2002.

47. Boice, *Two Cities, Two Loves*, 7.

48. "Books Published by James Montgomery Boice," in *The Life of Boice*, 46.

49. Eugene K. Betts, "Missions at Tenth, 1968–2000," in *The Life of Boice*, 16–19.

50. Rosemary Jensen, "Bible Study Fellowship International," in *The Life of Boice*, 34–35.

51. R. C. Sproul, "Foreword," *The Doctrines of Grace*, 9.

Chapter 6 A Church for the Twenty-First Century

1. Charles H. Spurgeon, as quoted in a prospectus from Holy Trinity Church, Chicago.

2. Donald Grey Barnhouse, "Isaiah 55:11," *Holding Forth the Word, 1927–1952*, as adapted by James Montgomery Boice in *Making God's Word Plain: One Hundred and Fifty Years in the History of Tenth Presbyterian Church of Philadelphia* (Philadelphia: Tenth Presbyterian Church, 1979), 104.

3. Barnhouse, as recounted in Boice, *Making God's Word Plain*, 104–5.

4. See David Bebbington, *Evangelicalism in Modern Britain: A History from the 1730s to the 1980s* (Grand Rapids: Baker, 1989), 2–3.

5. James Montgomery Boice, *Whatever Happened to the Gospel of Grace? Rediscovering the Doctrines that Shook the World* (Wheaton, Ill.: Crossway, 2001), 20–29.

6. See James Montgomery Boice, *What Makes a Church Evangelical?* Today's Issues (Wheaton, Ill.: Crossway, 1999), 19–27.

7. The theological errors of open theism are exposed in John M. Frame, *No Other God: A Response to Open Theism* (Phillipsburg, N.J.: P&R, 2001); Thomas R. Schreiner and Bruce A. Ware, eds., *Still Sovereign: Contemporary Perspectives on Election, Foreknowledge, and Grace* (Grand Rapids: Baker, 2000); and Bruce A. Ware, *God's Lesser Glory: The Diminished God of Open Theism* (Wheaton, Ill.: Crossway, 2000).

8. The doctrine of salvation in Christ alone is defended thoroughly in Donald A. Carson, *The Gagging of God: Christianity Confronts Pluralism* (Grand Rapids: Zondervan, 1996); and more briefly in Philip Graham Ryken, *Is Jesus the Only Way?* Today's Issues (Wheaton, Ill.: Crossway, 1999).

9. John Piper defends the biblical doctrine of imputation in *Counted Righteous in Christ: Should We Abandon the Imputation of Christ's Righteousness?* (Wheaton, Ill.: Crossway, 2002).

10. These doctrines are thoroughly explained in Boice, *The Gospel of Grace*.

11. John Calvin, quoted in Boice, *The Gospel of Grace*, 130.

12. Boice, *The Gospel of Grace*, 32.

13. For a full biblical exposition of these doctrines, see James Montgomery Boice and Philip Graham Ryken, *The Doctrines of Grace: Rediscovering the Evangelical Gospel* (Wheaton, Ill.: Crossway, 2002).

14. Harvie M. Conn, *The American City and the Evangelical Church: A Historical Overview* (Grand Rapids: Baker, 1994), 71, 73.

15. Dwight L. Moody, quoted in Conn, *The American City*, 60.

16. This idea is fully developed in James Montgomery Boice, *Two Cities, Two Loves: Christian Responsibility in a Crumbling Culture* (Downers Grove, Ill.: InterVarsity, 1996).

17. Augustine, *The City of God*, ed. Philip Schaff, Nicene and Post-Nicene Fathers, First Series, vol. 2 (Peabody, Mass.: Hendrickson, 1994), XV.1.

18. See Philip Graham Ryken, *City on a Hill: Reclaiming the Biblical Pattern for the Church in the 21st Century* (Chicago, Ill.: Moody, 2003).

19. Jacques Ellul, *The Humiliation of the Word*, trans. Joyce Main Hanks (Grand Rapids: Eerdmans, 1985).

20. R. Kent Hughes, *Disciplines of a Godly Man* (Wheaton, Ill.: Crossway, 1991), 106.

21. These themes are developed more fully in Philip Graham Ryken, ed., *The Communion of Saints: Living in Fellowship with the People of God* (Phillipsburg, N.J.: P&R, 2001).

22. See James Montgomery Boice, *Mind Renewal in a Mindless Age* (Grand Rapids: Baker, 1993).

23. These words of welcome are printed on the cover of Tenth's weekly bulletin. They were introduced by Dr. Di Gangi, who borrowed them from the City Temple Church in London, England.

Appendix 7 Music at Tenth

1. *Hymns of Praise*, 4th ed. (Philadelphia: Lippincott, 1867).

2. Information and quotations come from trustee and session minutes at the Presbyterian Historical Society in Philadelphia.

3. Address at Memorial Service in the Second Presbyterian Church, Philadelphia, November 2, 1930. Published in *Journal of the Department of History of the Presbyterian Church in the U. S. A.* 14 (December 1930): 151.

4. See Morgan P. Noyes, "Louis F. Benson, Hymnologist," in James Rawlings Sydnor, ed., *The Papers of the Hymn Society* XIX, which has provided much of the information given here on Benson.

5. See also William Chalmers Covert and Calvin Weiss Laufer, eds., *Handbook to The Hymnal* (Philadelphia: Presbyterian Board of Christian Education, 1935).

6. See James Montgomery Boice, ed., *Making God's Word Plain: One Hundred and Fifty Years in the History of Tenth Presbyterian Church of Philadelphia* (Philadelphia: Tenth Presbyterian Church, 1979), 56.

7. From the 1910 session minutes at the Presbyterian Historical Society in Philadelphia.

8. See Boice, *Making God's Word Plain*, 93.

9. Russell T. Hitt, "Barnhouse of Philadelphia," *Eternity* 26 (April 1975): 17, as quoted in Boice, *Making God's Word Plain*, 68.

10. Details about Dr. Barnhouse's involvement in music and the arts come from Donald Grey Barnhouse Jr., in personal correspondence to Paul S. Jones, April 4, 2003.

11. Tenth Church bulletin, October 17, 1943.

12. See Pauline Fox, abstract of "The Robert Elmore Collection at the University of Pennsylvania," a paper read at the Northeast Chapter of the College Music Society (April 17, 1993), 4.

INDEX

church architecture, 52, 68

Church of the Evangel, 69

Church of the Open Door (Los Angeles), 74

church planting, 167

City Center Academy, 13–14, 18, 126, 128, 130, 136, 215–17

City of God, 155

City Hall, 63

City Light, 127, 211

city ministry, 13–14, 127, 216

civil liberties, 44

civil rights, 106–7

Civil War, 59, 77

Clark, D. Marion, 130–31

Clowney, Edmund P., 104, 125

College of New Jersey, 37, 45, 50

Colman, Benjamin, 31

Columbia Bible College Choir, 203

Combs, Gilbert R., 197

communion service, 65, 68, 85

community, 161–62

compassion, 169–70

Concerto Soloists Chamber Orchestra, 207

Confession of 1967, 108–9, 115, 120, 182

congregationalism, 183

Congregationalists, 32

Congress on the Bible, 118

Conn, Harvie, 153

Conshohocken, PA, 137, 167

Consultation on Presbyterian Alternatives, 125

Continental Congress, 44–45

Conwell School of Theology, 116

Corbin, Carol, 205

Corbin, John, 205

Cornerstone Document (1828), 174–75

Cox, Harvey, 108

Cross, Robert, 36, 37

Crowe, Linward A., 127, 130

Culbertson, William, 96

Cullmann, Oscar, 114

culture, 143, 154, 155

Curtis, Gordon, 201

Curtis Institute of Music, 103, 202, 207, 210

Dallas Theological Seminary, 88, 93

Darby, John Nelson, 71

Darwin, Charles, 77, 78

Davies, Douglas, 198

Davis, John J., 104

Dawson, William, 203

Day, Ella E., 197, 198

Day, Frank Miles, 68, 80

deaconesses, 127

deacons, 170–71

Declaration of Independence, 45

definite atonement, 152

Deists, 30, 50

Delancey Building, 129

Delancey Place manse, 13, 102, 107, 115, 123, 136

Deliverance Evangelistic Fellowship, 128

depravity, 154, 155

DeWitt, John R., 66, 75, 176

Di Gangi, Mariano, 99–110, 115, 142, 176, 202–3

Dibble, Mel, 198

Dickinson, Jonathan, 37, 38

Dilworth, Walter H., 199

disabled, 171

discipleship, 164–66, 168

discipline, 28, 31, 164

dispensationalism, 71, 74, 75, 78, 93, 100

diversity, 161

divorce, 171

Doody, Daniel, 210

Dorcas Society, 64, 68, 105, 179

Duffield, George, 42–44, 45–46

Duncan, J. Ligon, 160

Earle, Elizabeth Porter, 197, 198

ecumenicity, 108

Edinburgh, 22, 32

Edwards, Jonathan, 35, 37, 49

Edwards, Morgan, 25

elderly, 171

elders, 150, 163–64, 183

election, 60, 151–52

Elliott, Thomas, 208

Ellul, Jacques, 159

Elmore, Robert, 103, 115, 200, 203–7, 213, 214

Emery, Walter, 203

Episcopalians, 48, 58

establishment, in Pennsylvania, 41–42

McIntire, Carl, 86–87
McKean, Thomas, 44
McLean Presbyterian
    Church (McLean,
    VA), 125
McNeil, John D., 70, 74,
    81, 176
McWherter, Rodney,
    201
means of grace, 190
Medical Campus Out-
    reach, 126
men's choir, 211, 213
Men's League, 68
Mercer, A. Singleton, 61
merchants, 56–57
mercy ministries, 126,
    169–71
Methodists, 47, 48
Metzger, Bruce, 113
Meyersohn, Kathe, 89
militancy, Barnhouse's
    retreat from, 93
Mission to North Amer-
    ica (MNA), 151
Mission to the World
    (MTW), 151
missions, 166–69
Modern Reformation
    magazine, 132
Moffitt, George, 101,
    111
Moody, Dwight L., 70,
    73, 74, 78, 154
Moravian church music,
    204
Moravians, 29, 47, 211
morning worship serv-
    ices, 129, 130–31
Moule, H. C. G., 78
Mount Herman, Calif.,
    118
Muhlenburg, Henry
    Melchior, 29

multicultural outreach,
    115–16, 128
Murphy, James, 61
music, 13, 102–3, 115,
    134, 159, 161,
    193–214

narcissism, 157, 161,
    164, 165, 169, 172
National Council of
    Churches, 94, 106
National Union Pres-
    bytery, 120, 188
Nazi Germany, 89
New Brunswick Pres-
    bytery, 33, 36
*New Collection of War
    Hymns*, 197
New Jerusalem, 155
New Light-Old Light
    division, 49, 77
new members, letter to,
    178–80
"new perspective" on
    Paul, 145
New School Presbyteri-
    ans, 50–51, 53–55, 58,
    59, 77
New Side Presbyterians,
    36–38, 42, 43
New York City, 51, 91
Nicks, Nancy. *See* Buck-
    lin, Nancy (Nicks).
Nicole, Roger, 116
Niebuhr, H. Richard,
    108
Ninth Presbyterian
    Church (Philadel-
    phia), 48

Ockenga, Harold John,
    11, 96, 112, 118
Old School Presbyteri-
    ans, 50, 53, 55, 77

Old Side Presbyterians,
    36–38, 43
Old World, 27
open theism, 144–45
Oratorio Choir, 211
organ, 102, 194–95, 196,
    199, 202
Ormandy, Eugene, 207,
    211
Orr, Lily, 198, 203
Orthodox Presbyterian
    Church, 86, 125
Overbrook, PA, 167
Overture L (UPCUSA),
    120, 121, 185
Owen, Robert Dale, 56

Packer, J. I., 104, 116,
    118, 132
Pan-Presbyterian Coun-
    cil, 70
Panic of 1857, 62
Park Street Church, 11,
    112
particular redemption,
    152
Pascoe, William H., 17,
    111
pastoral calling. *See* visi-
    tation.
pastoral care, 162–64
pastors, 163
Patterson Memorial
    Church, 69
Patterson, Morris, 61, 69
Patterson, Robert W., 17
Paxton Boys, 39–40
Paxton, James D., 67,
    176
Payne, J. Barton, 118
Pemberton, Israel, 40
Penn, William, 22, 29
Pentecost, J. Dwight, 93
perseverance of the
    saints, 152–53

pew rents, 68, 80, 179
Philadelphia
    Presbyterian origins,
    22–25
    church planting in,
    167
    see also Tenth Pres-
    byterian Church, as
    urban church.
Philadelphia Academy
    of Music Chorus, 205
Philadelphia Bible Insti-
    tute, 93
Philadelphia College of
    the Bible, 105, 116,
    134
Philadelphia College of
    the Bible Chorale,
    203
Philadelphia Conference
    on Reformed Theol-
    ogy, 116, 132, 138,
    149, 208
Philadelphia Eagles, 135
Philadelphia Leadership
    Foundation, 130
Philadelphia Orchestra,
    200, 207
Philadelphia Presbytery,
    28–29, 82–85, 94, 98,
    99–100, 122–23
Phillips, Richard D., 132
Pittsburgh Offensive,
    127
Plimpton, Robert, 207
Pontiac's Rebellion, 39
Poole-Connor, E. J., 93
post-Christian culture,
    156–58, 161, 165, 172
post-conservative evan-
    gelicalism, 144–46
postmodernism, 156,
    157
pragmatism, 157
prayer, 160, 162, 190

prayer meetings, 65, 82
preaching, 30, 158–59,
    165
precentor, 197
predestination, 119
premillennialism, 71
Presbyterian Board of
    Education, 51
Presbyterian Church in
    America, 125–26,
    128, 150
Presbyterian Church in
    the U.S.A., 86, 175
Presbyterian Journal,
    The, 125
Presbyterians, Presbyte-
    rianism, 150–51, 163,
    181–83, 189
    and American Revo-
    lution, 44–46
    Barnhouse on, 94
    and French and
    Indian War, 39–41
Prince, Thomas, 34
Princeton Seminary, 11,
    37, 47, 53, 62, 66, 70,
    75, 113
prison inmates, 171
Psalm of a Pilgrim People
    (Elmore), 207
Psalm of Redemption
    (Elmore), 206
Puritan literature, 116

Quakers, 22–23, 29, 32,
    39–41, 48

racial reconciliation,
    171
racism, 107
radio, 71, 81–82, 83, 88,
    90, 105, 117, 136
Ralston, George, 48, 174
Ramm, Bernard, 96, 122

Redeemer Presbyterian
    Church (New York
    City), 129
Reformation, 143, 145,
    146–49, 214
Reformed Presbyterian
    Church, Evangelical
    Synod, 125–26
Reformed theology, 10,
    60, 64, 72, 75
Reicke, Bo, 114
relativism, 145, 156–57,
    159, 164, 168, 172
relevance, 157
religious freedom, 44,
    122
religious toleration, 29
Revelation magazine,
    90–91, 117
revivalism, 49–51, 68,
    72, 78
revivals, 70
Richards, T. Richard,
    104
righteousness, 148
ritualists, 58
Robinson, J. A. T., 108
Rojas, Deborah, 211
Roman Catholics, 48,
    144, 147
Ross, James B., 61
Rowland, John, 33
Rush, Benjamin, 44
Ryken, Philip Graham,
    14, 131, 137–38, 176,
    211

Sabbath school, 64, 65,
    179, 197
sacraments, 160
St. Enoch's Presbyterian
    Church (Hamilton,
    Ontario), 100, 101
salvation, 145–46
sanctification, 119

Philip G. Ryken (D.Phil., Oxford University) is senior minister of Tenth Presbyterian Church, Philadelphia. He has written fourteen books and edited three. Among the former are *City on a Hill: Reclaiming the Biblical Pattern for the Church in the 21ˢᵗ Century* (2003). Among the latter are *The Communion of Saints: Living in Fellowship with the People of God* (2001). He also coedited *Give Praise to God: A Vision for Reforming Worship: Celebrating the Legacy of James Montgomery Boice* (2003). His academic specialties are the Reformation and theology, post-Reformation Calvinism and Puritanism, homiletics, and C. S. Lewis.

Allen C. Guelzo, Grace F. Kea Professor of American History and Dean of the Templeton Honors College at Eastern University, received the 1993 Albert C. Outler Prize in ecumenical church history for *For the Union of Evangelical Christendom* (1994) and the 2000 Lincoln Prize for *Abraham Lincoln: Redeemer President* (2000). Previously he taught at the Theological Seminary of the Reformed Episcopal Church.

William S. Barker (Ph.D., Vanderbilt University) is professor of church history emeritus at Westminster Theological Seminary. He taught at Covenant Theological Seminary (1972–1984), serving as president during his last seven years. Before joining Westminster's faculty in 1987, he edited the *Presbyterian Journal* for three years. He has written *Puritan Profiles* (1996) and coedited *Theonomy: A Reformed Critique* (1990).

Paul S. Jones (D.M., Indiana University) is organist and music director of Tenth Presbyterian Church and chair of the department of music at Philadelphia College of Bible. He composed the fourteen hymns included in *Hymns for a Modern Reformation* (2000), the lyrics to which were written by James Montgomery Boice.